The Embodied Analyst

The Embodied Analyst brings together the history of embodied analysis found in the work of Freud and Reich and contemporary relational analysis, particularly as influenced by infant research. By integrating the "old" embodied and the "new" relational traditions, the book contributes to a new clinical perspective focusing on form and process rather than content and structure – the "how" rather than the "what" and the "why." This perspective is characterized by a focus on movement, emotional interaction, and the therapist's own bodily experience in the analytic encounter.

Jon Sletvold presents a user-friendly approach to embodied experience, providing the history, theory, training, and practice of embodied experience and expression as a way of expanding clinical attention. Starting with a Spinozan view of the embodied mind, *Part One: History of Embodied Psychoanalysis* presents an overview of the history of the field in the works of Freud and Reich as well as a look at the Norwegian Character Analytic tradition. *Part Two: Conceptual Framework and Clinical Guidelines* explains how clinical interaction can be navigated based on the embodied concepts of subjectivity, intersubjectivity, and reflexivity. *Part Three: Embodied Training and Supervision* presents innovative approaches to training in emotional communication inspired by the performing arts. The book ends with a consideration of the embodied analyst in the twenty-first-century consulting room.

Capturing key aspects of a transitional movement in the development of psychoanalysis and psychotherapy, *The Embodied Analyst* is ideal for those working and training in psychoanalysis and psychotherapy.

Jon Sletvold is a Faculty, Training, and Supervising Analyst at the Norwegian Character Analytic Institute. He is former chair of the Psychotherapy Speciality Board of the Norwegian Psychological Association and is co-editor of two previous books.

"An invaluable contribution, *The Embodied Analyst* bridges psychoanalytic cultures and countries, substantially and impressively advancing contemporary attempts to integrate non-verbal and body-based experience in relational psychoanalytic theory and practice. Sletvold enriches the relational literature in his discussion of these dimensions in the work of Freud and his often-excluded disciple, Wilhelm Reich. Further enhancement is offered in his discussion of Scandinavian analysts who were influenced by Reich, illuminating the often misunderstood and inaccurately represented historical roots of including the non-verbal dimension in treatment. Using evocative clinical material throughout, Sletvold also offers a model for embodied clinical training and supervision." – *Frances Sommer Anderson, PhD, SEP. Editor*, **Bodies in Treatment: The Unspoken Dimension (*2008*)**

"The Embodied Analyst is an outstanding contribution to our understanding of the non-verbal and affective aspects of the analytic process. Within the psychoanalytic world, Wilhelm Reich is primarily recognized for the role that his seminal book on character analysis played within the development of the ego psychology tradition. By focusing more broadly, however, on his thinking about embodiment, Sletvold has managed to synthesize a lost aspect of Reich's legacy with a contemporary relational perspective on transference and countertransference, as well as recent insights into the change process emerging from mother-infant developmental literature. The result of this synthesis is rich in both theoretical and technical yield. It's also a fascinating and engaging read." – *Jeremy D. Safran, PhD, Past-President of the International Association for Relational Psychoanalysis and Psychotherapy and Co-Founder and Co-Chair of The Sandor Ferenczi Center at The New School*

"Norwegian psychoanalysis has long understood that being human involved living in a body, something that many others have managed to overlook. In this groundbreaking book, Jon Sletvold brings a contemporary reading of the best of Wilhelm Reich's theories of character analysis to such diverse influences as affect theory, cognitive neuroscience, infancy research and an array of contemporary psychotherapies. He thus weaves a vivid, immediate *and* scholarly picture of how we live our histories and psychologies through our *embodied subjectivity*. This book will change every analyst's practice for the better." – *Stephen Seligman, DMH, Clinical Professor of Psychiatry, University of California, San Francisco, Joint Editor-in-Chief,* **Psychoanalytic Dialogues,** *Training and Supervising Analyst, San Francisco Center for Psychoanalysis and the Psychoanalytic Institute of Northern California*

"In this lucid, judicious, and important book, Jon Sletvold integrates material from contemporary neuroscience, attachment and infant research, philosophy, and the history of psychoanalysis to give his reader an analyst for the twenty-first century. Through his reading of Freud's body ego and affect theory, as well as Reich's character analysis, Sletvold revisits the corporeal foundations of psychoanalytic thought and creates links among ideas that have often been perceived as incompatible. He further contextualizes these theories in light of more recent work on intersubjectivity in various fields and demonstrates their pragmatic importance with illuminating stories from his own work with patients and training analysis. Finally, Sletvold's consistently undogmatic, intellectually open, and compassionate explication of the implicit and explicit dynamics between analyst and patient is a pleasure to read." – *Siri Hustvedt*

Relational Perspectives Book Series
Lewis Aron & Adrienne Harris
Series Co-Editors
Steven Kuchuck & Eyal Rozmarin
Associate Editors

The Relational Perspectives Book Series (RPBS) publishes books that grow out of or contribute to the relational tradition in contemporary psychoanalysis. The term *relational psychoanalysis* was first used by Greenberg and Mitchell (1983) to bridge the traditions of interpersonal relations, as developed within interpersonal psychoanalysis and object relations, as developed within contemporary British theory. But, under the seminal work of the late Stephen Mitchell, the term *relational psychoanalysis* grew and began to accrue to itself many other influences and developments. Various tributaries – interpersonal psychoanalysis, object relations theory, self psychology, empirical infancy research, and elements of contemporary Freudian and Kleinian thought – flow into this tradition, which understands relational configurations between self and others, both real and fantasied, as the primary subject of psychoanalytic investigation.

We refer to the relational tradition, rather than to a relational school, to highlight that we are identifying a trend, a tendency within contemporary psychoanalysis, not a more formally organized or coherent school or system of beliefs. Our use of the term *relational* signifies a dimension of theory and practice that has become salient across the wide spectrum of contemporary psychoanalysis. Now under the editorial supervision of Lewis Aron and Adrienne Harris with the assistance of Associate Editors Steven Kuchuck and Eyal Rozmarin, the Relational Perspectives Book Series originated in 1990 under the editorial eye of the late Stephen A. Mitchell. Mitchell was the most prolific and influential of the originators of the relational tradition. He was committed to dialogue among psychoanalysts, and he abhorred the authoritarianism that dictated adherence to a rigid set of beliefs or technical restrictions. He championed open discussion and comparative and integrative approaches, and he promoted new voices across the generations.

Included in the Relational Perspectives Book Series are authors and works that come from within the relational tradition and extend and develop the tradition, as well as works that critique relational approaches or compare and contrast them with alternative points of view. The series includes our most distinguished senior psychoanalysts along with younger contributors who bring fresh vision.

The Embodied Analyst

From Freud and Reich to relationality

Jon Sletvold

Routledge
Taylor & Francis Group
LONDON AND NEW YORK

First published 2014
by Routledge
27 Church Road, Hove, East Sussex, BN3 2FA

and by Routledge
711 Third Avenue, New York, NY 10017

Routledge is an imprint of the Taylor & Francis Group, an informa business

© 2014 Jon Sletvold

British Library Cataloguing-in-Publication Data
A catalogue record for this book is available from the British Library

Library of Congress Cataloging-in-Publication Data

Sletvold, Jon.
The embodied analyst : from Freud and Reich to relationality / Jon Sletvold.
    pages cm
  1. Psychoanalysis. I. Title.
BF173.S8754   2014
150.19'5—dc23   2013033348

ISBN: 978-0-415-85618-8 (hbk)
ISBN: 978-0-415-85619-5 (pbk)
ISBN: 978-1-315-83279-1 (ebk)

Typeset in Times
by Apex CoVantage LLC

Printed and bound in the United States of America by
Edwards Brothers Malloy

Contents

Concluding remarks and future directions   155

Preface

In *The Embodied Analyst: From Freud and Reich to Relationality,* I describe key aspects of what I believe is a significant transitional moment in the unfolding of the relational tradition. This transformation in thought and strategy pivots on *expanding the scope of analytic attention* to embrace, apart from what the patient tells the analyst, also the form and impact of the communication, i.e., the tonality and rhythm of speech, gaze and posture, muscle activity in the face and body, and feelings of our own body.

This transition has been occurring over the past few years and can be seen in the theoretical and clinical writings of many contemporary analysts and therapists nested in various theoretical persuasions. I understand this shift as an expansion of, rather than a substitution for, preceding psychoanalytic and psychotherapeutic theory and practice. Traditionally, we have used symbolized and verbalized images revealing unconscious meanings in dreams, slips of tongues, and associations to understand transference and countertransference experience. The words of the patient and the reverie of the analyst have been the material of the psychotherapeutic process.

This widening of perspective, however, draws the attention of the analyst beyond verbal-symbolic sources of unconscious meaning to "something more" (Stern et al., 1998). It is a return to a bodily source of unconscious meaning, originally described by Freud, but elaborated later by Wilhelm Reich. I call this widened focus on the embodied dimension of the analytic interaction "attending to *embodied experience and expression.*" I refer here to experiences and expressions that are not necessarily verbalized but which nevertheless are rich in affective impact. These affective meanings often defy conceptual representation for long periods in the life of patients and therapists and/or of the therapeutic process. They are more about the *how* than the *what* and *why* of analytic interaction, signals often "hidden in plain view" (Stern, 2010, p. 3).

Unfortunately, Freud's early thoughts on the matter and the subsequent contributions of Reich regarding embodied experience were generally ignored by the psychoanalytic and wider psychotherapeutic community. With the impact of infant observation research in the last decades of the twentieth century, and parallel developments in theoretical and clinical perceptions of the interactive dimensions of treatment (represented by various models of intersubjectivity), there is a burgeoning interest in psychoanalysis and, indeed, in psychotherapy more generally, in the impact of embodied experience. In this text, I bring together the – partly unknown – history of embodied analysis found in aspects of Freud's work and particularly in Reich and some inspired by him, with contemporary relational analysis, especially as it is influenced by infant research. By integrating an "old" embodied and a "new" relational tradition, I hope to sharpen the clinical perspective by redirecting attention toward form and process rather than content and structure, in other words, from the "what" and "why" to the "how." This perspective is also characterized by attention to movement, rhythm, timing, and micro-moment emotional interaction; a focus D. N. Stern (2010) recently has termed "dynamic forms of vitality."

While this approach is garnering increasing attention at conferences and in books and journals, many analysts and therapists still narrate clinical process (and I assume conduct treatment) with only minor attention on the patient's and the analyst's embodied registrations and communications. While such signals can be subtle and often difficult to apprehend, I have found that trainee and practicing analysts and therapists can develop a sensitivity to embodied experience/expressions and use these observations in various therapeutic ways, just as one learns to attend to the latent meaning of verbalization.

To avoid any confusion about what this book is about, I also need to say what it is *not* about. It is not primarily about the body. It is not about the body as object. This is not to say that I don't find the body (as object) interesting and important. Numerous authors have written about different aspects of the body (biological as well as cultural), and rightfully so. But this is not one of those books. Neither is it primarily about how body and mind relate, even if it does present a distinct perspective on this ancient and weighty philosophical and theological question. The book is about *the mind*, specifically *the body in the mind, the embodied mind*, about how the mind is shaped by the feeling and sensing of our own and other people's moving bodies.

The form of the title – *The embodied analyst* – is not accidental. The book is more concerned with the analyst/therapist than the patient or groups of patients (particular diagnostic groups). There are a lot of good books on therapeutic methods for different groups of patients, a growing number of which include a focus on the body. This book does not intend to replace them, but rather be a supplement. I have two reasons for focusing on the analyst/therapist. One is that I, for a long time, have been involved in the training and professional nurturing of therapists/ analysts. The second is that the results of research on psychotherapy indicate that the most decisive factor in determining the outcome of therapy is the therapist (Rønnestad & Skovholt, 2013; Norcross, 2011; Wampold & Brown, 2005).

Above all, however, it is a book about psychoanalysis and psychotherapy. I hope it will make my views on the use of embodied experience/expressions plain and of use to clinicians. While not a manual as such, it does offer a perspective and a set of strategies for use in the clinical process. Let me summarize my strategy for navigating clinical interaction with a focus on continuous embodied experience/expression.

I see the mind (the minding process) as basically an ongoing process of registering, feeling, and sensing (in ways I would describe as intuitive and generally nonreflective) what is happening and changing in our body as we continually interact with our environment (with particular interest in other human beings). This continuous internal processing of feelings and sensations registers as a sense or "feeling of what happens" (Damasio, 2000). Attending to this process as it is felt within us is what I call "attending to *embodied experience*." Attending to the same process as it can be observed in others I call "attending to *embodied expressions*." When I sometimes (for reasons of economy) write embodied experience or expression for short, it will usually imply both *experience and expression*.

The psychoanalytic situation is, as Balint formulated it, "essentially a Two-Body Situation" (1952/1985, p. 235). It is therefore of vital importance that observations include both oneself and the other, i.e., both analyst/therapist and patient. Sensations and feelings derived primarily from our own bodily reactions constitute in my terminology the *embodied self-experience*. I shall also refer to these sensations by the term *embodied subjectivity*. In Chapter 6, I elaborate my conception of embodied subjectivity/self and argue that Freud (1923) hit the nail on the head when he said, "the ego is first and foremost a bodily ego."

However, in interaction with others (including psychoanalysis and psychotherapy), we not only register our own bodily reactions but also the effects of the emotional expressions of other(s). This impression is shaped by our unique capacity as humans to simulate and imitate the experience of the other. An expanded conception of imitation which includes embodied identification is therefore critical for understanding intersubjectivity as something no longer based on a cognitive conception of Theory of Mind. I refer to this conception of intersubjectivity as *embodied intersubjectivity*.

I speak of *intersubjectivity* as the ability to experience (feel, sense) some of the mind processes of others. This is consistent with the way the term has been used in developmental psychology and in psychoanalysis as it has been informed by infant research. However, it is different from its use by Stolorow (2011) and his group: "For us," he writes, "*intersubjective* denotes neither a mode of experiencing nor a sharing of experience, but the contextual precondition for having any experience at all" (p. 23n*). Neither definition, in my view, is better or more correct. However, I do find it useful to conceive of intersubjectivity in terms of an ability to experience the emotional state of the other by way of identification and imitation, and consequently as a capacity for *mutual recognition* (Benjamin, 1990). I think this is a most important dimension of analytic interaction, both for the patient and for the analyst/therapist, as I shall seek to demonstrate throughout this text. So, in my use, a meeting of two (embodied) *subjectivities*, for example analyst and patient, can be characterized either by a law or a high degree of (embodied) *intersubjectivity*, understood as a law or a high degree of shared experience and mutual recognition.

The ability to experience both similarities and differences between our own body states and those of others constitutes the basis for the registration of significant affective experiences that emerge in a relationship. These registrations take place without the involvement of reflective thought or traditional forms of symbolic representation. These nonverbalized registrations, I will argue, are critical for our ability to navigate analytic interaction.

However, embodied identification and imitation are also pivotal to reflective thought by making it possible to keep the perspectives of both oneself and the other in mind, and thereby to *disengage from a one-track relationship with the environment* (Hobson, 1998). The ability to experience both similarities and differences emerges as a precondition of the capacity for reflexive functioning or mentalization. This view of reflexivity as something emerging from an interaction between embodied subjectivity *and* intersubjecitivity I term *embodied reflexivity.* I also refer to this capacity as *dialectical objectivity* (Aron, 1996).

Taken together, these separate but interwoven and interacting aspects of embodied experience – embodied subjectivity, intersubjectivity, and reflexivity – explain why I find attention to embodied experience to have such a great potential to enrich psychoanalysis and psychotherapy.

While I see sense of self as the inner feeling of our emotional body state, I use *character* to denote this same emotional body state as observed from the outside. The way *character* is used in the world of play acting and theater illustrates this point. A character on a stage is observed by and communicates with an audience while also interacting with the other characters. Character in this way denotes a person's characteristic way of self-regulation *and* interactive regulation as observed and experienced by others. Using the terms *character* and *self* in this way also relates to my use of the terms *emotions* and *feelings*. Emotion can be observed from the outside, while feelings are the inner felt state of our body. And as I see *affect* as a convenient concept for both emotion and feeling, I see *personality* as a convenient concept for character *and* self, the totality of individuality, both from the outside and within. Corresponding to the distinctions between feeling/emotion and self/character, *intersubjectivity* refers to the interpersonal or relational field as felt on the inside, while *interaction* refers to the same field as observed from the outside.

Character analysis, psychoanalysis, and psychotherapy

In this book, *psychoanalysis* and *psychotherapy* are used more or less interchangeably, as are the shorter couplings *analysis/analyst* and *therapy/therapist.* This is something many contemporary writers do, among them the Boston Change Process Study Group (2010). I shall explain my understanding of these terms later, but before I do, I would like to say something about the lesser known term *character analysis.*

The book is based on a particular character analytic tradition (described in Chapters 2 and 4), and presents what I refer to as a character analytic perspective. Its foremost theorist was Wilhelm Reich (1949/1972). He was one of many talented young psychoanalysts who worked closely with Freud in the 1920s. Although character analysis represented a new departure, everyone, not least Freud himself, saw it as innate to psychoanalysis. It was only with the split between Reich and the International Psychoanalytic Association that character analysis distanced itself from psychoanalysis. Links remained, though. An important aspect of Reich's work was that he came to see neurosis first and foremost as *character neurosis*, whereas Freud had elaborated mostly on *symptom neurosis*. The part in *Character Analysis* (1949/1972) where Reich suggests that symptoms are best understood in the context of a neurotic character has been studied in great detail by analysts. And it was probably this aspect of Reich's work that inspired him to name his new approach character analysis. This diagnostic aspect of character analysis would forever be an integrated part of psychoanalysis, common to all schools of psychoanalysis. Diagnostic character analysis became foundational to all psychoanalytic thinking about diagnosis; today, however, many psychodynamic therapists are probably unaware of its basis or origin in the work of Reich. Wallerstein wrote the following in *Psychodynamic Diagnostic Manual*:

> The major shift in psychoanalytic clinical and therapeutic concern from the symptom neuroses that were the prototypical illnesses of Freud's day to current concern with the varieties of character, character problems and character neuroses, inaugurated in modern form with Wilhelm Reich's landmark book, *Character Analysis* (1933). (Wallerstein, 2006, p. 397)

The character analytic diagnostic perspective distinguishes a psychoanalytic understanding of mental disorders from psychiatric and behavioral/cognitive views which still consider symptoms as the basis for mental health diagnostics (McWilliams, 2011; PDM Task Force, 2006).

This book is, however, primarily about therapeutic character analysis. The diagnostic aspect of character analysis is an implicit, rather than explicit, topic. Therapeutic character analysis privileges, as previously stated, *form* over *content*, *the how* over *the what*, and it does so by attending above all to the emotional expression of the body. After the splits within psychoanalysis and between psychoanalysis and psychotherapy, this therapeutic aspect of character analysis was kept alive and developed mainly by psychotherapists who no longer considered themselves psychoanalysts. *Embodied analysis* in my parlance then seeks to express in a single concept the embodied perspective on psychoanalysis and psychotherapy, whether or not it is rooted in the historical concept of character analysis.

This brings me back to my use of the words *psychotherapy* and *psychoanalysis*. A conceptual distinction between psychoanalytic or psychodynamic psychotherapy on the one side and psychoanalysis on the other didn't emerge until after the Second World War (Aron & Starr, 2013). This in my view was very unfortunate.

I agree with Aron and Starr in that the distinction has been detrimental to the whole field, psychoanalysis and psychotherapy. There was never any scientific support for the notion that psychodynamic psychotherapy was different from psychoanalysis. All of the divergent views that existed within what was considered the psychodynamic psychotherapy community also existed in what was considered psychoanalysis. Psychodynamic and psychoanalytic therapies have never been differentiated on the basis of separate theories. It was a construction, not a discovery, and the time is ripe for deconstruction.

This said, I still find it useful to operate with two separate terms, psychoanalysis and psychotherapy. For one thing, some psychotherapies do not consider themselves psychodynamic therapies, particularly the behavioral and cognitive therapies. And over the last century, it became increasingly common to refer to long-term, intensive therapies as analysis and short-term therapies as therapy. Somewhat akin to this, it has become established practice to refer to shorter training (one to two years) as psychotherapy training and longer training (four to seven years) as analytic training (Stern, 2009). An important point for me is that the long-term analytic training – not least the character analytic training that I myself am involved in – tends to focus on developing the candidate as a person and on their personal/training analysis. Shorter psychotherapy training tends to focus more on therapeutic technique. The view that is argued for in this book puts more stress on the personal, professional development of the therapist/analyst than on what traditionally has been considered methods and technique.

Another aspect of this is that psychoanalysis as it is commonly used has a *broader* sense than psychotherapy. *Psycho and character analysis* is, to my mind, psychotherapy *and* psychology. This is particularly true of developmental psychology and the theory of the embodied mind. The word (psycho) *therapy* draws attention mainly to therapeutic technique, process, and result. Books and journals on psychoanalysis cover every aspect of the human condition; books, journals, and research on psychotherapy focus mainly on – therapy.

All the same, the process of change does not seem to differ according to whether the treatment is considered therapy or analysis, or whether it is affiliated to one or the other school. I am not saying therapies do not differ as a consequence of the therapist's theory and technique. What I am saying is that the process of change might be the same. Some psychotherapy relationships work, some don't (Norcross, 2011). And it is my belief that change processes are affected to a great extent by the nonverbal body-emotional interaction between patient and therapist, whether conscious attention is paid to this interaction or not. The aspiration of this book is simply to help psychotherapy relationships work more often.

In my view, the historical divisions both within psychoanalysis and between psychoanalysis and psychotherapy were and remain particularly harmful. I hope this book can be one of many contemporary texts that contribute to a healing of these divisions.

The structure of the book is as follows. The notion of the embodied mind is explained in the introductory chapter. The first section of the book (Chapters 2 to 4) presents a historical review of embodiment in psychoanalysis and psychotherapy. The second section (Chapters 5 to 9) describes and discusses a contemporary conceptual framework to guide clinical attention. It is illustrated with clinical cases. In the third section (Chapters 10 and 11), I present a training strategy aimed at sensitizing therapists to embodied experience and expression. Finally, the concluding chapter draws some implications of the presented views and considers future directions.

To repeat, the purpose of this text is not to suggest a new school or method of embodied psychoanalysis/psychotherapy. The overall purpose of the upcoming chapters on history, theory, practice, and training is to expand and sensitize clinical attention to embodied experience and expression in psychoanalysis and psychotherapy.

Acknowledgments

This book has become a reality thanks to the strong and enduring support of the editors of the Relational Perspectives Book Series, Adrienne Harris and Lewis Aron. In the book's formative years, Lew gave me unstinting support and astute advice on how to make it a readable "story." During the final process of completion, Adrienne's commitment to the project and advice on structure made the book a much better read than it otherwise would have been.

The dedicated engagement of the editorial team at Routledge, Taylor & Francis Group was another factor in securing the book's realization. Their commitment was among several others personified by Christopher Spring in the early stages, by Susannah Frearson's skillful and pleasant assistance and cooperation in the final stages, and by publisher Kate Hawes, who chaperoned the book from start to finish.

The original idea for a book with approximately the same title was Steven Knoblauch's. We had in fact planned to write it together. After a while, however, we realized it would be best if we parted ways. By then, I had already drafted important parts of the present book, parts which Steven had read and commented on in detail. The book, therefore, owes much to his ideas and effort.

If this book appears to be written in good English – and I think it is – it is thanks to the work of my dedicated English language consultant Christopher Saunders. I am very grateful, Chris, for your thorough reworking of my Norwegian-English.

Thanks to friends and colleagues who have read and given valuable response to different parts of the text: George Downing, Jeremy Safran, Sue Shapiro, Stephen Seligman, Turid Nylund, Anne Kulseng Berg, Marianne Børstad, Per Anthi, and Svein Haugsgjerd.

Thanks also to my colleagues in the early years of the Norwegian Character Analytic Institute, where many of the ideas in this book were first formulated, especially Turid Nylund, but also Per Harbitz, Rita Østensen, Vera Børsum, Thor Ole Kjos, Jon Jørgensen, Else Arnesen, Peter Lohne, Erling Dugstad, Margrethe Øglænd, Atle Austad, and numerous other faculty members, and, not to forget, candidates taking part in training seminars, supervision sessions, and training analysis.

Last, but not least, I owe a debt of thanks to my patients who, over a period of 40 years, entrusted me with their unique life experiences.

A special thanks to Lars Sletvold and Ingrid Walbye Sletvold: to Lars for widening my philosophical perspective, and to Ingrid for giving me a granddaughter, Mari, and an opportunity, once again, to be part of "the interpersonal world of the infant" – an important reference for the perspective developed in this book.

Some material in the chapters in this book appeared in its early stages in *The Journal of the Norwegian Psychological Association* and in the articles below. All material is used by permission.

Sletvold, J. (2011). "The reading of emotional expression": Wilhelm Reich and the history of embodied analysis. *Psychoanalytic Dialogues,* 21, 453–467.

Sletvold, J. (2012). Training analysts to work with unconscious embodied expressions. *Psychoanalytic Dialogues,* 22, 410–429.

Sletvold, J. (2013). The Ego and the Id revisited. Freud and Damasio on the body ego/self. *The International Journal of Psychoanalysis*, 94, 1019–1032.

Chapter 1

The embodied mind

The object of the idea constituting the human mind is the body

(Spinoza)

It is my fundamental belief that experience is essentially embodied experience. I see the mind, or better the minding process, as a continuing process of registering, feeling, and sensing (in ways I shall describe as intuitive and generally nonreflective) what is happening and changing in our body as we interact with our environment (with particular interest in other human beings). This internal processing of feelings and sensations registers as a sense or feeling of what is happening. My belief challenges the Cartesian conception of body and mind as separate realms or entities. Conceptualizing mind/body as mind *and* body is still common in psychoanalytic writing, even if it may not be intended for the most part. I therefore set out in this chapter what we might see as a Spinozan alternative to the Cartesian conception.

From the vantage point of post-Cartesian psychoanalysis, Stolorow (2011) and his coworkers have importantly criticized the idea of the isolated mind: "[o]ne isolated mind, the analyst, is claimed to make objective observations and interpretations of another isolated mind, the patient" (p. 20). They developed phenomenological contextualism to reunite the mind with its context, above all the outer world. From my Spinozan perspective, I emphasize just as strongly the need to transcend the separation of the mind, not only from the world, but also from the body. The focus of this chapter is actually more on *the body in the mind* than on *the world in the mind*. The notion of the contextualized mind is already widely accepted, at least in relational circles. The notion of the embodied mind might not be as widely accepted as yet.

Toward a psychoanalytic conception of the embodied mind

Bruce Reis recently made the following observation:

> A revolution is underway. Disciplines as diverse as philosophy, neuroscience, linguistics and developmental psychology are redefining what it means to be

human by sharing their respective knowledge bases, synergistically creating radically new conceptions of subjectivity and intersubjectivity. (2009, p. 565)

Reis speaks of a "wide-ranging theoretical synthesis . . . bringing new ways of thinking to psychoanalysis." Consistent with the movement Reis describes, I shall be looking at the advantages of making use in clinical practice of research and theoretical formulations in fields related to psychoanalysis and psychotherapy, such as philosophy, neuroscience, and developmental and experimental psychology. I draw on these ideas to demonstrate the kind of emerging conceptual imagery or metaphors that help me integrate embodied experience in psychoanalysis. I begin with a clinical observation published in 1960 by Marion Milner:

> [The] inner ground of being, as a real psycho-physical background to all one's conscious thoughts can be directly experienced by a wide focus directed inwards. [This] kind of attention deliberately attends to sinking itself down into total internal body awareness, not seeking at all correct interpretations, in fact not looking for ideas at all although interpretations may arise from this state spontaneously. (Quoted in Wallin, 2007, p. 338)

Milner's advocacy of this kind of (countertransference) attention to embodied experience came at a time when psychoanalytic culture lacked a theoretical framework to appreciate its value, and was unprepared to fathom the implications of what she was reporting. I want to consider a conceptual framework for twenty-first-century psychoanalysis enabling the kind of experience Milner was reporting. I start with something Freud wrote in 1898:

> I am . . . *not at all inclined to leave the psychology hanging in the air without an organic basis.* But apart from this conviction *I do not know how to go on, neither theoretically nor therapeutically* and therefore must behave as if only the psychological were under consideration. (Masson, 1985, p. 326, my italics)

Even if Freud – temporarily – had to give up his ambition to achieve an organic basis for psychoanalysis, he didn't forsake it altogether. Note for example what he wrote later on in *The Ego and the Id*: "The ego is first and foremost a bodily ego" (p. 26). What exactly Freud meant by this formulation remained, however, at best unclear and because of that, conceptions of ego and self in psychoanalysis in the twentieth century for the most part had no room for embodied experience. It is fascinating to consider how the ego of ego psychology, the self of self psychology, and the self-states of contemporary relational thought remained largely "hanging in the air without an organic basis," contrary to Freud's intentions and views as presented in *The Ego and the Id*.

In this chapter, I shall be looking at theoretical developments that have contributed to a grounding of the mind in the body in ways that Freud and others after him were not privy to when they formulated their ideas. For example, in the past few decades, neuroscientists have formulated new models to explain how a sense of self and other might emerge from embodied experience. New ways of understanding, ways which Freud the neurologist could only contemplate in part, are now becoming increasingly tenable.

Spinoza, Merleau-Ponty, Damasio, and Stern

But first I need to take a big step backward in time, to Spinoza, who was the first to formulate a clear alternative to Descartes' theory of body/mind. I shall then ask how Merleau-Ponty managed to situate the body – as opposed to sensation and reason – at the center of human experience (perception). By positioning the body at the center of experience, Damasio can explain how emotions and feelings constitute the core and source of embodied experience. I also introduce the work of Daniel N. Stern on vitality affects and forms of vitality, and how it expands our understanding of embodied affectivity. Taken together, the ideas of Spinoza, Merleau-Ponty, Damasio, and Stern justify closer clinical attention to affective, embodied experience. I end the chapter with a consideration of the reluctance that still seems to exist around the idea of the embodied mind.

A Spinozan alternative to Cartesianism

Damasio (2003) drew renewed attention to the remarkable fact that Spinoza, writing only some 30 years after the publication of Descartes' *Meditations on First Philosophy* (1641/1992), formulated a distinctive alternative to Descartes' view of the relationship between mind and body. In his *Meditations*, which Descartes dedicated to the "Dean and the Doctors of the Sacred Faculty of Theology at Paris" (p. 13), he claimed to have demonstrated "the existence of God and the distinction of the human soul from the body" (p. 12). Contrary to this view, Spinoza described in *The Ethics* (1677/1982) the human mind or soul (depending on the translation) as the *idea of the human body*. "The object of the idea constituting the human mind is the body and the body as it actually exists" (*The Ethics*, Part II, from the proof following Proposition 13). Spinoza saw the body *and* the external world as the basis of the mind. "The human mind does not perceive any external body as actually existing except through the ideas of the modification (affections) of its own body" (Proposition 26). In condensed form, Spinoza here explains why attention to embodied experience is so essential to the navigation of analytic interaction – and everyday life.

With the Cartesian view of body and mind as separate realms remaining the dominant view until recently, Spinoza's alternate view, on the other hand, was heavily suppressed for centuries. He was excommunicated by the Jewish Synagogue in Amsterdam, condemned by Christian and political leaders all over Europe, and even attacked by the nonbeliever Voltaire.

Commenting on the fate of Spinoza, Damasio (2003) wrote: "Darkly, through the glass of his unsentimental and unvarnished sentences, Spinoza apparently had gleaned an architecture of life regulation along the lines that William James, Claude Bernard, and Sigmund Freud would pursue two centuries later" (p. 13). And almost 300 years later, philosophers would again formulate the view that the human body interacting with the external world grounds what we call mind. Building upon the phenomenology and existentialism of Husserl (1913/1989a, b) and Heidegger (1926), Merleau-Ponty argues that the seat of perception (mind) is to be found in our own body.

In *Phenomenology of Perception* (1945/1996), Merleau-Ponty starts out by discussing the traditional views of philosophy and psychology on how we come to know the world: empiricism and rationalism. The common point of departure for these conceptions is consciousness. Both, Merleau-Ponty argues, represent second-hand abstractions. Neither empiricism nor rationalism can explain how we come to perceive the world first hand. "Pure sensation . . . is the 'last effect' of knowledge . . . and it is an illusion . . . that causes us to put it at the beginning" (1945/1996, p. 37). At the beginning, he argues, is our own body. "It is a fact that I believe myself to be first of all surrounded by my body, involved in the world, situated here and now" (p. 37).

According to Merleau-Ponty, it is only from a given bodily position (real or imagined) that we can perceive anything at all. We can't just see (or imagine) a house, we must see (or imagine) it from a specific bodily position. What we perceive will vary depending on whether we see the house from one side or another or from above. In Merleau-Ponty's words,

> My body is the fabric into which all objects are woven, and it is, at least in relation to the perceived world, the general instrument of my "comprehension". . . . It is my body which gives significance not only to the natural object, but also to cultural objects like words. . . . The word "hard" produces a sort of stiffening of the back and neck, and only in a secondary way does it project itself into the visual or auditory field and assume the appearance of a sign or word. (p. 235, 1945/1996)
>
> In short, my body is not only an object among other objects, a nexus of sensible qualities among others, but an object which is *sensitive to* all the rest, which reverberates to all sounds, vibrates to all colours, and provides words with their primordial significance through the way in which it receives them. . . . We are not, then reducing the significance of the word, or even of the percept, to a collection of "bodily sensations" but we are saying that the body, in so far as it has "behavioural patterns," is that strange object which uses its own parts as a general system of symbols for the world, and through which we can consequently "be at home in" that world, "understand" it and find significance in it. (pp. 236–237)

Merleau-Ponty points to a fundamental distinction between, on the one hand, the "objective body" and mental representations, images of the body as object – the two Cartesian bodies – *and*, on the other, the body, "which is *sensitive to* all the rest." One of the problems psychoanalysis has had with the body derives to a great extent from a conception of it as a physical or nonphysical entity, flesh and blood versus imaginings and fantasies – echoes of Cartesian dualism. In Merleau-Ponty's vision of embodiment, the body exists for us first and foremost as immediate experience, "the object which is *sensitive to* all the rest." Only at a second remove do we form conceptions, physical and/or mental, of the body.

Merleau-Ponty's basic argument, then, is that we come to know ourselves and the world in which we live not from "sensation" nor from "objective thought," but from "the pre-objective realm" constituted by the experience of our own body. This is also his starting point for considering how we get to know other selves, a view that presages current positions:

> What we said about the body provides the beginning of a solution to this problem [how we get to know other selves]. The existence of other people is a difficulty and an outrage for objective thought (p. 346). . . . If my consciousness has a body, why should other bodies not "have" consciousness? Clearly this involves a profound transformation of the notions of body and consciousness. As far as the body is concerned, even the body of another, we must learn to distinguish it from the objective body as set forth in works on physiology. (p. 351)

As the passage below will show, Merleau-Ponty's explanation of intersubjectivity also pre-echoes the results of developmental research on alter-centric participation (Bråten, 1998b) and infant imitation (Meltzoff & Moore, 1995). On this reading, it is from our own body that we come to understand the existence of other minds. He writes,

> Here again I have only the trace of a consciousness which evades me in its actuality and, when my gaze meets another gaze, I re-enact the alien existence in a sort of reflection. There is nothing here resembling "reasoning by analogy." . . . A baby of fifteen months opens its mouth if I playfully take one of its fingers between my teeth and pretend to bite it. And yet it has scarcely looked at its face in a glass, and its teeth are not in any case like mine. The fact is that its own mouth and teeth, as it feels them from the inside, are immediately, for it, an apparatus to bite with, and my jaw, as the baby sees it from the outside, is immediately, for it, capable of the same intentions. "Biting" has immediately, for it, an intersubjective significance. It perceives its intentions in its body, and my body with its own, and thereby my intention in its own body. (p. 352)

Referring to Husserl and his statement that the perception of others is like a coupling phenomenon, Merleau-Ponty adds: "The term is anything but a metaphor. In perceiving the other, my body and his are coupled (p. 118). . . . It is as if the other person's intention inhabited my body and mine his" (p. 185). Merleau-Ponty here presages a view of intersubjectivity that has recently been given the term *intercorporeity*, inspired by the discovery of so-called mirror neurons, as a basis for embodied "knowing" of others (Gallese, 2009). And Reis (2009) made the following relevant connection, stating that "there is also a crisscrossing of bodies, the other and my own. Merleau-Ponty . . . called this a *chiasmatic* relation, wherein my body and the body of the other are both instances of the same corporeal process that runs throughout the sensible/sentient world" (pp. 571–572).

Merleau-Ponty's reading of intersubjectivity more than half a century ago also anticipated current relational views concerning the therapeutic action of psychoanalysis. He wrote:

> Psychoanalytical treatment does not bring about its cure by producing direct awareness of the past, but in the first place by binding the subject to his doctor through new existential relationships. It is not a matter of giving scientific assent to the psychoanalytical interpretation, and discovering a notional significance for the past; it is a matter of reliving this or that as significant, and this the patient succeeds in doing only by seeing his past in the perspective of his co-existence with the doctor. (1945, p. 455)

Contemporary conceptions of the embodied mind

In recent years, psychoanalysis and psychotherapy have drawn on research in neuroscience and experimental psychology that contributes greatly to our understanding of how minding processes are rooted in the body (Beebe & Lachmann, 2002; Cozolino, 2002; Fonagy, Gergely, Jurist, & Target, 2002; Gallese, 2009; Hobson, 2002; Hurley & Chater, 2005; Kaplan-Solms & Solms, 2002; LeDoux, 1996; Lichtenberg, Lachmann, & Fosshage, 2002; Panksepp, 1998; Schacter, 1996; Schore, 1994, 2003a/b; Solms & Turnbull, 2002). In particular, the ideas put forward by Portuguese-American neurologist Antonio Damasio (1994, 2000, 2003, 2010) resonate well with the perspective developed in this book. Sharing with Merleau-Ponty the notion of experience and perception as grounded in the body, Damasio adds significantly to our understanding of emotions and feelings as constituting the core of embodied experience.

Much of modern dualistic thinking, not least in science, rather than steering a course between mind and body distinguishes between mind and brain on the one hand, and the rest of the body on the other. But it is not only the separation of mind and brain that is mythical, says Damasio in response to this way of thinking. "The mind is embodied, in the full sense of the term, not just embrained" (Damasio, 1994, p. 118). Emotions, feelings, thoughts, fantasy, and memory are woven together *within* our bodies, he maintains. This view flows into a conception of feelings and thoughts as formed *between* bodies, a process Gallese (2009) terms *intercorporeity*.

Body, emotions, feelings

Critical to Damasio's work is his conceptual distinction between embodied emotions and subjective feelings. This distinction also helps us understand relations between unconscious and conscious processes (see Chapter 6 for further discussion of this issue). More than 100 years ago, William James (1890/1983) suggested that

> [o]ur natural way of thinking about . . . emotions is that the mental perception of some fact excites the mental affection called emotion, and that this latter state of mind gives rise to the bodily expression. My theory, on the contrary, is that *the bodily changes follow directly the perception of the exciting fact, and that our feeling of the same changes as they occur* IS *the emotion.* (p. 1065; italics in original)

In *Descartes' Error* (1994), Damasio refers to neurological data related to emotional disorders that accompany various neurological diseases and injuries. The nature of these disorders hinges precisely on the extent to which, and in what manner, the parts of the nervous system which keep the brain informed of body states are damaged.

James's theory suggests that the whole body is involved when we feel and sense. This is different from maintaining that some sense organs, along with their neural pathways and dedicated regions of the brain, are sufficient to create feeling. Of course, James didn't have the benefit of the scientific data available today; most of it didn't see the light of day until some 100 years after James wrote those lines. This may partly explain why it took so many years for James's theory to gain acceptance. It is interesting to note the correspondence between James's theory, Damasio's data, and Merleau-Ponty's formulations, all of which point to *the body itself as constituting our basic perceptual system.* "In the beginning there was no touching, or seeing, or hearing, or moving along by itself. There was rather *a feeling of the body* as it touched, or saw, or heard, or moved" (Damasio, 1994, p. 232). This conception of perception as fundamentally embodied received cogent support from the experimental psychologist Gibson (1979) in his *ecological theory of perception.* Damasio (1994) suggests that nature, in its effort to ensure the survival of the body, stumbled upon a highly effective solution, "*representing the outside world in terms of the modifications it causes in the body proper*" (p. 230, italics in original).

In this perspective, feelings are internal sensations, or "images" of the body's internal landscape, a landscape populated by heart, lungs, intestines, muscles, skin, etc. Changes in the condition of these organs coincide with changing in emotional states and are variously experienced as changes in feelings. This conception of the emotions is not self-evident and rarely experienced in a conscious way (particularly not in quotidian patterns of activity) because our sensation of the body and its myriad of possible sensations (for example cold, pain, and softness experienced simultaneously) tends to be swallowed up by impressions of things extrinsic to the body, a landscape, a tune, a smell, or taste. Feelings, then, "qualify" something else. And because this "something else" claims most of our attention, it is difficult to grasp our feelings as the registration of an embodied, emotional, interactive moment.

Nonetheless, as Wallin (2007) recently reminded us, Marion Milner, writing in 1960, realized at an early date the clinical value of "concentration of the body" and attention to "whole body awareness." Here in more detail:

> I noticed the astonishing changes in the quality of one's perceptions, both of oneself and the outside world, that the deliberate use of a wide rather than narrow focus of attention brings . . . [the] inner ground of being, as a real psycho-physical background to all one's conscious thoughts . . . can be directly experienced by a wide focus directed inwards. . . . [This] kind of attention deliberately attends to sinking itself down into total internal body awareness, not seeking at all correct interpretations, in fact not looking for ideas at all – although interpretations may arise from this state spontaneously. (Milner, 1960/1987, p. 236)

When Milner was publishing her work, this kind of thinking was far from mainstream, but she gives a vivid description of how a deliberate immersion, a "sinking . . . down into total internal body awareness," stimulates the emergence of feelings and ideas.

Unconscious emotions, conscious feelings, and vitality affects

The respective perspectives of Spinoza, Merleau-Ponty, James, and Damasio suggest how extrinsic stimuli affect the state of the body without our knowledge. These bodily changes constitute our *emotional body states,* states that are always changing, not least when prompted by an encounter with another. Emotional body states are so multiple, simultaneous, multi-layered, and complex that they only partially become represented in conscious awareness. They remain for the most part *unconscious emotions.*

Emotional body states can reach consciousness, Damasio (1994) suggests, when these bodily changes are sensed and felt together with an image of the object that precipitated them. In this sense, consciousness emerges as a recognizable sensation of something happening in the body in response to an interaction. We cannot entertain a conscious image of an object, Damasio writes in *The Feeling of What Happens: Body, Emotion and the Making of Consciousness* (2000), without first having reacted emotionally/bodily to it. We experience nothing without foregoing changes in the body. Emotions (embodied expressions) come before feelings (subjective experiences). The way Damasio uses the word *emotion*, i.e., to signify the observable but often unconscious bodily changes, I find both clarifying and useful. Echoing Damasio, I also speak of *feeling* to signify subjectively felt, often conscious sensations. This important conceptual distinction is found in several European languages in addition to English. Norwegians, for instance, differentiate between *beveget* or *rørt* (moved) on the one hand and *føle* or *kjenne* (feel, sense) on the other; the first denotes observable expressions of affect, the second the subjective impression. Damasio (2010) recently introduced the idea of *primordial feelings* for the very first registrations of our body state, for example pleasure/pain, occurring prior to changes caused by an object. I return to this idea in Chapter 6 when I discuss Freud's and Damasio's view of ego/self.

Damasio (1994, 2003) refers to changes within the body as the "body-loop." At this physiological level of bodily events, changes are mapped in the parts of the brain devoted to sensory input from the body (the somatosensory cortices), constituting the immediate neural substrate from which feelings proceed. But changes in the somatosensory cortices may occur without foregoing changes in the body. Damasio terms this the "as if body-loop." Mood-changing substances, i.e., drugs and alcohol, act by creating such "as if bodily states" in the somatosensory cortices. Feelings are not necessarily therefore a mirror image of the body's state. Phylogenetically, this function may have been advantageous: not sensing the pain of a life-threatening injury may have increased chances of survival. On the other hand, we know from clinical experience what the disadvantages of dissociation can be to psychic well-being. Even though I see feelings basically as "images" of body states, I think it is important to keep in mind the complexity of the relationship between embodied states and feelings; it is not necessarily linear, a point which is critical for grappling with clinical questions concerning dissociation and embodied states.

Daniel Stern (1985) expanded our understanding of affective experience with the idea of *vitality affect*. He would later elaborate this concept, calling it among other things *feeling shapes* (Stern, 2004). More recently he wrote about *forms of vitality* (2010). Studying mother–infant interaction, Stern was struck by a continuous dimension of emotional experience, exemplified by the rate of acceleration of activity, or cross-modal rhythms such as a baby giggling and a mother matching the rhythm with a movement of her upper torso. This dimension is independent, but could act in the emergence of discrete feeling states such as happiness, anger, and fear. Rather than being distinct and discrete, vitality affects or forms of vitality are ever-changing *feeling shapes* reflecting the intensity, strength, and rapidity of the interaction. Stern explains:

> They are the felt experience of force – in movement – with a temporal contour, and a sense of aliveness, of going somewhere. They do not belong to any particular content. They are more form than content. They concern the "How," the manner, and the style, not the "What" or the "Why." (2010, p. 8)

I am struck here by the similarity with Reich's character analytic perspective: "Alongside the 'what' of the old Freudian technique, I placed the 'how'. . . . I learned in the course of time to comprehend the form of the communications themselves as direct expression of the unconscious" (1942/1978, p. 153). The kind of expansion of clinical attention that I am advocating is, above all, an effort to comprehend precisely what Stern now describes as *forms of vitality*. I share with Stern the belief that these forms contain literarily speaking the most *vital* aspects of human experience. Becoming aware of forms of vitality might, however, be no small challenge insofar as Stern characterizes this aspect of human experience as largely "hidden in plain view" (2010, p. 4).

Damasio (1994) introduced *background emotions* and *background feelings* to designate an aspect of affective life somewhat akin to Stern's vitality affects/ forms of vitality. While not identical to Stern's conceptions, Damasio too points to the ever-presentness of affective experience. These distinctions between discrete emotions and the continuous flow of affective experience are, as I see it, essential to the practice of psychoanalysis and psychotherapy, especially with regard to how we apprehend and deal with embodied experience/expressions. Patients will frequently, if not always, be aware of categorical feelings such as happiness, grief, anger, and fear. But in many cases, neither patients nor therapists will be aware of – or indeed trained to recognize and navigate – the experiences and meanings of what Stern originally called vitality affects. Here is a short clinical vignette to help make the value of using these distinctions more readily apparent.

Peter is talking about a discussion he had had with his wife the day before. He wonders which of them was the most unreasonable. Listening to him, I remain focused on the emotions conveyed by his facial expressions and physical posture. Rather than commenting on his account per se, I say "I get the impression that it feels important for you to sort this out . . .", and "It seems to me it feels unfair, considering that your wife said . . ." In the first comment, the vitality form "important" is given verbal expression; in the second, the quality feeling "unfair" is articulated. The point in both cases is that these emotional aspects had not been verbalized by Peter himself and may not have been consciously felt.

Peter's facial expression tells me immediately whether my choice of words describes his implicit feelings. If they don't feel right to him, he will usually correct me and substitute the right word(s). In either case, something has been made more conscious, and Peter stays in command of his emotional life.

A condition of this approach is sensitivity to changing facial expressions. Emotions revealed by facial expression are often on the verge of breaking into consciousness. The road to consciousness is literally shorter from the face than from other parts of the body. An approach like this tends to intensify a process of emotional awareness and promotes the patient–therapist alliance as the patient feels apprehended and understood.

Feelings, thoughts, words, and "the intention unfolding process"

What the above clinical vignette also shows is that experience has an emotional *and* a cognitive component. There are no thoughts without feelings, and no feelings without thoughts. Hobson (2002) puts it like this in his account of *the cradle of thought*: "In the account I have given, thoughts are only gradually distilled out of the attitudes and intentions that are fundamental to relatedness between the infant and the world. One implication of this is something that Vygotsky stressed: every thought contains a transmuted element of feeling" (p. 258). *Descartes' Error* (Damasio, 1994) is essentially about how crucial an ability to feel our own emotional body state is to rational decision-making.

Stern and his colleagues in the Boston Change Process Study Group (2008) recently introduced the concept "intention unfolding process" in an effort to grasp how verbal thought apprehends emotional body events and images.

> In spontaneous speech, there is something in mind that wants expressing. Let us call this "something in mind" an image, in the broadest sense of the term. The image can be an idea, a movement, a gesture, an affect, a vitality affect, a background feeling. . . . There is an intention . . . to link the image to words. . . . This is the "intention unfolding process". . . . This process, which usually takes several seconds, is dynamic, unpredictable, very messy, and widely distributed in the body; it usually involves all analogous conscious and unconscious bodily happenings. This nonlinear dynamic process is perhaps what makes us human. (p. 137)

All that is nonverbal contributes to the process – "the affects, 'the background feelings' from the body, the 'vitality affects,' physical discomfort, mood, the state of subconscious motivational systems (hunger, sleep, sex), ambient sensations, immediate past history, and so on" (p. 139). "The bodily concept is activated when words are used, or words can be activated when the sensory motor schemas are experienced" (135).

The group's thesis takes the ideas developed by Merleau-Ponty, Damasio, and Hobson a step further. According to their formulation, during the emergence of the reflective-verbal from the embodied, "the reflective, the implicit, and the disjunction between the two, make up one intuitively grasped package" (p. 143). The idea of the reflective-verbal, the implicit (embodied), and the disjunction between the two constituting a whole is, I think, an important idea and can help us overcome our deeply engrained cultural tendency to valorize one or the other of these realms of experience. Later (in Chapter 8), I consider more closely how the verbal-reflective feeds on and changes embodied experience, though we can see the process in action in the vignette where the therapist's verbal comments bring about an immediate change in the patient's body. It is not only about the ability of the therapist to read emotional expressions; it is also about the ability of spoken words to change emotional body states.

I end this introductory chapter on the embodied mind by attempting to answer why psychoanalysis has found it so difficult to conceive of the body as the core of the mind.

The reluctance to accept the embodied mind

Despite the increasing evidence for the body as constituting the basis of the mind, the idea of mind and self as things apart from the body is still very much alive. Why is there so much reluctance in psychoanalysis and psychology in general to conceptualize the mind as an embodied phenomenon? I find Totten's (1998) reflections illuminating.

> As Lacan, Reich, Freud, Winnicott and others all recognize in their different ways, *what is initially a "body ego" tends powerfully to identify itself with the mental, and to identify the mental with itself*. . . . Clarifying the philosophical weaknesses of this position is not really enough. More than a theory, this is an *experience*: a positioning of the subject as mental rather than bodily, which needs to be understood analytically, as an over determined choice. The "mental ego" is clearly a common experience in our culture but, equally clearly, not a universal, permanent and total experience (or we could hardly observe it). (pp. 176–177, my italics)

Orbach (2004) adds a further consideration:

> Bodies in the current psychoanalytic session are adjuncts to mental processes: sometimes they stimulate affects, sometimes they become diseased, sometimes they represent memory – the body as elephant – sometimes they are seen as deeper and more truthful (this would be a Jungian or Reichian notion) or they are seen as a theatre, as Joyce McDougall . . . does, as a stage on which the troubles of the psyche are acted and inscribed. But mindedness to the body as a body which is speaking for itself and its difficulties is peculiarly absent. (p. 21)
> It (the body) has become almost everything else but a breathing, living, desiring body. In the post-Freudian, post-instinctual body along with losing the sexually pursuant body that marauds and must be tamed for civilization and art, we seem to have lost the body *as body*. (p. 22)

Damasio (2000) refers to the advantage of concentrating resources on the images that describe problems in the outside world. But skewing the perspective like this, he argues, comes at a cost. It tends to prevent us from sensing the origin and nature of what we call self. Things, he suggests, might have been different sometime,

> perhaps at some magic brief time between Homer and Athens, lucky humans would have perceived in an instant that all of their amusing antics were about

life and that underneath every image of the outside world, there stood the ongoing image of their living bodies. . . . I suspect they were able to sense more about themselves than many of us, the unforewarned, are able to sense these days. I marvel at the ancient wisdom of referring to what we now call mind by the word *psyche* which was also used to denote breath and blood. (pp. 29–30)

Spinoza saw the mind as the idea of the changes or affections of our own body, but the human mind, he added, "perceives not only the modification of the body, but also the ideas of such modifications" (Proposition 22, *The Ethics*, Part II). Commenting on this notion, Damasio says,

once you form an idea of a certain object, you can form an idea of the idea, and an idea of the idea *of the idea*, and so forth. All of this idea formation occurs on the mind side of substance, which, in the current perspective, can be largely identified with the brain-mind sector of the organism. (2003, p. 215)

Recalling Totten's (1998) observation – "what is initially a 'body ego' tends powerfully to identify itself with the mental, and to identify the mental with itself" (p. 176) – one reason we so easily see mind and self as purely mental phenomena might be because we as humans so easily form *ideas of ideas*. If so, it is another reason to pay more deliberate and systematic attention to the body in the mind.

However, as we will see in the next chapter, concepts of an embodied mind were actually very present in the minds of those who founded psychology and psychoanalysis a little more than 100 years ago.

Part I

History of embodied psychoanalysis

Chapter 2

The history of embodied analysis
Freud and Reich

All mental states are to some degree "affective", and not one of them is without its physical manifestation.

(Freud)

Character analysis developed the reading of emotional expression.

(Reich)

This historical review will show that efforts were made to embody psychoanalysis from its very inception. I begin by looking at concepts of embodiment found in Freud's early writings, and then trace the reemergence of analysis of body communication/experience linked to Freud's discovery of the transference, and the growing emphasis that ensued on the analysis of emotional communication in the analytic situation. A particularly distinct expression of this development is Reich's stressing of the importance of analyzing the latent negative transference. His subsequent development of consistent resistance analysis and character analysis ultimately leads to the point where he defined character analysis as "the reading of emotional expression."

Embodiment in Freud's early writings

Attention to the embodied dimension of the psychoanalytic interaction has often been looked upon as deviation from the Freudian view. It is therefore a somewhat ironic historical fact that Freud, early in his career, developed an excellent ability to read the emotional expression of the body, believing it to offer a way "to read the mind." This should not be surprising if we recall that Freud was a neurologist and had studied hysteria extensively. "Hysterics," he concluded, "suffer mainly from reminiscences" (Breuer & Freud, 1893/1895/1955, p. 7). According to Freud, hysterical symptoms should be understood as affect-motor memories of traumatic experience, not as the result of hereditary weakness.

In an article from 1890 (wrongly dated 1905 in the standard edition of Freud's works [henceforth S. E.]), Freud explores the possibility of a scientifically (as alternative to religious) based psychotherapy. *Psychic Treatment*

(Soul Treatment) elaborates extensively on the possibility of reading the mind from the expression of the emotions in the body.

> A man's states of mind are manifested, almost without exception, in the tensions and relaxations of his facial muscles, in the adaptations of his eyes, in the amount of blood in the vessels of his skin, in the modifications in his vocal apparatus and in the movements of his limbs and in particular of his hands. (Freud, 1890/1953a, p. 286)

These physical changes, Freud adds, stand in the way if one wishes to conceal one's mental state from other people. "But they serve these other people as trustworthy indications from which his mental processes can be inferred and in which *more confidence can be placed than in any simultaneous verbal expressions that may be made deliberately*" (p. 286, my italics). Freud is probably referring to the thinking of James and Lange when he writes: "In certain mental states described as 'affects', the part played by the body is so obvious and on so large a scale that some psychologists have even adopted the view that the essence of these affects consists only in their physical manifestations" (p. 287).

Freud describes the pervasive bodily changes that result from persistent affective states of a distressing nature, while, "[o]n the other hand, under the influence of feelings of joy, of 'happiness', we find that the whole body blossoms out and shows signs of a renewal of youth" (p. 267). Not only does he emphasize strong affects, but mental processes generally, as manifested in somatic changes.

> The affects in the narrower sense are, it is true, characterized by a quite special connection with somatic processes; but, strictly speaking, all mental states, including those that we usually regard as "processes of thought", are to some degree "affective", and not one of them is without its physical manifestation or is incapable of modifying somatic processes. (p. 288)

In his case histories in *Studies on Hysteria*, Freud describes how he often bases his judgment of the patient's state more on a reading of the emotional expression of the body than on what the patient is saying. A passage from his first note on Frau Emmy von N, May 1, 1889, can serve as an illustration.

> This lady, when I first saw her, was lying on a sofa with her head resting on a leather cushion. She still looked young and had finely-cut features, full of character. Her face bore a strained and painful expression, her eyelids were drawn together and her eyes cast down; there was a heavy frown on her forehead and the naso-labial folds were deep. She spoke in a low voice as though with difficulty and her speech was from time to time subject to spastic interruptions amounting to a stammer. She kept her fingers, which exhibited a ceaseless agitation resembling athetosis, tightly clasped together. There were frequent convulsive tic-like movements of her face and the muscles of her

neck, during which some of them, especially the right sterno-cleido-mastoid, stood out prominently. Furthermore she frequently interrupted her remarks by producing a curious "clacking" sound from her mouth which defies imitation.

What she told was perfectly coherent and revealed an unusual degree of education and intelligence. This made it seem all the more strange when every two or three minutes she suddenly broke off, contoured her face into an expression of horror and disgust, stretched out her hand towards me, spreading and crocking her fingers, and exclaimed, in a changed voice, charged with anxiety: "Keep still! – Don't say anything! – Don't touch me!" (Breuer & Freud, 1893/1895/1955, pp. 48–49).

As we see, Freud gives as detailed a description as possible of the patient's affect motor expression. He also mentions that *Frau Emmy von N* talks and tells, but he does not dwell on what she actually says. Instead, Freud describes *the way* she talks, "in a low voice as though with difficulty" and further, "What she told was perfectly coherent and revealed an unusual degree of education and intelligence." At the end of the note, Freud does tells us what the patient says, but these verbal utterances turn out in his reading to be integrated parts of an emotional expression. "[S]he . . . contoured her face into an expression of horror and disgust, stretched out her hand towards me, spreading and crocking her fingers, and exclaimed, in a changed voice, charged with anxiety: 'Keep still! – Don't say anything! – Don't touch me!'" As I mentioned in Chapter 1, this integrated bodily-emotional and verbal expression has recently been termed an "intention unfolding process" by the Boston Change Process Study Group (2008) in an effort to catch how emotional body states, images, and words coalesce into a single integrated expression.

The way Freud at this point privileges *the body's emotional expression and the form of the verbal communications, rather than their contents* is highly remarkable in light of forthcoming developments. Nevertheless, his initial ambition to develop an embodied psychology and psychotherapy is reflected in many of his early works, not least *Project for a Scientific Psychology* (Freud, 1895/1950). It falls outside the scope of this historical review to discuss the vicissitudes that led Freud to temporarily abandon his goal, and instead develop a theory and method that mainly relied on the interpretation of the contents of verbal associations and dreams. Writing to Fliess on September 22, 1898, however, he asserted,

> I am not at all in disagreement with you, not at all inclined to leave the psychology hanging in the air without an organic basis. But apart from this conviction I do not know how to go on, neither theoretically nor therapeutically and therefore must behave as if only the psychological were under consideration. (Masson, 1985, p. 326)

So Freud turned his mind to dreams, fantasy, and the interpretation of symbolic representations. *The Interpretation of Dreams* (Freud, 1900/1966) initiated a period during which Freud, contrary to his earlier focus on trauma, came to focus on dreams and fantasies as the expression of unconscious sexual drives and wishes. This change of focus is clearly reflected in the case of "Dora" (Freud, S. E., vol. VII). But this exclusive focus on a purely mentalist psychology didn't last long. With the importance of transference to analytic therapy gradually dawning on him, he was once again, slowly but surely, being drawn back to the emotional expression of the body. And as I will show, it was a more consistent exploration of transference that prompted Reich years later to "read the mind" by "reading the emotional expression."

As early as 1911, in "The handling of dream-interpretation in psycho-analysis" (Freud, 1911/1958a), Freud warns analysts against letting dream interpretation interfere with the ongoing analytic process. And with his papers on technique the following years (1912/1958a/b; 1913/1958c; 1914/1958d and e) he was clearly expanding psychoanalysis beyond dream analysis into transference analysis. Yet to be clear, even as Freud's emphasis shifted to the patient's emotional engagement with the analyst, symbolic representations in the form of the unfolding of verbal associations were still considered to be the primary material for analysis. While the interpretation of symbolic representations is well suited for dream analysis, it is not always the form in which the transference is communicated and verbal formulations are therefore less well suited for grasping and working with the transference as it is enacted in the clinical interaction. Important aspects of the transference will often not be expressed verbally but rather by means of the kind of bodily expressions Freud so clearly had described earlier.

This inconsistency in method came to be Reich's (1949/1972) point of departure in his development of the character analytic technique, exemplified first by his work on the so-called latent negative transference. This transference came to be seen by Reich as a prime example of an emotional attitude in the patient that typically was not symbolized and expressed in words, and thus often overlooked by analysts. He also pointed to serious practical consequences when lack of trust in the analyst the patient could manifest in early stages of an analysis was not analyzed. According to Reich, the analysis would either be terminated prematurely or become superficial because the analysis of the latent negative transference was not undertaken.

Reich and the reading of emotional expression

It was a more consistent exploration of the bodily manifestations of the transference that led Reich to rediscover the possibility of "reading the emotional expression." By the time Reich had started studying psychoanalysis around 1920, it was firmly established that the primary material to be analyzed was the patients' verbalized free associations, dreams, and other symbolic expressions. In 1952, Kurt R. Eissler interviewed Reich for the Sigmund Freud Archives, asking his opinion of Freud. Eissler states initially that he would like Reich to tell him everything he knows, observed, and thought about Freud. Reich's reply starts like this:

> Well, that is quite a big order. I know a lot about Freud. I would like to start with a basic theoretical difference in the approach of psychoanalysis and my

work, not to propagate my work, but to explain how I saw Freud. Psycho-analysis, as you well know, works with words and unconscious ideas. These are its tools. According to Freud, as I understood him, as he published it, the unconscious can only be brought out as far back as the Wortvorstellun-gen (verbal ideas) when the "word images" were formed. In other words, psychoanalysis cannot penetrate beneath or beyond the second or third year of life. Psychoanalysis is bound down by its method. It has to stick to that method which is the handling of associations and word images. Now, *character analysis developed the reading of emotional expression.* Whereas Freud opened up the world of the unconscious mind, thoughts, desires, and so on, I succeeded in reading emotional expressions. Until then, we couldn't "read the mind". We could only connect verbal associations. (Higgens & Raphael, 1967/1972, pp. 3–4, my italics)

Reich in this way contrasted his character-analytic method as the reading of emo-tional expression with Freud's method as the handling of associations and word images. On the basis of this comparison, Reich concluded that because psychoanal-ysis was restricted to connecting verbal associations, it could not "read the mind." Much psychoanalytic writing reflects the accuracy of this characterization of the state of psychoanalytic technique as it was taught in the 1920s and 1930s and still at the time Reich gave this interview. But historical irony emerges here. When Reich contrasts his approach with Freud's, he emphasizes "the reading of emotional expres-sion," whereas Freud's approach is considered only to allow one to connect verbal associations, not "to read the mind." This is a historical paradox in light of Freud's early focus on the emotional expressions of the body, from which "mental processes can be inferred and in which more confidence can be placed than in any simultane-ous verbal expressions that may be made deliberately" (Freud, 1890/1953a, p. 286).

While there obviously is a history of interest in the significance of embodied emotional expression running from Freud through Reich to contemporary authors, analysts lost interest temporarily following Reich's disenchantment with psychoanalysis (Jacobs, 2005). One of the purposes of this chapter is to contribute to a healing of this historical rupture by supplying a conceptual bridge between past and present theorizing.

Basic elements of character analysis as developed by Reich

I review here the basic elements of the character analysis Reich developed between 1925 and 1935. In the first part of that period, Reich headed the seminar on psy-choanalytic technique in Vienna. The seminar was particularly focused on the latent negative transference. Here, Reich draws on his personal experience.

[I]t was not until a patient told me, some months after the termination of an unsuccessful analysis, that he had never trusted me that I learned to appreciate the danger of the negative transference that remains latent. That patient had recalled beautifully for a year and a half in a good positive transference. . . . Most of our meetings at the Vienna seminar were also concerned with the negative transference, especially the latent transference. In short, we see that this was not the blind spot of one analyst. Failure to recognize the negative transference appears to be a general occurrence. Undoubtedly, this can be traced back to our narcissism, which makes us highly receptive to compliments but quite blind to all negative tendencies in the patient unless they are crudely expressed. (1949/1972, p. 25)

Reich came to identify the latent negative transference as a secret resistance, not expressed in the content of words, but rather in the form of the communication, in "the way the patient speaks, looks at and greets the analyst, lies on the couch, the inflection of the voice, the degree of conventional politeness which is maintained" (p. 49).

To begin with: what is meant by "analytic material"? This is usually taken to mean the patient's communications, dreams, associations, slips. Theoretically to be sure, it is known that the patient's behaviour is of analytic importance; but unequivocal experiences in the seminar show that the patient's behaviour (manner, look, language, countenance, dress, handshake, etc.) not only is vastly underestimated in terms of its analytic importance but is usually completely overlooked. At the Innsbruck Congress, Ferenczi and I, independent of one another, stressed the therapeutic importance of these formal elements. *As time went on, they became for me the most important fulcrum and point of departure for the analysis of character.* (1949/1972, p. 31, my italics)

Reich explains how his approach was not without problems and challenges, especially as it provoked protest and anger in the patient. If the analyst did not get stuck in emotionless associations, if he refused to be content with dream interpretations and instead attacked the character defenses concealed in the patient's attitude, then the patient would often become angry.

At first, I did not understand this reaction. The patient would complain about the emptiness of his experiences. But when I pointed out the same emptiness in the nature of his communications, in his coolness, in his grandiloquent or hypocritical nature, he became angry. He was aware of the symptom, a headache or a tic, as something alien. *But his character was the person himself.* He was disturbed when it was pointed out to him. What was it that prevented a person from perceiving his own personality? After all, it is what he is! Gradually, I came to understand that it is the entire being that constitutes the compact, tenacious mass which obstructs all analytical efforts. The patient's whole personality, his *character*, his individuality resisted analysis. But why? *The only explanation is that it fulfils a secret function of defence and protection.* (1942/1978, p. 131) *The entire world of past experience was embodied in the present in the form of character attitudes. A person's character is the functional sum total of all past experiences.* (p. 128)

The form of the communication as direct expression of the unconscious

Psychoanalysis at that time adhered to a rule of interpreting the material in the sequence in which the patient offered it (Reich, 1942/1978, p. 151). Reich suggested that resistances should be dealt with systematically, starting with the resistance closest to the psychic surface and of particular contemporary importance. The neurosis, he urged, should "be undermined from a secure position" (p. 151). Direct interpretations of unconscious instinctual material could only disrupt this work and should therefore be avoided. "The patient first had to establish contact with himself before grasping the connections between his various neurotic mechanisms. As long as the armour remained in place, the patient could at best achieve only an intellectual comprehension of his situation" (p. 151). Reich addressed this problem by emphasizing attention to embodied communication. He explained:

> One thing I was sure about, however, was that the character-analytic technique was a considerable step forward toward the mastery of severe, encrusted neuroses. The stress was no longer on the content of neurotic fantasies but on the energy function. Since the majority of patients were incapable of following the so-called basic rule of psychoanalysis, i.e., "to say everything which comes to mind," I ceased to insist on it. Instead, I used as my points of attack not only what the patient communicated but everything he offered, in particular the way in which he made his communications or was silent. Even silent patients revealed themselves, expressed something which could be gradually unravelled and mastered. *Alongside the "what" of the old Freudian technique, I placed the "how"*. I already knew that the "how", i.e., the form of the behaviour and the communications, was far more important than what the patient told the analyst. Words can lie. The expression never lies. Although people are unaware of it, it is the immediate manifestation of the character. *I learned in the course of time to comprehend the form of the communications themselves as direct expression of the unconscious.* (1942/1978, pp. 152–153, my italics)

With this shift in attention from "what" to "how," Reich found that intellectual understanding of the unconscious was superseded by the patient's immediate perception of his own expression. This made it more difficult to conceal an affect behind words. "The patient no longer talked about his hate – he experienced it" (p. 153).

What Reich points out again and again is that the expressive form of a communication, e.g., how it is expressed in the body and the voice, is at least as important as the verbalized content. Most recently, Daniel Stern (2010) has expanded his idea of vitality affects to include what he terms *forms of vitality*, and states: "They are more form than content. They concern the 'How,' the manner, the style, not the 'What' or the 'Why'" (p. 8). These dynamic forms of vitality, he argues, are the most fundamental of all felt experience. Form and process as opposed to content have drawn growing attention in contemporary relational thinking, especially as it has been informed by infant research. For example, Beebe and Lachmann write:

> Psychoanalysis is currently seeking an expanded theory of interaction. Organizing principles of interaction can be discerned when mother and infant are viewed as a system. . . . [W]e propose that these principles can illuminate *how interactions are organized at the nonverbal level in adult treatment. These organizing principles of interaction describe self- and interactive process not dynamic content.* (2002, p. 33, my italics)

And Reich commented on interactions at the nonverbal and the verbal levels in the following way:

> The ideas of orthodox psychology and depth psychology are chained to word formations. However, the living organism functions beyond all verbal ideas and concepts. Human speech . . . is not a specific attribute of the living organism, which functions long before a language and verbal representations exist. (1949/1972, p. 358)

Reich's theorizing here resembles and presages contemporary views on the relation between body, emotions, and language. The Boston Change Process Study Group (BCPSG) (2007) argues that previous psychoanalytic theory had got the surface/depth distinction upside down. "[W]e assert that the local level, where implicit relational knowing is enacted, is the foundational level of psychic life. . . . In brief, implicit relational knowing is based in affect and action, rather than in word and symbol" (p. 3). In Chapter 8, I return in some detail to how we today can conceptualize the relation between a "local" affect motor and a verbal reflective level of experiencing.

Sensing others' emotions through "plasmatic" imitation

In a letter to his former wife, psychoanalyst Annie Reich, in 1935, Reich refers to his *"ability to sense others' emotions before they have manifested themselves; that is what made me a character analyst"* (1994, p. 19, my italics). Reich's final important contribution to character analytic technique is, in my view, his explanation of how it is possible "to sense others' emotions before they have manifested themselves" (p. 19).

> *We work with the language of facial and body expression.* Only when we have sensed the patients' facial expression are we in a position to comprehend it. We use the word "comprehend" here to mean quite literally to know which *emotion* is being *expressed* in it. (1949/1972, p. 362)

Such sensing of the patient's emotions comes about, Reich suggested, through a process of inner automatic imitation.

The patient's expressive movements involuntarily bring about *an imitation* in our own organism. By imitating these movements, we "sense" and understand the expression in ourselves and, consequently, in the patient. Since every movement is expressive of a biological condition, i.e., reveals an emotional condition of the protoplasm, the language of facial and body expression becomes an essential means of communicating with the patient's emotions. As I have already pointed out, human language *interferes with* the language of the face and the body. When we use the term "character attitude," what we have in mind is the *total expression* of an organism. This is *literally* the same as *the total impression* which the organism makes on us. (1949/1972, p. 362)

Very few, even among Reich's own disciples, grasped the full implications of what he was suggesting. The only analyst to formulate a similar view, to my knowledge, is Freud. In a footnote to his discussion of identification in *Group Psychology and the Analysis of the Ego* (Freud, 1921/1955) he states, "A path leads from identification by way of imitation to empathy, that is, to the comprehension of the mechanism by means of which we are enabled to take up any attitude at all towards another mental life" (p. 110n2). The German text makes it clear that this "mechanism," according to Freud, is the only one that makes it possible to know the mental life of another person.[1] Michael Franz Basch (1983) later elaborated on Freud's view:

A given affective expression by a member of a particular species tends to recruit a similar response in other members of that species. As Freud (1921) suggested, this is done through the promotion of an unconscious, automatic, and in adults not necessarily obvious, imitation of the sender's bodily state and facial expression by the receiver. This then generates in the receiver the automatic response associated with that bodily state and facial expression, which is to say the receiver experiences an affect identical with that of the sender. (Basch, 1983, p. 108)

And recently, Gianni Nebbiosi and Susanna Federici-Nebbiosi reported the following from their work on rhythmic and empathic listening with the body:

For many years now, we have been using the tool of miming our patients in order to obtain a better understanding of them. This was done for the purpose of using a knowledge that resides in the analyst's body and of which he is completely unaware. (2008, p. 224)

This embodied understanding of the basis of empathy and intersubjectivity proposed by Freud, Reich, Basch, and Nebbiosi and Federici-Nebbiosi has only been accepted in recent years, facilitated by studies of innate imitative ability in newborns (Meltzoff & Moore, 1995) and the demonstration of a mirror neuron system in humans (Rizzolatti, Fogassi, & Gallese, 2001; Gallese, Eagle, & Migone, 2007; Gallese, 2009). Chapter 7 is devoted to a theoretical and clinical exploration of this embodied understanding of intersubjectivity.

Reich and the relational turn in psychoanalysis

Despite his understanding of the embodied basis of emotional communication and intersubjectivity, Reich cannot be considered a relational analyst by contemporary standards. His attitude is that of the omniscient analyst who is able to objectively tell the patient the truth. But he was definitely one of the first analysts to see psychic structure, character, as the result of relational conflict, of conflict constituted at the interface of inner and outer worlds.

In *Character Analysis* Reich has a chapter on the basic conflict between need and outer world. In every case that is analyzed deeply enough, he says, one will find not the antithesis between love and hate, not the antithesis between eros and the death instinct, but the antithesis between ego and the outer world. "[T]he *first* impulse of *every* creature must be to establish contact with the outer world" (p. 271). In the chapter on *Psychic Contact and Vegetative Current*, where he expands on the talk he gave at the Lucerne Congress in 1934, Reich writes, "The psychic process reveals itself as the result of the conflict between instinctual demand and the external frustration of this demand. Only secondarily does an inner conflict between desire and self-denial result from this initial opposition" (p. 287). Without a working knowledge of these theories, Reich says, it is impossible to understand the results of character-analytical research.

The following quotes illustrate how Reich advocated several positions that have later become integral parts of contemporary, particularly relational psychoanalysis. One of these positions concerns the patient's experience of the analyst's subjectivity (Aron, 1996).

> Many psychoanalytic rules had an inherently and strongly taboo character, which merely reinforced the patient's neurotic taboos in the sexual realm. Such, for instance, was the rule that the analyst should not be seen – should remain, so to speak, a blank sheet of paper upon which the patient inscribed his transference. This procedure did not eliminate but rather reinforced the patient's feeling that he had to deal with an "invisible", unapproachable, superhuman. . . . Under such circumstances, how could the patient dare to express his human criticism? All the same, the patients had a way of knowing about the analysts. But with this kind of technique, they seldom expressed what they knew. (1942/1978, p. 154)

Another position which is foundational to this text is Reich's positive view on movement in the analytic situation.

> Another rule was that the patient was only supposed "to remember", but never "do anything". I was in agreement with Ferenczi in rejecting this method. There could be no doubt that the patient should be "allowed to do" also. Ferenczi got into difficulties with the association because, having a good intuition, he allowed the patients to play like children. . . . I overcame my reserve

toward the patient's actions and discovered an unexpected world. At the base of the neurotic mechanism, behind all dangerous, grotesque, irrational fantasies and impulses, I discovered a simple, self-evident, decent core. (p. 155)

Reich's character analysis was originally intended to offer a consistent method of analyzing resistance, and has largely been seen as something of a confrontational approach. In this respect, Nic Waal (1958), who worked closely with Reich in Oslo, writes that some of Reich's patients became either crushed or obsessively oppositional or projective by his active therapy. But she adds that many were rescued from severe personality problems. In the following passage, she reports on her experience of Reich's confrontational approach in her own treatment with him.

I could stand being crushed by Reich because I liked truth. And strangely enough I was not crushed by it. All through this therapeutic attitude to me, he had a loving voice, he sat beside me and made me look at him. He accepted me and crushed only my vanity and falseness. But I understood at that moment that true honesty and love both in a therapist and in parents is sometimes the courage to be seemingly cruel when it is necessary. It demands, however, a great deal of the therapist, his training and his diagnosis of the patient. (Waal, 1958, p. 43)

In my opinion, the confrontational aspect is only one aspect of character analysis. It can and should entail an empathic approach, as Nils Strand, a prominent character analyst in Norway in the last part of the twentieth century and my own training analyst, highlighted.

You can never identify too much with people you want to help. But you can forget you are doing it, and that is no good. . . . Competent psychotherapy is dependent on the therapist's sensitivity, and contact with one's sensitivity. No therapist, no human being for that matter can be too sensitive. What is decisive is the strength to contain the sensitivity. (Strand, 1991, p. 165, my translation)

The split between Reich and IPA

The split between Wilhelm Reich and the International Psychoanalytic Association (IPA) happened around the time of the 13th IPA Congress in Lucerne, August 1934. Before the Congress, Reich had lost his membership and had to attend the Congress as a guest. He presented his paper on *Psychic Contact and Vegetative Current. A Contribution to the Theory of Affects and Character-Analytic Technique* (1949). There has been a lot of conjecture about how Reich lost his membership of the German Psychoanalytic Society. Hitler had just seized power, and the political climate in Germany was problematic to say the least. Reich may well have been seen as dangerously mixing psychoanalysis and left-wing politics, rather than attacked for his psychoanalytical views as such, which, at the time, were not particularly controversial (Sharaf, 1983). He was excluded from the Communist Party at about the same time, a consequence of his views on *The Mass Psychology of Fascism* (1946/1988).

At the Lucerne Congress, the Norwegian delegation (Harald Schjelderup, Ola Raknes, and Nic Hoel [later Waal]) argued for Reich's right to stay within IPA, and offered him membership of the Norwegian Society. Professor Schjelderup invited Reich to Norway to teach character analysis and conduct his planned psycho-physiological experiments. Reich stayed in Norway from 1934 to 1939. His seminar on character analysis was attended by most of the Norwegian analysts of the time.

Towards the end of his Norwegian sojourn and especially after relocating to the U.S., Reich lost much of his interest in character analysis. His impatient mind went on to explore what he believed was the biophysical core of the neurosis. In Norway, he founded what he called character analytic vegetotherapy, renaming it later orgontherapy following his 1942 discovery of what he believed was cosmic orgone energy (orgone, from orgasm and organism). Reich saw this phase of his work as "a decisive step, for it means that we have left the sphere of psychology" (1949/1972, p. 358). Its discussion falls outside the scope of this book however.

Character analysis after Reich internationally

Most of Reich's followers in Norway and the U.S. tried more or less enthusiastically to keep pace with his thinking. Most IPA analysts, on the other hand, had ceased taking him seriously, and some even thought he was unhinged. So, in spite of being one of the most influential psychoanalytic writers and teachers of his time, Reich and character analysis are seldom mentioned in the psychoanalytic literature. There are some notable exceptions, among them Kernberg's (1984) and Schafer's (1983) chapters on character analysis and David Shapiro's (1965, 2000) books on neurotic styles and character dynamics. Other contributions are reviewed by Jacobs (2005).

Spezzano's (1993) work on affect in psychoanalysis and Josephs' (1995) on relational character analysis address directly the relational implications of character analysis. Both in their way acknowledge the value of integrating character analysis and relational psychoanalysis. There are historical similarities between character analysis and interpersonal analysis according to Spezzano. He writes,

> There is a clear parallel in Reich's argument to Sullivan's (1940) later warning that the content of all talking is intended as much to disguise as to communicate. What is really going on with the patient, however, will be revealed despite himself in his mannerisms and in the form of his communications. In many ways, interpersonal psychoanalysis has carried on the tradition of character and resistance analysis with more determination than any other school has. (p. 202)

Josephs (1995) introduces the term empathic character analysis, and explains,

> Character analysis as it was practiced by Wilhelm Reich could be said to be unempathic. Yet there is nothing intrinsic to character analysis per se that makes it incompatible with an empathic stance if empathy is understood as encompassing attunement to multiple, unconscious, and conflicting points of view within a mutually evocative dyad. (p. xxiii)

The basic assumption of the character analytic perspective is, in my opinion, that emotions and the unconscious are expressed immediately in bodily action and imagistic symbolization (Bucci, 2005; Fosshage, 2005) and only at a remove on the verbal/conceptual level. Recently, new models have emerged that highlight and integrate this perspective in light of contemporary relational analysis. Bucci (1997) has formulated a multiple code theory of emotional processing covering three basic modes, the verbal symbolic, nonverbal symbolic images, and the sub-symbolic, the latter constituting the body-based affective core of emotion schemas.

Lichtenberg, Lachmann, and Fosshage (2002) integrate neurobiological arguments (Edelman, 1992; Damasio, 2000) with a contemporary psychoanalytic conception of the self and conclude that consciousness is created in two momentous steps.

> The linking of very early memory maps with a current perception create primary (Edelman) or core (Damasio) consciousness – a state of being mentally aware of things in the world in the form of here-and-now lived experience. The second step, a linking of symbolic memory, linguistically organized concepts, and representation of self, create higher order consciousness. In higher order (Edelman) or extended (Damasio) consciousness, concepts of self, past, and future can be connected to here and now awareness. (p. 15)

An overarching assumption, they say, has until recently remained unchallenged: "communication means talking, and other forms of communication, bodily posture, somatic symptoms, and varieties of 'acting out' or 'enactments,' constituted either resistances to, or pathologies of free association," before adding that this conception "is a remnant of time prior to the recognition of procedural learning as an equal partner with symbolized or episodic memory in the communication between any partner, whether mother and infant or analyst and patient" (Lichtenberg, Lachmann, & Fosshage, 2002, p. 57).

The Dyadic Systems Model of Beebe and Lachmann (2002) distinguishes the explicit and the implicit realms. The model's conceptual and visualized separation of the verbal and emotional forms of communication and experience enables the study of nonverbal, body-emotional regulation in its own right. At the same time, it allows for an explicit consideration of the relation between verbal and emotional processing. An additional strength of the model is that it draws attention to both self-regulation and interactive regulation. Some of the rich possibilities of the model are demonstrated in Beebe and Lachmann (2002) and subsequently in *Forms of Intersubjectivity in Infant Research and Adult Treatment* (Beebe, Knoblauch, Rustin, & Sorter, 2005).

The distinction between body-emotional and verbal-conceptual experience and communication might even be reflected in the fundamental anatomy of the brain. After assembling an impressive body of developmental and neuro-scientific research, Schore (1994, 2003a, 2003b, 2011) suggests that while the left hemisphere is dominant for language and conscious, verbal-conceptual reasoning, the right hemisphere seems to be dominant for emotions, body, and image-based communication, unconscious processing, and the body-based self. On this basis, Schore (2003b) portrays psychotherapy as a direct right brain-mind-body to right brain-mind-body exchange. Schore makes a further conceptual distinction not only between interactive regulation and self-regulation, but also between self-regulation and *auto* regulation; reserving the term *auto regulation* for processes that go on only in one's own body, whereas self-regulation will often have an interactive element as well.

And most recently, Geltner (2012) in his book on *countertransference analysis and the use of feeling in psychoanalytic technique* has written about *language* and *feelings* as the two channels of human communication: *cognitive communication* and *emotional communication*. He elaborates particularly on *objective countertransference*, borrowing the term from Winnicott (1949) and defining as follows: "Objective countertransference is a feeling that is induced in the analyst by the patient's emotional communications and is a repetition of a feeling that originated in the patient's emotional life history" (p. 23). Feelings originating in the analyst's own life history are what Geltner refers to as *subjective countertransference*. In this text, I use the terms *induced* and *personal countertransference* correspondingly, following a suggestion by Downing (1996).

Uniting these new models is their recognition and clarification of the slowness of verbal communication compared to the split-second speed of communication at the body-emotional level. This central feature is clinically illustrated and elaborated by Knoblauch (2000). He describes *verbal discrete-state exchanges* as slower and unidirectional and *non-verbal continuous-process exchanges* as rapid and bidirectional, and illustrates the clinical value of attending to a continuous emotional process. In *Body Rhythms and the Unconscious* (2005) and subsequent papers (2008, 2011), Knoblauch performs concrete and detailed analyses of micro-moments of body-emotional exchanges, and how these exchanges can facilitate reflection and verbalization. I consider these analyses of micro-moments as supplementary to the more global perspective on embodied interaction conceptualized and illustrated in this book.

In a book titled *The Present Moment*, Stern (2004) highlights the distinction between *the lived story* and *the told story*, that is, life as it is lived moment by moment in contrast to how it is verbally narrated afterwards. This is one more way of illuminating the distinction between the verbal-reflective and body-emotional domain. Stern pays special attention to the temporal aspect of emotional experience. The present moment takes between one and 10 seconds, he suggests, and composes a lived story.

> The present moment that I am after is the moment of subjective experience as it is occurring – not as it is later reshaped by words (p. xiii). . . . What is shared in a moment of meeting is an emotional lived story. It is physically, emotionally, and implicitly shared not just explicated. The notion of "vitality affects" and "shared feeling voyages" . . . were needed to give substance to the idea of a shared lived story. (pp. xvi–xvii)

Experiences contained in present moments, Stern emphasizes, occur in parallel with the exchange of language during a session. He calls special attention to direct and implicit experience because it has been relatively neglected. "With an emphasis on implicit experience rather than explicit content, therapeutic aims shift more to the deepening and enriching of experience and less to understanding its meaning" (p. 222). Stern's ideas echo those of Reich when he wrote that a consequence of the character analytic approach is that "intellectual understanding of the unconscious was superseded by the patient's immediate perception of his own expression" (1942/1978, p. 153).

I conclude this chapter on the history of embodied analysis by repeating Reich's words: "Alongside the 'what' of the old Freudian technique, I placed the 'how.' I already knew that the 'how,' i.e., the form of the behaviour and the communications, was far more important than what the patient told the analyst" (1942/1978, p. 153). And as already pointed out, in his latest book, Daniel Stern (2010) uses almost the same words to describe *forms of vitality*: "They are more form than content. They concern the 'How,' the manner, the style, not the 'What' or the 'Why'" (p. 8). These dynamic feeling shapes, Stern goes on to argue, are the most fundamental of human experience. I agree with Seligman (2011) here: this is a matter that points to a direction essential to pursue for future research and clinical psychoanalysis.

In the next chapter, I explore the difference between a psychoanalytic perspective, building in part on Reich's character analysis on the one hand, and bodywork therapies inspired by Reich's vegetotherapy and orgone therapy on the other.

Note

1 "Von der Identifizierung führt ein Weg über die Nachamung zur Einfülung, das heisst, zum Verständnis des Mechanismus durch den uns überhaupt eine Stellungnahme zu einem anderen Seelenleben ermöglicht wird" (Freud, Gesammelte Werke [G. W.], 13, 1991, 121n2).

Chapter 3

Character analysis and Reichian body-work

While Reich's contribution to an embodied psychoanalysis, notably his development of character analysis, is central to the history foundational to this text, this
is not how most people remember Reich. He is probably best known – and more
controversial – both within the field of psychoanalysis and more widely for his
development of the libido theory into what he termed first sex-economy and later
orgone theory, and therapeutically for his vegetotherapy and orgone therapy. An
important aspect of my review of history is to clarify the difference between a
psychoanalytic perspective, building in part on Reich's character analysis on the
one hand, and body-work therapies inspired by Reich's vegetotherapy and orgone
therapy on the other. This chapter is dedicated to this question.

It falls outside the scope of this book to explore the many different forms of
neo-Reichian body-work therapy inspired by Reich's later work. However, it is
important to be aware of a principal difference between Reich's psychoanalytic
and psychotherapeutic work and what he later referred to as "bio-physical" therapy, not least because it will help clarify how the perspective upon which this
text is built might differ from some of the therapies called body-oriented psychotherapy or body-psychotherapy.

I will take as my starting point a discussion that ensued following the publication of *The Rooting of the Mind in the Body* by Fonagy and Target (2007a). Attachment research, they wrote, in its alliance with an abstract cognitive science, has
underrated bodily experience and now needs to return to physical experiences of
attachment. In their conclusion, Fonagy and Target emphasize that they "wished
to draw attention to the way style in speech, thought, and relationships may be
determined by an underlying, unifying coding system of embodied images or procedural memories of experiences rooted in bodily experiences." But this way of
stating an important question must not be understood, they add, "as an argument
for a neo-Reichian body-oriented psychotherapeutic perspective" (p. 432). In a
subsequent letter to the editor of *JAPA*, the Norwegian psychoanalyst Per Anthi
(2007) questioned their advice.

> At this point, it is necessary that they amplify what they really mean by a neo-
> Reichian perspective. Do they refer to Reich as vegetotherapist or orgone ther-
> apist? Or do they refer to his character analytic technique developed during

the decade 1928–1938? Many have problems in distinguishing between Reich, on the one side, with his grandiose scientific visions, his radical political statements, and his growing paranoia and, on the other side, with his real contribution to psychoanalytic technique.

Reich's focus on nonverbal expressions and bodily based phenomena contain information of early significant experiences and are therefore in Anthi's opinion highly relevant to Fonagy's and Target's discussion of how the mind is rooted in the body. After explaining in some detail the benefits of character analytic technique, Anthi concludes:

> It is true that Reich's original character analytic technique needs to be modified and improved, but not by ignoring Reich's important emphasis on the somatic aspects of character analysis. In this way, Fonagy and Target avoid the possibility to achieve a better understanding of some of the questions they raise.

In their response Fonagy and Target thank Anthi for a scholarly and interesting letter and express, among other things, the following:

> Dr. Anthi's remarks concerning Reich are well taken. Reich's early work on character analysis is truly groundbreaking. In addition to the discovery of personality disorder and Axis II of the *DSM* (before any such ideas were commonly discussed in psychiatric or psychoanalytic discourse), Reich's writing on character analysis still offers very helpful insights on technique. It is valuable indeed to be reminded of this first phase of Reich's work.

Fonagy and Target conclude by expressing the hope that their letter will serve to correct an underestimation of the importance of Wilhelm Reich's contribution. This discussion between Anthi and Fonagy/Target reflects in my opinion some confusion in the fields of psychoanalysis and psychotherapy following Reich's development of what he first called "vegetotherapy" and later "orgone therapy." It was a therapy Reich (1949/1972) himself considered – and in my view rightly so – a biophysical therapy, not a psychotherapy. It was probably the biophysical development of Reich's work Fonagy and Target had in mind when they made their remark about "neo-Reichian body-oriented psychotherapeutic perspective." Anthi here helps to sort out this confusion, but also highlights a frequently made mistake concerning the relevance of Reich's work to psychoanalysis and psychotherapy.

Psychotherapists inspired by Reich's work developed different therapeutic approaches, combining psychodynamic psychotherapy and aspects of Reichian and other forms of body-work (biophysical therapy techniques). In Norway and in some parts of Europe, this approach to therapy was as previously described termed character analytic vegetotherapy, preserving Reich's original terminology. Other variations in Europe went under the name of Biosynthesis (Boadella, 1987) and Biodynamic Analysis (Boyesen, 1976). In the U.S., the most widely known form has been Bioenergetic Analysis (Lowen, 1975).

Commenting on these post-Reichian developments Einar Dannevig (1995a) wrote that Wilhelm Reich's character analysis developed from Freudian psychoanalysis as a verbal method for reworking the patient's resistance to the analytic process. He further stated that what in Norway came to be known as character analytic vegetotherapy was the consequence Reich and his Norwegian students drew from the fact that the so-called character resistance obviously also manifested itself in neuromuscular hyper- and hypo-tensions. He continues:

> As his [Reich's] interest more and more was drawn to his cosmology and natural philosophy, the so-called orgone theory, he left character analysis and turned to a biophysical form of therapy, where the word and psychology had little place. Regrettably, most of his students followed him more or less wholeheartedly. Apart from Harald Schjelderup in Norway and Tage Philipson in Denmark none of his students took a clear position for character analysis. This in my opinion has created many confused and confusing therapies and therapists. (1995a, p. 1, my translation)

For my own part, I wrote that "the field of body oriented psychotherapy has much to gain by getting rid of the historical misunderstandings manifest in the field's biologisms. And instead take as its theoretical point of departure the psychology of non-verbal emotional behavior and bodily expression, or in other words Character Analysis" (Sletvold, 1996, p. 10).

So, I think, in agreement with Anthi and Dannevig, it is important to distinguish between character analysis and the later biophysical developments in Reich's thinking. In her groundbreaking paper on the body in psychoanalysis, *The Embodied Analyst in the Victorian Consulting Room*, Sue A. Shapiro (1996) addresses this issue. The first analysts to recognize the potential of the body on its own terms, she writes, were Reich and Ferenczi. In her view, Reich, in his classic work on character analysis, "come[s] close to integrating an understanding of mind and body" (p. 310). Referring to the criticism subsequently leveled at Reich's work, the result, she says, is that "direct attention to and manipulation of patients' bodies have been thoroughly condemned by psychoanalysts, and the heirs to his theories, including Lowen's bioenergic work . . . have been marginalized" (p. 310). Reich, like Freud, Shapiro further underlines, was a one-person theorist. Reich's omission of his own body and emotional state, in her opinion, reduces the applicability of his views to a specifically psychoanalytic inquiry. I agree with Shapiro in her evaluation of Reich as a basically one person/one body theorist. But in my opinion, it is possible to extend Reich's one-body perspective into a two-body perspective with great emphasis on the analyst's own embodied experience, hence my title, *The Embodied Analyst: From Freud and Reich to Relationality*. However, the confusion created by the combination of psychotherapy and elements of physical therapy still marks the field known as body-psychotherapy or similar names. I find Shapiro's (1996) analysis of the problems connected to the manipulation of the patient's body in a psychotherapeutic setting very much to the point. With great precision, she identifies the basic unanalyzed problem in therapies involving physical manipulation of the patient's body.

> Current research cited by Damasio corroborates my personal criticisms of bioenergetics – putting your face or your body into certain positions or configurations triggers certain emotions. The bioenergetic therapies I have seen mistake these created emotions for the release of real pent-up emotions. Their own impact in generating these emotions is not routinely explored. So although the patient is seen as a body and a mind, the patient is a reactive object, *a body that is being pushed to have certain experiences, not a body that is moving itself.* (p. 310, my italics)

The danger of confusing released with created emotions identified by Shapiro is a challenge for therapies using techniques that are directly aimed at changing emotional body states. These challenges were recently illustrated and discussed by Cornell (2009) and Shapiro (2009). Cornell opens his article *Stranger to Desire: Entering the Erotic Field* with these words: "Elizabeth and I lay on our backs, side by side on the carpet of my office. We were in close proximity to each other, but our bodies did not quite touch" (p. 75). Cornell then asked Elizabeth to notice any impulses within her body in relation to his and, if she wished, to explore any of those impulses through movement between her body and his. In her commentary, Shapiro describes her own bodily reaction as she read Cornell's article as anxious, tight, breath held. She put it into the following words:

> *I don't want to do this, why are you making me, I trust you but this feels weird and scary and I don't think I will feel any impulse, but what if I do? What do you want from me? What are you feeling in your body?* (p. 94)

In her discussion, Shapiro points to the problem Ferenczi (1933/1955) termed "the confusion of tongues" between children and adults, and finds it problematic to address early experience with the technique described by Cornell because "even though the infant's sensory experiences clearly penetrate and inform later sexual experiences, this influence goes both ways" (Shapiro, 2009, p. 96). She highlights her point with this question: "Under what circumstances do two adults lie down next to each other on the floor?" (p. 97).

Shapiro clarifies her own position with regard to the various body-oriented therapies, of which there is an enormous variety.

> If someone is out of touch with her body as Cornell describes Elizabeth to be, there are many alternative approaches to increasing her awareness of bodily sensations, of exploring her sexual experiences and capacities, that are less emotionally risky for both Elizabeth and Cornell. (2009, p. 99)

Shapiro agrees with Cornell that states of corporal awareness and opening are of importance to personality development, attachment styles, and sexuality. Indeed, all therapists would benefit greatly not only by studying microanalyses of mother-infant videotapes, but also by experiencing their own particular sensorimotor infrastructure and the powerful emotions that arise when this structure is addressed. "Currently, psychoanalytic training does not require a study of one's physical self equivalent to a personal analysis" (Shapiro, 2009, p. 100).

According to Shapiro's experience of engaging the body in psychoanalysis, one doesn't have to act on the patient's body in order to increase his or her awareness of his or her body. Much can be done through "a deep exploration and attunement to one's own physical sensations while in the presence of an other. Immediate and literal physical interactions with the analyst are rarely necessary" (2009, p. 100). Shapiro at the same time expresses as her belief that all treatments, whether or not there is touch, involve body-to-body communication. She and I share the belief that the more we, as therapists, are able to tune in to these experiences in ourselves and become aware of changes in our patients' bodies, the more we have to work with. "Our bodies speak incessantly. We are unconsciously processing this corporal speech all the time" (Shapiro, 2009, p. 100).

Shapiro states further that while body therapies that involve physical contact and psychoanalytic therapy are two modalities that do better separately than together, she has

> over the years, become increasingly comfortable giving patients a hug or finding some way of being in physical contact. . . . When someone is exceedingly dissociated, I might place a hand on his or her knee or a back when I am as certain as I can be that my touch is welcome and will not cause further dissociation. (2009, pp. 99–100)

Shapiro sees this supportive or grounding touch as different from bodily action aimed at opening up new experiences and behaviors. The questions Shapiro takes up are, in my opinion, important questions that we need to discuss and clarify as part of the unfolding considerations of embodiment in psychoanalysis and psychotherapy. These questions should not, in my opinion, be avoided as taboo or approached dogmatically, but with the kind of open-mindedness that the exchange between Cornell and Shapiro exemplifies.

Downing (1996) addresses this issue, giving the terms experiential and internal body techniques to interventions aimed at exploring embodied experience and ongoing movement. This is in contrast to what he calls external body techniques, where the therapist acts upon the patient's body either with his hands or by instructing the patient to make certain movements or adopt certain positions. It is the use of such external body techniques that has been characteristic of body-psychotherapies. In particular, several innovative new approaches to the treatment of trauma have emerged from body-psychotherapies, and should be recognized (Levine, 1997; Rothschild, 2000; Ogden, Minton, and Pain, 2006). *Bodies in*

Treatment (Anderson, 2008) includes many significant papers describing a whole range of "body techniques."

In this text, I will not be using external body techniques in the clinical illustrations presented and discussed. The work I present is about what Shapiro (1996) describes as "a body that is moving itself," rather than "a body that is being pushed to have certain experiences." But, I am not encouraging a taboo against external body techniques in psychotherapy and psychoanalysis. (History does not underpin the constructiveness of taboos.) The considerations above are meant to sharpen therapists' awareness of the difference and borderland between, on the one hand, ongoing bodily emotional interaction that is part of the process in any case, and, on the other, experiences that are more or less the result of interventions suggested by the therapist. As Shapiro points out, current research, explaining that experience is partly an image of the body's physical state, makes it easier to focus this issue. There is an important difference between changes brought about in the body by words and emotional communication, and by physical means. While reactions created by words and bodily emotional communication only work through associated emotional meanings, physical body movements additionally elicit emotional experiences as a consequence of the purely physical changes. In Shapiro's formulation, "putting your face or your body into certain positions or configurations triggers certain emotions" (p. 310).

Clinical and scientific advances over the last decades in the body-mind field create a new basis for evaluating the relationship between embodied psychoanalysis/psychotherapy on the one hand, and bodywork on the other. In the next chapter, I explore what Scandinavian, especially Norwegian, analysts and therapists have added to Reich's thinking about embodied character analysis. I also review recent developments in psychomotoric physiotherapy (Fadnes, Leira, & Brodal, 2010) focusing on movement and balance. Given a growing recognition of movement as foundational in psychoanalysis and psychotherapy, a new common ground with body therapies can emerge centered on "a body that is moving itself."

Chapter 4

The Norwegian character analytic tradition

The royal road to the unconscious is not the dream but the behavior.

(Schjelderup)

As we saw in previous chapters, Reich (and his work) became a *persona non grata* in the IPA community. Reich, for his part, lost much of his interest in psychoanalysis and character analysis toward the end of his stay in Norway and especially after relocating to the U.S. Yet the idea of embodied character analysis was not totally lost. Indeed, in Norway it remained a respected point of view, not least thanks to the efforts of the psychologist and analyst Harald Schjelderup and the Danish psychiatrist and analyst Tage Philipson. Both in their separate ways took an autonomous position on embodied character analysis. Both forfeited their friendship with Reich along with membership of the IPA.

After the Second World War, Schjelderup continued as chairman of the Norwegian Psychoanalytic Society, but it was no longer recognized by the IPA, which suspected it of a Reichian bias. Ola Raknes (1970) remained a loyal supporter of Reich and of his work in the U.S. Nic Waal pioneered child psychotherapy in Norway. Schjelderup, Philipson, Raknes, and Nic Waal were all popular training analysts in the postwar era. Some of their pupils founded in 1972 the Forum for Character Analytic Vegetotherapy. In 1999, the forum established the Norwegian Character Analytic Institute. The work of these four analysts, plus that of a fifth, Trygve Braatøy, will be explored in this chapter, as will the roles of the Norwegian Psychoanalytic Society and the Norwegian Character Analytic Institute in the formation of embodied analysis in Norway.

Harald Schjelderup

Schjelderup studied physics and experimental psychology before becoming professor of philosophy in 1922, at the age of 26. He studied psychoanalysis in Vienna from the middle of the 1920s, and in 1928 he became the first professor of psychology in Norway.

Schjelderup had probably heard about Reich in Vienna in the late 1920s. However that may be, after Reich fled to Denmark in 1933, Schjelderup invited him and other Jewish analysts to attend a meeting in Oslo, scheduled for the 1934 Easter break. As stated earlier, Schjelderup rallied behind Reich at the Lucerne Congress, and organized facilities for him to work at Oslo University when his Danish work permit expired. Schjelderup's enthusiasm for character analysis informs an article he published in 1936 where he writes: "The royal road to what is known as the unconscious is not the *dream* but the *behaviour*. . . . In my opinion character analysis represents the most important advance in psychotherapy since Freud" (1936, p. 649, my translation).[1] His enthusiasm was obviously shared. In March 1935, Reich writes to his girl-friend Elsa Lindenberg,

> My darling, my Elschen,
>
> I am in a great mood again. I just arrived home at 1 a.m. from a seminar evening at which Schjelderup gave an excellent report on a character-analytic case. It was the first time in the twelve years that I have been fighting alone for my technique that another person has reported on a case in a manner in which I recognize my work, my battles and struggles. To be quite honest with you, I was a bit touched. (Reich, 1994, p. 35)

Schjelderup's independent position

While the character analytical technique excited Schjelderup, he disagreed with what he termed the *sexualistic* theories of both Freud and Reich. He proposed a theory of neurosis centered on suppressive discipline during childhood and traumatic experiences of every kind. To Schjelderup, neuroses derived essentially from the helplessness and the anxiety caused by the traumatic event or circumstance. After comparing "the analytic methods," he concludes that analyses of hysteria and anxiety neurosis could start with Freudian free association technique, though in most cases he found a combination of character analysis and "muscular analysis" to be the most effective approach. "Practical and reliable application of these methods requires us, however, to relieve them of the special theory of neurosis invested in them by Reich, and give them a new design" (1941/1988, p. 84, my translation). This position offended Reich, and as far as I am aware, they ceased to have contact following Reich's August 1939 letter to Schjelderup just after arriving in New York.

> Now that I have relocated to New York I must approach you with a request that has important consequences for clearly delineating the existing views in psychological research. The most important changes and amendments in the development of psychology took place during the last six years in Scandinavia. On the theoretical side they have been grouped together under the concept "sex economy", and on the practical side they come under the heading

of "character-analytic vegetoterapy". At the core of these changes lies my orgasm theory, which asserts on the basis of clinical experience that disturbances in the autonomic vegetative functioning of orgastic experience constitute the core mechanism that produces and maintain the source of energy for all types of psychological disorders. Character armouring and muscular armouring have been detected and formulated as the most important result of this disruption in the equilibrium of sexual energy. One can have whatever views one wishes on this subject. You have on several occasions publicly disassociated yourself not only from orgasme theory but also from my sociological explanation of the origin of sexual suppression, which is essential for character analysis. Since I am responsible for the cohesion and also for the further development of my theory, with all its consequences, I must ask you to refrain in the future from calling your technique "character analysis". (1994, pp. 238–239)

Reich reiterates his theoretical convictions and ends the letter by extending his best wishes, "certain that you will not refuse to help clarify scientific views" (p. 240).

So while Schjelderup had a high opinion of character analysis, he was critical of Reich's theoretical and experimental work. Adopting an independent position both in relation to Reich and the IPA, he developed a rather unique relational perspective in the 1930s, criticizing both Freud and Reich for overestimating the role of sexual drive and underestimating the effects of real trauma.

During the analysis of neurotics you really find a lot of infantile sexual tendencies, sexual fantasies, and things that point in the direction of the oedipal complex and the castration complex. On closer enquiry it turns out that these sexual complexes, at least in many cases, are not the cause of the neurotic disturbance, but that their strong development to the contrary is an effect of inhibitions brought about in other ways. It turns out that every general inhibition of activity and impulsivity has an effect also on the sexual development and brings disturbances in the ability to fully experience sexuality as adults. (1941/1988, p. 101, my translation)

Prior to the outbreak of the Second World War, Schjelderup was associate editor of *Internationale Zeitschrift für Psychoanalyse*, the official organ of IPA of which Freud was editor-in-chief. During the Nazi occupation of Norway, he led the resistance of academics and staff at the University of Oslo and was arrested and interned. After the war, he continued as chair of the Norwegian Psychoanalytic Society. By then, however, the Society had been excommunicated by the IPA for its alleged Reichian bias. The Society was reinstated in 1975, a year after Schjelderup's death. Schjelderup's postwar work includes important research on the lasting effects of psychoanalytic treatment (1955). This was probably the first major longitudinal study of psychoanalytic patients.

Schjelderup's focus on the patient's subjectivity

Schjelderup's view of the therapeutic action of psychoanalysis as experiential rather than interpretative can be seen in an article he wrote on the personality-changing processes of psychoanalytic treatment. "In preference to theoretical explanations, some illustrative examples will give a clear idea of *the emotional processes in the analysis – not as interpreted by the analyst, but as experienced by the patient*" (1956, p. 51, my italics).

The following is from one of his examples, an analysis of a female patient who suffered from a severe compulsion neurosis. The patient's feeling that others were always preferred culminated in a particular episode, "a turning-point in her development." At this point, Schjelderup lets his patient continue in her own words.

> I have had what has surely been the most frantic and worst night of the whole analysis. . . . The full realization that mother rejected me. . . . I suppose I was between three and four years of age – there was nothing dramatic – but I staked everything: "listen to me, mother!". . . She didn't slap me; but I felt the complete rejection and her hostility. . . . I went up to my brother's room . . . cried and cried till I was worn out. . . . When I went out again, the only option I could see was not to need anybody – since then I have been in a panic lest I should grow fond of anyone . . . I have raged against you for dragging me into this . . . Not until quite recently have I experienced myself in the analysis like that, as quite little. This has got to the bottom of it all . . . all that wishing to be a man, and the sexual difficulties, are secondary, a result of the destructive effect of my rejection. (1956, p. 58)

In this and other illustrations of the analytic process Schjelderup focuses on how the experience of the patient unfolds without offering his interpretation. So in emphasizing the importance of the patient's own experience, as a coauthor with the analyst, he foreshadows contemporary intersubjective and relational understanding. The quotation also illustrates his view that sexual problems are often secondary rather than the primary causes of neurosis. He lets the patient herself formulate the connection between her main symptoms and the infantile conflict in this way.

> I hated mother because she had rejected me – I could have burnt her, set fire to everyone – there wasn't a thing I wouldn't have done – later, under the influence of the compulsion, I had to prove that I had done nothing wrong – but I had such a sense of guilt for wanting to do it – I can see the connection now. (p. 58)

Schjelderup's global analysis

Unconscious infantile conflict can be expressed in three ways, Schjelderup believed: through neurotic symptoms and symbolic representations; through character formation; and finally through the development of distinct bodily, muscular, and respiratory patterns. He wrote:

> An unresolved infantile conflict has thus "offshoots," and in a variety of ways it exerts an influence upon later development. Schematically we can distinguish between three different aspects, or lines, of this development: One line goes in the direction of symbolic representation of the unconscious in dreams, neurotic symptoms, and other "automatic behaviour." A second line leads to formation of character, and a third to muscular behaviour. These are abstractions, of course. Man is a unity. And character structure, experience, and muscular behaviour cannot be treated as separate components. (p. 49)

"Classical" analysis, Schjelderup goes on to say, centers on symbolic representation while a more direct beginning is possible by addressing character attitudes or muscular behavior. This principal distinction between the analysis of symbolic and nonsymbolic representations has only been revived, as far as I can see, in recent years in the models proposed by Beebe, Knoblauch, Rustin, and Sorter (2005), Bucci (2005), Knoblauch (2000), Stern (2004), and others reviewed in the previous chapter.

Summing up his view on the therapeutic action of psychoanalysis Schjelderup states that even though character analysis and vegetotherapy are spoken of as fundamentally new in psychoanalysis, "what we have are special developments of technical viewpoints which find their natural place within the *global analysis* . . . into which psychoanalysis has increasingly developed" (1956, p. 50). By global analysis, Schjelderup is referring to an integration of "the analytic methods," but also to "a complete reorganization of the field of personality."

> An emotional "breakthrough", accompanied by the revival of the underlying conflicts, is often a great relief, but it does not itself effect a lasting change. . . . Only gradually does a real rectification take place. This rectification is a very complex process: reconditioning of earlier emotional reactions, working through of infantile cravings, admission of new feeling and fancies, and the understanding of connections which have previously been inaccessible to the patient's adult reason. Actually what takes place is a complete reorganization of the field of personality, as the dynamic conditions are changed. A decisive part is played by the change in the patient's spontaneous *self-feeling*, and together with this the change in the spontaneous *relation to other people*. (p. 60)

One analytic method cannot be regarded as more correct than the others, according to Schjelderup, and none of the different forms of analysis is, generally speaking, any more suitable than one of the others. In this way, he presaged contemporary research according to which no particular method or technique seems to be decisive for therapeutic change. And there is also a similarity between his analytic attitude and contemporary relational thinking on tolerating complexity, uncertainty, and ambiguity. This is Schjelderup:

In some cases of compulsive neuroses and set "character neuroses," which are hardly accessible to the more "classical" analysis, a "character-analytic" or "muscular" technique may prove more effective. But what is more important than a specific technique is a high degree of elasticity and tolerance on the part of the analyst. Any dogmatism and one-sidedness in his attitude hinders that liberation and integration of personality which is the goal of analysis.

The main principle governing the analytic treatment seems, therefore to be the same, even if there may be great differences as regards the purely technical form of procedure. *The corrective emotional experiences in the transference situation play a centrally important role.* (pp. 50–51, my italics)

Tage Philipson and embodied identification

When Tage Philipson, a young Danish psychiatrist, traveled to Berlin in 1933 to meet Reich, it was only to learn that he was too late: Reich had already fled to Denmark. Back in Copenhagen, Philipson soon started studying with Reich, and the two became good friends. He worked closely with Reich in the early days of vegetotherapy. Reich had come to see muscular armoring as functionally identical with the character armor, the term he had given to character defenses. As a consequence of this understanding, Reich started to palpate tense muscles much like a physiotherapist, focusing especially on respiration with a view to eliciting the so-called orgasm-reflex. The orgasm-reflex was proof, he believed, of achieved orgastic potency and successful analysis. But although verbal analysis and body-work proceeded together, Philipson was concerned about the approach's dualistic nature, the continued separation of mind and body. He therefore started to explore ways to integrate the new focus on the body with character analysis.

Building on Reich's notion of inner "plasmatic" imitation, Philipson developed a theory of embodied identification (1951). He came to see embodied identifications as crucial for the development of neuroses.

When the more superfluous neurotic traits are dissolved . . . it turns out that patient's expression and appearance are marked by such an accurate rendering of the parent, most often the mother, who played the major part in the developmental arrest, that you as therapist can describe the person concerned. (Philipson, 1951, p. 2, my translation)

These identifications come about, according to Philipson, because of a tendency in children to unconsciously identify with the bodily attitudes of parents they least tolerate. He argued that bodily traits that were seen as hereditary could just as well be a result of such identifications. Philipson began imitating his patients. Marit Nordby (2009, personal communication) started analysis with Philipson in the early 1950s. She recalls how at one point in her analysis she suddenly recognized her own mother in the way Philipson was sitting, and became aware that she was unconsciously, and much against her own wish, adopting her mother's way of sitting on the edge of the chair.

In his exploration of embodied identification, Philipson looked for a "common denominator" expressing both the patient's character and physical attitude. This common denominator could sometimes be the name of an animal like fox or cat, or a relational term like peacekeeper, suggestive of the type of family role expected of and played by the patient.

> This – the common denominator – is nothing you come to by using your head. You have it some place within yourself, and the more you are able to function in contact with the patient, the more you are able to "to live within" him, really make yourself identical with him, then this – the common denominator – comes by itself. And it is from this position you really succeed with the treatment." (Quoted in Strand, 1991, p. 165, my translation)

Philipson found that the verbal naming of this common denominator functioned best when the patient coined the term. Nils Strand (1991), who studied with Philipson in the 1950s, has explained the importance of identification with the patient.

> You can never identify too much with people you want to help. But you can forget you are doing it, and that is no good. . . . Competent psychotherapy depends on the therapist's sensitivity, and [the therapist's] contact with his sensitivity. No therapist, no human being for that matter, can be too sensitive. What is decisive is the strength to contain the sensitivity. (p. 165, my translation)

In reviewing Philipson's conception of embodied identifications in light of recent developments in psychoanalysis and interpersonal neurobiology, Andersen (2007) discusses embodied identifications in relation to conceptions of projective identification and empathy and points to possible clinical advantages of being able to differentiate these embodied countertransference experiences in the analytical situation. The contributions of Philipson and Andersen are consistent with Racker's (1968) discussion of concordant identificatory processes. Philipson's theory of embodied identification also in many ways presages recent theorizing by neuroscientists and developmental researchers. Referring to research on mirroring mechanisms, Gallese (2009) writes,

> All of these intriguing findings link to our understanding of broader contours of intersubjectivity, clarifying how social identification has a multilayered embodied basis. . . . The discovery of mirror neurons provide a new empirically based notion of intersubjectivity, viewed first and foremost as intercorporeity . . . as the main source of knowledge we gather about others. (p. 523)

Love and sexuality

Philipson's thinking took another crucial step when he came to see love, not sexuality, as the basic factor in the development of character and neurosis. Reich was, as we have seen, at least as committed to "the sexual etiology of the neuroses," the libido theory, as Freud. However, like Freud he often spoke of love instead of sexuality in his writings. Although Reich could write about "the deeply buried needs for love . . . in every person" (1942/1978, p. 168), he could not tolerate Philipson's view on the primacy of love. Their friendship and their working relationship ended. Philipson was very upset by the breach, but continued his work and edited a two-volume book titled *Kærlighedslivet* [Love Life] (1952). The role he ascribed to love resembles what we today see as the role of attachment. Philipson died in 1961 at 53 years old. Nils Strand (1991) worked to preserve and expand Philipson's legacy in Norway. In the 1980s, he became the author's training analyst and teacher of character analysis.

Nic Waal

Nic Waal (also known as Nic Hoel after her first husband) was one of several Norwegian students of psychoanalysis in Berlin around 1930. Her training analyst there was Salome Kempner. Nic Waal also became one of Norway's first child psychiatrists. From 1934 onwards, she was among Reich's most committed students. She describes her experience of the situation after the split with IPA.

> Reich, who, was now excluded, went fanatically over to one side, while the orthodox therapists went to the opposite. Reich kept a rigid frame of reference, forgetting Freud's own campaign that "libido is sexuality but not genitality." But in this fighting Reich detected the nonverbal communication through bodily language, which later became a part of modern thinking. The orthodox therapists were in the same way, on their side, as rigid, forgetting Freud's first writings. Reich went on describing erotic sexuality and loving sexuality in neurosis. (1958, p. 43)

Writing this in 1958, Nic Waal was possibly exaggerating the case when she said that "nonverbal communication through bodily language" had already become a staple of modern thinking. She gives, however, a very positive evaluation of her own treatment with Reich compared to her previous therapists. Before starting in therapy with Reich, she had been treated by Schjelderup (while he was a classical analyst) and Fenichel in addition to Kempner.

> Finally I started to get treatment from Reich, and he detected at once – quite unlike my previous therapists, that I had used a lively and vital eroticism as a defense against aggression and depression. He detected at once also that I had

severe problems around aggression, that I was falsely kind and a false "yes-sayer". It was a terrible revelation, but I knew he was right. (Waal, 1958, p. 43)

Nic Waal also valued Reich's development of vegetotherapy, but grew critical of his orgone and cosmic energy theories. Above all, she felt that to evaluate these theories she would have to start a completely new training in physics and biology. Instead she wanted to devote her energy to child psychiatry in Norway. Commemorating Reich, she summarizes her experience of him like this.

> As a leader he combined in former days good leadership with a democratic attitude to his pupils. . . . Later he changed. The more the official fight went on, the more he became a hierarchical leader and a very dominant one. . . . My opposition, which was apt to come, was looked upon as treachery or cowardliness. (Waal, 1958, p. 46)

During the 1950s until her death in 1961, Nic Waal made an enormous contribution to child psychotherapy and child psychiatric teamwork in Norway (Waal, 1955). She established a psychiatric institution for children known today as Nic Waal's Institute. Indeed, this is where many of the first generation of clinical psychologists in Norway received their clinical training.

Her most specific contribution was the creation of a body-oriented diagnostic method known as *Nic Waal's Somatic Psychodiagnostic Method* (Grieg, Rasmussen, & Waal, 1957), based among other things on evaluating the patient's reactions to the passive movement of the limbs. Later in this chapter I shall describe her efforts to save Jewish analysts and children from Nazi persecution.

Ola Raknes

Ola Raknes, originally a philologist with a dissertation in the psychology of religion, also studied psychoanalysis in Berlin around 1930. His training analyst was Karen Horney. A couple of years after Reich's arrival in Oslo, Raknes started in therapy with him. This therapy was probably one of the first where Reich practiced consequently his new vegetotherapy. For Raknes, the experience was very positive. Indeed, it marked a turning point; from then on he remained a devoted student of Reich for the rest of his life. His devotion is evident in his book *Wilhelm Reich and Orgonomy* (1970). The following passage gives an impression of his position.

> [I]t seems as if there was no other way of discovering this basis of health – free biological pulsation – except through psychoanalysis, character analysis, and orgone therapy – this was, at least the way taken by the research. Personally, I do not think that this long road will be necessary in the future. I think that a biotherapy which directly aims at freeing biological pulsation will be

both the shortest and the most secure way of healing the biopathies, particularly the neuroses. (Raknes, 1970, p. 128)

Raknes was, to my knowledge, the only Norwegian analyst influenced by Reich who came to consider himself an orgonomist. He practiced vegetotherapy, which he also called biotherapy, until his death in 1975. However, he was a warm and tolerant person who, unlike Reich, did not require his students to accept every one of his views. He came to be an influential figure in the mental health field in Norway in the 1950s and 1960s, especially among young psychologists. I think it is also fair to say that his radicalism made other Reichian analysts and therapists in Norway seem more mainstream.

A special feature of vegetotherapy, as it was practiced by Raknes and some of his students was that patients were treated in their underwear, and sometimes completely naked. And most remarkably, some of his female patients, including psychologists and psychotherapists, were given vaginal massage as part of their treatment. What prompted Raknes to perform vaginal massage I don't know. To my knowledge, Reich never practiced nor recommended it. However, Starr and Aron (2011) have discovered recently that genital stimulation had been more or less standard treatment for female hysteria for 2,000 years, culminating in the final decades of the nineteenth century. (Recently also shown in the movie *Hysteria*.) It was not therefore a new Reich-inspired invention. However, vaginal massage, the more widely known practice of having the patient undress, and the theoretical rationale of liberating repressed sexuality, created controversy around Raknes and his students. But it also seems like such methods were more easily accepted in the sexually puritanical and "innocent" 1950s than it became later.

Trygve Braatøy: Psychoanalysis and Physiotherapy

A review of Reich's influence on psychoanalysis and psychotherapy in Norway must acknowledge the work of the psychiatrist and psychoanalyst Trygve Braatøy. He was a contemporary of Schjelderup, Philipson, Waal, and Raknes. His training analyst was Otto Fenichel, and he did not consider himself a student of Reich. However, he valued Reich's character analytic technique, but he rated Freud very highly as well. And he was particularly inspired by Ferenczi's work. Braatøy was deeply interested in finding ways to include bodily phenomena in psychoanalysis, and he described several ways in which this could be done, not least in his *Fundamentals of Psychoanalytic Technique* (1954a), published in the U.S. The reception of this book within the "official" psychoanalytical community is worth noting (Knutsen, 2012). In a review in *International Journal of Psychoanalysis* Markillie (1955) gave the book a pasting. Braatøy, the reviewer maintained, had misunderstood central aspects of analytic thought; the title of the book should have been the one that was also on the cover, "A fresh appraisal to the methods of psychotherapy."

It worried Braatøy that psychoanalysts had become listeners rather than observers. Observing and making use of visual information were essential, he said, to Freud's discoveries in Studies on Hysteria. He quotes Freud:

> In such cases, the patient states that he has no associations, and is right. One will guard oneself against being in the wrong if one makes a rule of *not letting the face play of the patient who lies quietly on the coach out of one's sight.* One learns without difficulty to separate the psychic ease, when a reminiscence does not occur, from the tension and signs of affect called forth in the patient by the defense against reminiscences coming to the surface. (Quoted in Braatøy, 1954a, p. 111, my italics)

Too much stress, Braatøy suggested, had been laid on Freud's view that it should be celebrated as a "triumph for the treatment if he [the therapist] can bring about that something that the patient wishes to discharge in action is disposed of through the work of remembering" (Freud, 1914/1958d, p. 153). Formalized in psychoanalytic technique, this attitude had focused the psychoanalyst's attention too one-sidedly on the patient's words or lack of words.

> It has made them into listeners – not observers. My analyst, Otto Fenichel, sat in a low chair behind the head of the couch where he could not see my face. When I questioned him about this, he argued that he was so trained in listening to patients that, by their words, their way of speaking or of not speaking, he could accurately gauge the emotional tension in them. (Braatøy, 1954a, p. 110)

Braatøy did not find his analyst's answer satisfying. Freud had extensive training in neurology, he said, before he developed psychoanalysis. It was a kind of clinical experience that many later analysts lacked. It had enabled Freud to describe the meaning of hysteria and nervous disorders "*not* with the help of the patients' verbal information *but on the basis of* the neurologist's detailed and precise description of *the differences between the organic and the hysteric movements*" (Braatøy, 1954a, p. 111).

Braatøy speculated further on the reasons why visual information was so comprehensively ignored in psychoanalysis and psychotherapy. Was it because psychoanalysts, being "intellectuals," were listeners and talkers rather than observers, he wondered. But then he added,

> It has also to do with surprises and shocks in Freud's early psychotherapeutic work when some of the patients suddenly overstepped the boundaries of the therapeutic relationship. These shocks were undoubtedly serious in a work which had (and has) continually to be conducted on the borderlines of accepted morality. With this background, it is easy to understand that, in teaching, Freud felt inclined to stress as rules and regulations the limits set to the patients' movements and actions. (1954a, pp. 111–112)

Braatøy was concerned with the limitations imposed on psychoanalytic under-standing by the lack of visual information in psychoanalytic literature. It was due, he believed, to the restriction of movement connected with technical rules and tra-ditions. Braatøy illustrates the impact of this tradition by citing Ferenczi's paper on *Technical Difficulties in the Analysis of a Case of Hysteria* (Ferenczi, 1919/1950). Far into the treatment, Ferenczi still felt it necessary to adhere to the classic rules regarding movement and failed therefore to observe what he could have seen in the first hour on the couch: that this female patient invariably lay with her legs crossed. "But only after all this time did an accidental glance at the manner in which she lay on the sofa convince me that she kept her legs crossed during the whole hour" (Ferenczi, 1919/1950, p. 120). This at last – after two unsuccessful attempts at analysis – opened up for an exploration of the patient's sexual conflict.

Braatøy noticed that candidates starting training often found it strange and dif-ficult to be seated out of sight of the patient, while senior analysts seemed to be quite comfortable with this arrangement.

> Some overworked, aging analysts feel the deep chair behind the patient's couch not a prison but as a position where from which he at last can whisper to his deceased mother the famous epitaph: "Now you have peace – and so have I." If one asks such a person to change, to look in addition to listening, to rearrange the situation if need be, one may provoke intense irritation. (1954a, p. 116)

So Braatøy argued that analysis and psychotherapy should not be restricted to comments on verbal utterances, but should be extended to nonverbal behavior as well. This expansion of analytic attention to include bodily reactions he felt was important because it activated and enlarged the therapist's field of vision. "In intellectual and intellectualizing patients it is helpful because this direct approach may break or go beneath the play of words which goes on over and around such chronic and habitual tensions" (1954a, p. 121). These – intellectual – patients will at first tend to react with irritation – "don't pick on me," while more hysterically inclined patients will immediately welcome comments on body behavior.

> They will feel the sensitive approach to their postures as a liberation because they are constitutionally "performers." They are not intellectuals interested in verbal expressions and communications; they more closely resemble athletes, dancers, actors. Their basic need is immediate action and bodily expression. Breaking the tension in relation to movement and action in analysis means, therefore, returning in a more analytic way to the clientele originally respon-sible for the first psychoanalytic discoveries. (1954a, p. 121)

Hysterical patients, Braatøy observed, rarely come to psychoanalysis on their own initiative because they do not believe that pains or bodily tensions can be talked away. "They are right. Psychoanalysis acts in such cases by liberating emo-tions, breaking tense postures, permitting forbidden movements" (1954a, p. 121).

"Reformulating psychoanalysis from these non-verbal angles will break a dam between industrial medicine, psychosomatics, the clientele of osteopaths, physiotherapists, and psychoanalysis proper" (p. 121).

A biological view allows one to understand the mind as a function of the body, Braatøy noted, and in clinical work one discovers that repression, inhibition, defense, and resistance equate with bodily tension.

> Seeing this, the analyst will further discover that influencing the patient's attitudes and postures – as far as they are determined by tensions inappropriate to the situation – is essential to an understanding of how psychoanalysis acts. It acts by changing the attitude (posture) of the patient. This *(physio)therapeutic work* [my italics] has always been an integral part of psychoanalysis. In classic psychoanalysis, it goes on from the beginning of the first hour to the end of the last *with the help of the couch*. But remember: the couch is an instrument, not a commandment. (1954a, pp. 116–117)

In more ordinary psychoanalytic cases, Braatøy says, he waits until the patient has settled down to a characteristic way of behaving during the session, and especially when this behavior appears to repeats itself "like a broken record," before communicating somatic observations to the patient. He may start by asking, "Are you aware that you're always keeping your legs crossed (eyes focused; fingers fidgeting with your tie; head turned to the left)?" (1954a, p. 144). With patients whose general tension is so great that it more or less blocks them completely, including their ability to express themselves verbally, Braatøy might immediately comment on the tension and interpret it in terms of fear, anxiety, and embarrassment. And he might permit the patient to sit up or make other changes.

> If these adaptations do not give sufficient help, I change the analytic procedure into something resembling direct physiotherapy. With passive movements, and concentration on local muscular tensions, I try to help the patient relax while at the same time release his breathing. This is likely to call forth emotional outbursts – laughter, crying – and with the help of this catharsis vocalization can lead to verbal information. (1954a, p.144)

There is a striking resemblance between Reich's technical leap from character analysis to vegetotherapy and Braatøy's advocacy of "psychoanalytic physiotherapy." The difference is that Braatøy argues purely technically, making no reference to Reich's sex economy theory.

Commenting more generally on physiotherapy and osteopathy, Braatøy made the following observation: "Every physiotherapist and osteopath receives confessions and more or less intimate information during treatment. Nobody seems to know that this is *because* of the treatment, because this aspect is not included in the theory of the manipulations" (1954a, p. 144).

Collaboration with physiotherapist Adel Büllow-Hansen

Instead of continuing his own physiotherapeutic work, Braatøy started working systematically with the physiotherapist Adel Büllow-Hansen. Together they
founded psychomotor physiotherapy, which became an officially recognized and
influential specialty in Norwegian health care (Bunkan, 2003; Ekerholt, 2010).
Michael Heller gives a broad review of developments in Norway in the borderland
between body-work and psychotherapy in what he refers to as *The Golden Age of
Body Psychotherapy in Oslo* (Heller, 2007a/b, 2012).

A promising new development took place recently as a result of the work of
psychomotor physiotherapists Britt Fadnes and Kirsti Leira, and neuroscientist
Per Brodal (2010). From focusing directly on respiration and muscular tension
(much as in vegetotherapy), they promote awareness of minute body movements
(proprioception) and balance. Awareness and control of the body's rhythmic
movement improves bodily and mental balance and frees up respiration spontaneously (Fadnes, Leira, & Brodal, 2010).

It should also be noted that Braatøy inspired a form of body psychotherapy
in Denmark called Biodynamic Analysis. This group developed a very extensive
method of testing the body's muscular tensions and correlating muscular hypo and
hyper tension patterns with character structure (Marcher & Fish, 2010). Braatøy's
work has had a lasting effect, above all, on the development of psychosomatic and
psychomotor physiotherapy in Norway and body psychotherapy in Denmark. But
his influence on mainstream psychoanalysis and psychotherapy in the 1950s and
1960s, as well as later on, is limited. The *zeitgeist* was not in favor of the body-
based and character analytic views of people like Braatøy and Schjelderup, it was
in favor of the ego psychology of Hartman.

The Norwegian Psychoanalytic Society

Psychoanalysts Per Anthi and Svein Haugsgjerd (2013) and the historian Harard F.
Nilsen (2013) have recently reviewed the history of the Norwegian Psychoanalytic
Society in the years 1933 to 1945, with a special emphasis on the efforts of Norwegian analysts to rescue Jewish and left-wing Austrian and German analysts from Nazi
persecution. The essential elements of the story are as follows: In February 1933, Hitler was appointed *Reichskansler*. By April, the *Gleichschaltung* laws were passed,
requiring all professional organizations to be *judenfrei*. As most of the members of the
German Psychoanalytic Society were Jewish, a mass emigration of psychoanalysts
took place, first from Germany and later from central Europe. It was in this climate
that Schjelderup invited a group of German Jewish psychoanalysts to Oslo during
Easter 1934 to discuss the idea of immigrating to Norway. The meeting took place at
Schjelderup's Department of Psychology at the University of Oslo and among those
present were Otto Fenichel, Wilhelm and Annie Reich, George Gerö, Edith Gyömrö
(Glück), Lotte Liebeck (later Bernstein), Stefi Pedersen, Edith Jacobson, and Nic

Waal. They drafted a resolution condemning fascism and anti-Semitism to be read at the IPA Congress in Lucerne in August. In the summer of 1934, the Austrian/German emigrant group of psychoanalysts in Oslo consisted of Wilhelm Reich, Otto Fenichel, Stefi Pedersen, Lotte Liebeck, Paul Bernstein, and several others. Another political refugee was Willy Brandt, future chancellor of Germany, who socialized and worked politically with the group, in particular Reich (Anthi & Haugsgjerd, 2013).

Following Edith Jacobson's arrest by the Gestapo on October 24, 1935, her former training analyst, Otto Fenichel, worked with an extensive network of politically committed analysts to campaign for her release from custody. In November 1935, as a consequence of Fenichel's campaign, Ernest Jones, then president of IPA, sent Nic Waal on secret missions to Berlin, Prague, and Vienna to assess Jacobson's condition. In Vienna she tried to persuade Anna Freud, seemingly in vain, that Jacobson was a genuine psychoanalyst and not a political militant. After falling seriously ill in prison, Jacobsen was released in 1938 for treatment in a hospital. On April 3, Ola Raknes traveled to Leipzig with a pledge to marry Jacobson, entitling her to an emigration permit. In the event, the permit was denied. Further efforts of several Norwegian analysts and others enabled Edith Jacobson to flee Germany in 1938 (Anthi & Haugsgjerd, 2013).

On April 9, 1945, Germany invaded Norway. The Norwegian army tried to fight the occupants. The analysts Trygve Braatøy and Johannes Landmark participated as army doctors, and Landmark was killed in combat on May 1, 1940. At the very start of the occupation, *Reichspsychiater*, Prof. Mattias Heinrich Göring, Hermann Göring's cousin, arrived in Norway to regulate the psychoanalytical profession. Chairman of the Norwegian Psychoanalytic Society, Harald Schjelderup, made the decision to dissolve the society. Learning from the experience of the German Psychoanalytic Society and Berlin Psychoanalytic Institute under the Nazi regime, Schjelderup decided to remove or destroy the archives and any sensitive information. During the first two years of the war, Schjelderup organized the resistance movement at the University of Oslo. In 1943, he was arrested by the Gestapo, imprisoned, and sent to a concentration camp.

In October 1942, all registered Jews in Norway were arrested and shipped off to Stettin, Poland; their final destination would be Auschwitz. Paul Bernstein was one of them. He died in Auschwitz. In November 1942, a raid took place on Jewish women. In an escape masterminded by Nic Waal, 15 young Jewish orphans, sent to Oslo after the annexation of Sudetenland, managed to flee to Sweden. Associates of the Norwegian Society, Stefi Pedersen, Lotte Bernstein, and Nina Hackel, escaped in the same operation. Other Jews were saved by being taken into hospitals with false identities and medical conditions for later escape to Sweden. The chief psychiatrist at Ullevål Hospital in Oslo, Haakon Sætre, collaborated closely with analysts before and during the war, especially referring many patients to the non-medical analyst Schjelderup. Sætre was arrested by the Gestapo and executed on February 8, 1945, for hiding Jews in his psychiatric ward (Anthi & Haugsgjerd, 2013).

After the war, it was learned that the Norwegian Society had been excluded from the IPA during the war. The official explanation was that it had not paid fees between 1940 and 1945. In 1953, the Norwegian Society tried to re-join the IPA at the Congress in London, but the application was refused. In the words of the president of the IPA, Heinz Hartmann, "A group of psychoanalysts in Norway has asked to be accepted as a Component Society. Among them are a few who do not practice analysis, but something else – a new technique" (1954, p. 278). Braatøy reacted strongly to Hartmann's allegations and presented a short history of the Norwegian Society. He emphasized "the difficulty of breaking off cooperation with certain members for scientific reasons in peacetime after having cooperated with them in times of extreme external danger during the war" (Braatøy, 1954b, p. 278). When Braatøy asked them to explain the exclusion of the Norwegian group, Hartmann said, "The decision is merely postponed until the Norwegian group reaches proper standards for membership" (1954, p. 278). What Braatøy might not have realized was that he himself and Schjelderup were the ones considered guilty of the "new technique" and of not adhering to "proper standards." In light of the history of the Norwegian analysts before and during the Second World War, the attitude and action of the IPA were, in my opinion, disgraceful and obnoxious.

In the decades after World War II, the Norwegian Psychoanalytic Society made repeated efforts to convince IPA that it was no longer under Reichian influence, but it was only in 1975 that it regained full membership (Alnaes, 1993). All the same, several members continued to attend to nonverbal expressions and bodily experience. This is reflected in the work of Killingmo (1990, 2007) and Anthi (1983, 1986, 1995, 2007), among others, though Reich and character analysis are not referred to frequently. Recently, this situation has changed. In a new textbook on psychoanalytic therapy, Gullestad and Killingmo (2013) describe their perspective as *relational character analysis*, explaining that they borrowed the term from Josephs (1995).

Anthi and Haugsgjerd (2013) summarize their own contemporary character analytic technique in the following way:

> If we neglect the basic tool of clinical science – our visual observations – our analytic practice could acquire an intellectual bias. Various forms of nonverbal behavior could be regarded as equivalents to free association. Psychoanalysis had always been a form of "vegetotherapy" in Freud's sense – that the treatment will not have effect unless the affects of the psychic conflict are mobilized (i.e. the vegetative nervous system). Besides, it might be useful to sit at the head of the couch in such a way that one could better observe the patient's different nonverbal behavior and investigate how these body-based phenomena suggest significant early experiences. Specific preverbal experiences, nonverbal expressions, or what we today call implicit and procedural manifestations, could be stored and take root in a given *way* of behaving, relating or speaking. Such specific formal behavior expressions could be explored by bringing the patient's attention to them, enabling the patient to associate

with their actual somatic sensations and body attitudes, thus experiencing them more concretely and tangibly. Norwegian analysts stress the importance of observing *how* verbal and nonverbal communications are expressed, assuming that the formal characteristics suggest their origin. Consequently, analysis of the specific formal qualities of the verbal and nonverbal material will often lead to the unconscious content of a given conflict. One may say that the integration of character analytic technique and the classical analytical approach represents a particular trait of Norwegian psychoanalysis. (2013)

What Anthi and Haugsgjerd are describing here is precisely the "new technique" that Hartmann referred to back in 1953 as the reason for refusing to renew the Norwegian Society's membership of the IPA. It was not until the 1975 IPA Congress in London, 30 years after the war and one year after the death of Schjelderup, that the Norwegian Society regained status as a component society of the IPA. In the intervening years, members of the Norwegian association did their best to convince the IPA that they were no longer practicing anything that deviated from IPA-approved standards. But, as we have seen, some members surreptitiously kept the character analytic approach alive, until today it can again be practiced in the open, and even be published in the official organ of the IPA.

Norwegian Character Analytic Institute

All the same, several members of the Norwegian Psychoanalytic Society were against making concessions to IPA standards. Ola Raknes, Nic Waal, and other members and candidates left the Society. One of those candidates was Einar Dannevig, whose contribution to the establishment of the Character Analytic Institute in the 1990s will be discussed below. Along with two others, he was instrumental in the creation of the Institute for Psychotherapy in 1962. Its mandate from the start was to provide training in psychoanalytic psychotherapy for work in public health institutions. Today it is a nationwide organization with 400 members and nearly 100 candidates. The Institute for Psychotherapy early on established connections with interpersonal analysis and the William Alanson White Institute in New York. It has on its faculty today several of the most prominent relational analysts in Norway, among them P. E. Binder (2009).

In 1972, the *Forum for Character Analytic Vegetotherapy* was formed by Einar Dannevig and other students of Raknes, Nic Waal, Philipson, and Schjelderup, with the purpose of keeping alive and developing the Reichian tradition in Norway. The group had originally formed around Raknes, who was still alive at the time (he died in 1975 at 88 years old). Only Raknes considered himself an orgonomist, however, and the group differed widely on other counts as well. Differences notwithstanding, in their own ways the members sought to integrate what they found of value in the Reichian legacy with later analytic developments, particularly existential and interpersonal analysis. Psychoanalysis and psychotherapy were increasingly regarded as separate entities from the 1950s (Aron & Starr, 2013), and as the founding members of the Forum had either left or chosen not to apply for membership in the Norwegian Psychoanalytic Society, most of them came to regard themselves as psychotherapists rather than analysts.

In Norway, *Character Analytic Vegetotherapy*, a term coined by Reich, came to mean various combinations of psychodynamic psychotherapy and Reichian body-work. Internationally, the best-known form of combined body-work and psychotherapy is probably *bioenergetic analysis*, developed by Alexander Lowen (1975). By the early 1990s, the concept of character analytic vegetotherapy had undergone a radical change. This was above all thanks to the work of Rolf Grønseth (1991, 1998) in the 1980s. Emphasis shifted from body-work to verbalizing the impression of the patient's bodily expression. In what he termed *existential* character analytic vegetotherapy, Grønseth dismissed every form of body-work. The therapist should instead focus on finding words for his or her impression of the patient's bodily presentation, thereby helping the patient to become aware of his or her bodily state and identity

The study of Reich's own writings on character analysis in light of Schjelderup's idea of a global analysis gave the Reichian legacy a new lease on life from the mid-1990s. For my own part, I came to see what Reich referred to as *not manifest emotions* as the very phenomenon Stern (1985) was indicating with his concept of *vitality affects*: "Stern sees the manner or form of performance as crucial for the infant's emotional experience in the same way as Reich sees it as crucial for the psychotherapist's experience of the clients' emotionality" (Sletvold, 1996, p. 5). The essence of character analysis, I therefore suggested, could be defined as *attending to not manifest emotions or vitality affects*. I concluded that paper as follows.

> In this way – taking character analysis as its point of departure – body oriented psychotherapy will again be firmly rooted in developmental psychology and psychoanalysis. The analysis of non-verbal bodily behavior becomes a natural extension of psychoanalysis, as the analysis of the transference once was an extension of dream-analysis. The peculiarities of each case and session should decide to which extent the stress should be put on dream, transference or muscular behavior. So my suggestion is that the field of body-oriented psychotherapies should see its natural place among the psychoanalytical therapies from which it once took its point of departure, as a considerable enrichment and vitalization of those therapies. (Sletvold, 1996, p. 10)

The Character Analytic Institute in Oslo was formally established in 1999. It merges character analysis, elements of body-work, and relational psychoanalysis (Mitchell, 1988; Aron, 1996; Stark, 1999). This synthesis was inspired by and facilitated above all by the work of Einar Dannevig and George Downing, independently of each other.

Dannevig had been a leading figure in the analytical and psychotherapy field in Norway for half a century. He had been in training analysis with both Raknes and Schjelderup in the 1950s. He was in contact with interpersonal psychoanalysis in New York from the 1960s and was a close friend of Gerard Chrzanowski. In the mid-1990s, Dannevig led two advanced seminars on character analysis, and remained an enthusiastic advocate of an integrative character analytic institute until his death in 2005.

As already mentioned, Dannevig, having trained with the Psychoanalytic Society in the 1950s, chose not to apply for membership. Throughout his career, he maintained a broad orientation, identifying himself equally as psychotherapist and psychoanalyst. This is reflected in a letter he wrote me dated October 29, 1995, as part of our discussion on the identity of the new character analytic institute.

> I believe psychotherapy is psychotherapy is psychotherapy. If someone's professional identity is attached to the Reichian tradition, it is probably adequate for him/her or them to call what they do character analysis, just as others call what they do psychoanalysis, existential analysis, interpersonal analysis, etc. For me, who belongs to them all, it is natural to talk about psychotherapy, analysis, and psychological treatment. Abroad I call myself a psychoanalyst because there it is an inclusive term. (My translation.)

Dannevig's influence also contributed to the explicitly relational orientation of the Character Analytic Institute from its very start. In the same letter, commenting on my first draft of the training program in which I used the word "technique" – referring to Freud's and Reich's technique papers – he wrote: "I hate seeing the word technique used to denote *any kind of interpersonal work*" (my italics) (Dannevig, 1995b).

George Downing, an American-trained psychologist teaching child and adult psychiatry in Paris, studied body-work in California and psychoanalysis and philosophy in Paris in the 1960s. In his book *The Body and the Word in Psychotherapy* (1996), he shows a number of ways in which body-work can be integrated with a psychoanalytic psychotherapy focusing on transference/countertransference experience. Regrettably, the book never appeared in English. Downing also argues, in line with Schjelderup's and Braatøy's earlier arguments, that body techniques should be relieved of the special theory invested in them by the Reichian tradition. His alternative framework draws extensively on infant and child development research on the one hand, and some of Ferenczi's seminal ideas on the other. (For a summary in English of his thinking on infant development, see Downing, 2004.)

The early 1990s saw the first of several yearly seminars chaired by Downing at the Forum for Character Analytic Vegetotherapy. These seminars above all explored the embodied dimensions of the transference/countertransference. Downing contributed to the integration of relational and embodied perspectives and inspired embodied ways of therapy training. His influence extends to the introduction of new models of developmental psychology, especially the work of Stern, Beebe, and Tronick, and of emotion theory, particularly the work of Damasio. In this way, Downing both theoretically and technically inspired the development of the training program at the Character Analytic Institute. In later years, Downing has developed a unique approach to Video Intervention Therapy (Downing, Wortmann-Fleisher, von Einsiedel, Jordan, & Reck, 2014), which he teaches in Oslo, throughout Europe, and in New York.

Whereas Anthi and Haugsgjerd (2013) describe their approach within the Norwegian Psychoanalytic Society as integrating the character analytic technique with the classical analytical approach, the Norwegian Character Analytic Institute is based on an integration of embodied character analysis and relational psychoanalysis. Given this theoretical basis, the Institute has particularly focused on developing embodied approaches to training. The training program explores ways to integrate embodied dimensions of the psychotherapeutic interaction within a psychoanalytical training program, with a special focus on the use of imitation. The program can be seen as a model for integrating attention to embodied experience with the more traditional focus on verbal-symbolic representations of experience. The structure and content of this program are presented and discussed in greater detail in the third section of this book.

Note

1 "Nicht der *Traum* sondern das *Verhalten* ist der Via Regia zum sogenanten Unbewussten." "Meiner Meinung nach bedeutet die Charakteranalyse den wichtigsten Fortschritt in der Psychotheraopie seit Freud." (Schjelderup, 1936, p. 649)

Part II

Conceptual framework and clinical guidelines

Chapter 5

Navigating clinical interaction

Memory and overview

Having introduced the idea of the embodied mind and reviewed aspects of the history of embodiment in psychoanalysis and psychotherapy, I intend in this section to discuss a contemporary perspective on working with embodied experience and expression. Hardly any of the ideas I shall be presenting are new. They were developed by analysts, theorists, and researchers over decades, even centuries. Much of the cited research does stem, however, from the last two decades. What I consider my contribution is the way I organize clinical attention into three main areas of embodied experience: 1. *self*; 2. *other*; and 3. *self with other*. I have the distinct impression that most clinical and theoretical discussions of attention to embodied experience in psychoanalysis and psychotherapy have tended to focus on only one or at most two of these areas.

This chapter is an introduction to and an overview of the section on conceptual framework and clinical guidelines. First I consider the fundamental importance of memory.

Memory: Past, present, and future

Memory has been at the heart of psychoanalysis from its inception. Freud's first grand discovery was, as we recorded previously, that "Hysterics suffer mainly from reminiscences" (Breuer & Freud, 1893/1895/1955, p. 7). Recently, Reis (2009) suggested that what Breuer and Freud referred to as reminiscences actually were what we today call implicit or affect motor forms of memory. And the phenomena Freud (1912/1958a) later described as transference deal specifically with memory's role in human relations; in Stern et al.'s (1998) terminology, implicit relational knowing. We cannot form an impression of a person without activating a lot of information stored in our memory. Some experiences, particularly traumatic events, cause spurious memory activation, leading us to believe, for instance, that the placid individual before us is in fact a dangerous villain, or vice versa.

James's theory of emotions has been criticized because while it can explain how we react when we meet a bear in the forest, it cannot explain Hamlet's prevarication. Taking issue with this criticism, Damasio (1994) found our bodily reactions were the same whether the stimulus was an external event or an activated memory.

In psychoanalysis, we take this for granted. The analytic challenge with respect to transference and countertransference is to evaluate the relative contribution of the therapeutic relationship in the present and the inputs from the patient's and therapist's memories.

Schacter (1996) offers an intriguing account of the revolution in memory research over the past decades. By integrating and comparing data from introspection, clinical observation, cognitive psychology, and neuroscience, it is now apparent that memory is not one coherent system, but a series of systems. It feels different to remember something (an episode), to know something (knowledge), and to know how to do something (a skill). This is not accidental; different neurophysiological processes are also involved.

We have an *episodic memory* for events associated with a time and place and a *semantic memory* containing what we know. Both these types of memory are connected to words and stored in what Freud termed the pre-conscious, and can be made conscious when needed. They are also termed declarative or explicit and constitute our *autobiographical memory*.

Additionally, there is *procedural* or *implicit memory*. It manifests itself through motor skills and bodily emotional reactions called *affect motor memories* by Downing (1996) and *emotional memories* by LeDoux (1996). Bråten (2000) suggests *e-motional memories*, embracing the dual emotive and kinetic connotations. The trauma researcher van der Kolk (1994) notes how the "the body keeps the score." Stern et al. (1998) proposed the term *implicit relational knowing*; it is also about ways of being together, they stress. But whatever the name, we are talking about a basic form of memory that is bodily, emotional, and relational, not symbolic and verbal. It is also worth noting the robustness of affect motor memory, and the corresponding fragility of episodic memory (Magnussen & Overskeid, 2003; Schacter, 1996). Some of the controversy over so-called false memories has been caused by not considering the big difference in reliability of these two aspects of memory. The affect motor memory of traumatic events will generally be reliable, as the body will hardly produce these reactions if "nothing has happened." The ability to recall traumatic events accurately in episodic memory will, however, vary greatly. And if the traumatic event happened during the first year or so of life, no episodic memory will have been stored in the first place. Freud highlighted this difference between the cognitive and the emotional aspect with respect to dreams: "If I am afraid of robbers in a dream, the robbers, it is true, are imaginary – but the fear is real" (1900/1966, p. 460).

In any case, memory per se is an elemental "backdrop" to all subjective experience, and will always be essentially emotional. "It is now clear that we do not store judgment-free snapshots of our past experiences but rather hold on to the meaning, sense, and emotions these experiences provided us" (Schacter, 1996, p. 5).

Semantic memory features acquired opinions and "truths" about ourselves. Cognitive therapy, as we know, specializes in modifying semantic memory. Episodic memory stores the events that took place in our past, which we usually take as constituting our autobiography. Those qualities of ourselves we designate by such terms as personality, character, and identity rest not least on implicit or unconscious relational memory expressed in affect motor responses. Strictly speaking, affect motor memory is also part of our autobiographical memory. In this light, clinical psychoanalysis and psychotherapy are about modifying our autobiographical and affect motor memory. And memory, I will add, is not only about the past; there are "memories" of the future too. One of the most important tasks of autobiographical memory is to inform our expectations of the future. Depression is often more attuned to "memories" of a miserable future than of a painful past.

The novelist Siri Hustvedt points to the bright side of our ability to form "memories of the future": *"Writing fiction is like remembering what never happened"* (2011, p. 187, my italics). She explains.

> Fictions are born of the same faculty that transmutes experience into the narratives we remember explicitly but which are formed unconsciously. Like episodic memories and dreams, fiction reinvents deeply emotional material into meaningful stories, even though in the novel, characters and plots are not necessarily anchored in actual events. (p. 195)

Hustvedt offers some very relevant reflections, personally and scientifically informed at the same time, on how autobiographic memory and the narrative self might rest on affect motor memory. "[B]odily, emotional expectations form the ground for the axis of discourse and the narrative self" (p. 192), and "I believe that meaning is crucially grounded in emotion. It makes sense that narrative . . . mimicking memory itself, focus on the meaningful and leave out the meaningless" (p. 189).

Freud early on pointed to an important difference between episodic memories, autobiographic memories, and affect motor memories. Episodic memories are formed in time – past, present, and future – in accordance with what he termed secondary process. Affect motor memories are "timeless," in accordance with the primary process governing unconscious mental processes. "This means in the first place that they are not ordered temporally, that time does not change them in any way and that the idea of time cannot be applied to them" (Freud, 1920/1955a, pp. 31–32). Hustvedt makes the following connection concerning creativity.

> Psychoanalysis has long known that we are strangers to ourselves, and that the idea of unconscious perception had been with us at least since Leibniz in the seventeenth century. All creativity . . . can be traced back to this timeless dimension of human experience or, I would say, *a dimension with sensorimotor timing, but not self-reflective time.* (2011, p. 194, my italics)

To trauma researchers van der Kolk and Saporta, traumatic experiences may be encoded at a sensorimotor level without localization in space and time, they therefore cannot be easily translated into symbolic language necessary for linguistic retrieval (1993). So while episodic memories tend to change and develop as they are retold, in accordance with Freud's principle of *nachträglichkeit*, traumatic, affect motor memories tend to stay the same until they hopefully become the object of a therapy informed by van der Kolk's (1994) discovery that "the body keeps the score."

Apart from autobiographical and affect motor memory, we have genetic or evolutionary memory (also referred to as temperament and instincts). In this respect, Hustvedt writes about how the "deeply established corporeal metrics, the sensory motor beats of self and other, merge with genetic temperament" (2011, p. 192). Genetic memory consists of our innate knowledge about our needs and how to relate with others at various stages of life. As I see it, this memory is an important ally in psychoanalysis and psychotherapy and an essential precondition of change. Psychoanalysis, in terms of reconfiguring our autobiographical and affect motor memories, entails in this respect harmonizing our autobiographical and genetic memories, making us more like what we are supposed to be.

When we conceive of change in psychoanalysis and psychotherapy in terms of reconfiguring memory, new experience becomes decisive. In the treatment of phobias, for instance, we know the importance of exposing the patient to the feared phenomenon. Most often in psychoanalysis, the need to experience human relationships in new ways will occupy center stage. Realizing we can interpret our past in new ways is not enough. We also need "corrective emotional experiences" (Alexander & French, 1946), fresh "moments of meeting," and new "implicit relational knowing" (Stern et al., 1998; Stern, 2004). Lichtenberg, Lachmann, and Fosshage (2002) in their spirit of inquiry put it this way:

> When guided by *a spirit of inquiry*, verbal and nonverbal psychoanalytic exchanges highlight both the autobiographical scenarios of explicit memory and the mental models of implicit memory as each memory system contributes to a sense of self, other, and self with other. *An analyst's and patient's affective coparticipation in the striving to explore, understand and communicate understanding creates an interaction that contributes, through gradual incremental learning, to new implicit relational knowledge.* (p. 82)

Let us keep in mind what Lichtenberg, Lachmann, and Fosshage remind us, that both memory systems – explicit, autobiographical memory and implicit, affect motor memory – contribute "to a sense of self, other, and self with other." As we proceed, I will focus on how we can conceive the emergence of "a sense of self" (Chapter 6), "a sense of the other" (Chapter 7), and "a sense of self with other" (Chapter 8), respectively.

The first, the second, and the third

My organization of clinical attention into these three main areas (self, other, and self with other) was originally inspired by the work of psychoanalyst Martha Stark[1] (1999) on *three modes of therapeutic action.* Based on Mitchell's (1988) analysis of the *relational-conflict, developmental-arrest,* and *drive* models, Stark describes the corresponding therapist stances as *authenticity, empathy*, and *objectivity*. The analyst, she argues, should not remain locked in one or the other of them, but be able to move between them. The therapeutic action of the objective, empathic, and authentic modes she describes as *enhancement of knowledge, provision of experience*, and *engagement in relationship*, respectively.

Historically, however, analysts have tended to idealize one or the other of these modes of therapeutic action. For a long time, the unquestioned ideal to emulate was the objectively interpreting analyst. Especially with the work of Kohut (1971), empathy and an understanding mode became increasingly valued. And finally, authenticity and a constructive use of the countertransference (the therapist's own feelings) became valued with the growth of interpersonal and relational analysis. Stark also refers to these three modes as *one-person, one-and-a-half-person*, and *two-person psychologies*. She sees the empathic position as a one-and-a-half person psychology because the person of the therapist is considered only in his empathic capacity and not as an authentic person with his own subjectivity.

I share with Stark the view that we need all these three modes, positions, and perspectives and that we should not idealize any one of them, but develop as best we can our (and our patients') capacity to function in and across all three. Throughout this text, I will refer to these modes by the terms *subjectivity, intersubjectivity*, and *reflexivity* or *objectivity*. I would add, though, that the concept of objectivity has changed considerably compared to its traditional meaning when seen in the perspective of embodied subjectivity and intersubjectivity. This I will elaborate on in Chapter 8.

I came to realize that these three basic perspectives emerging through the history of psychoanalysis also seem to constitute the structure of the embodied mind. Experience seems spontaneously to organize itself around the self, the other, and the self with other. The clinical and training guidelines that will be presented and discussed in the remainder of this book are all structured around these three embodied perspectives.

To help you get some personal experience of what these three positions might feel like, I suggest a small exercise. Imagine you are in a meeting with another person, patient or otherwise. Focus first on your own physical posture in this meeting. If you are in your office you might do this in your therapist chair. Pay special attention to your physical posture and way of moving at a moment of your own choosing. Then register what you feel and whatever ideas come to mind.

When you have a reasonably clear conception of what you are experiencing in your position move slowly to where the other person is positioned. Take some time to find the physical posture and manner of moving you intuitively feel are the other's in this same moment of this meeting. Give yourself again some time to register what you feel and what comes to mind in this particular position.

When you again have got some clarity on what you are experiencing in this second position, move slowly to a third position. This latter position (chair) should be at an equal distance to the two other positions, but somewhat to the side and facing them. In this third position look at the first and second positions, keep in mind what you experienced in both of them and let yourself form a picture of the meeting and how it seems to unfold.

Based on my own experience I am pretty sure that everyone who tries this exercise will find that they get three distinctively different experiences in the three positions, and that some are surprising and some not. Whatever you experience, I hope you can bring it with you and have it as an experiential background throughout this text.

Research findings, Daniel Stern (2000) suggests in his introduction to the second edition of *The Interpersonal World of the Infant*, strongly indicate that infants are born with separate but parallel information systems (perceptual, cognitive, and affective) for *self*, *other*, and *things*. Available evidence today gives no support to ideas like "normal autism," "primary narcissism," and "symbioses." The developmental challenge for humans is not separation of self from other, as this separation exists from the very beginning. The challenge becomes rather to develop broader and stronger bonds, attachments, and relations to others, and at the same time manage to balance these bonds with autonomy, authenticity, and individuality. The third challenge seems to be to develop a capacity for reflecting over similarities and differences between the states of self and other.

The three next chapters each explore one of these three areas. Taken together, they will hopefully stimulate the formation of images and clinical perspectives of practical use in an embodied approach to psychoanalysis and psychotherapy. My intention is to present this conceptual framework as a means of guiding clinical attention, to make it easier for you the reader to keep in mind that they are meant to constitute a single coherent perspective. What follows is a short synopsis.

We spontaneously tend to organize our perceptions of what is happening in our body as we interact with other human beings around the perceptual poles of self and other – poles of embodied experience to which I shall also refer as *embodied subjectivity* and *embodied intersubjectivity*. I call it the *polar* organization of experience because the one cannot be conceived of without the other. As many will agree, there can't be an "I" without a "you," and vice versa. Psychoanalysis was, however, particularly occupied with the self-side of this dialectic, as reflected in the prominent position of concepts like "ego psychology," "self psychology," and, more recently, "self-states." True to this tradition, I start with the self-side.

In Chapter 6, I examine the evolution of conceptions of self-experience from an embodied perspective with a particular emphasis on a rereading of Freud's *The Ego and the Id* (1923/1961a). Building on Freud's view of the ego as first and foremost a bodily ego, I explore contemporary perspectives, especially the arguments propounded by the neuroscientist Antonio Damasio.

Chapter 7 focuses on the experience of the other, on intersubjectivity. I use the term *intersubjectivity* to refer to our ability to experience (feel, sense) some of the mind processes of others, and to our capacity for mutual recognition (Benjamin, 1990) of these processes in one another. As noted previously, Stolorow (2011) and his group use the term somewhat differently: "For us, *intersubjective* denotes neither a mode of experiencing nor a sharing of experience, but the contextual precondition for having any experience at all" (p. 23n*).

Embodied intersubjectivity takes on a special quality for humans thanks to our capacity for alter-centric participation. Alter-centric participation presupposes an expanded conception of imitation to include what I term internal imitation or embodied simulation. I consider this to be a critical idea for an embodied understanding of intersubjectivity, no longer based on a cognitive conception of theory of mind.

In Chapter 8, my conception of embodied subjectivity and intersubjectivity further emerges as a pivotal precondition for reflective thought and use of symbolic language, what I term *embodied reflexivity*. Key here is the ability to disengage from a one-track relation with the environment, which makes it possible to keep the perspective of both self and other in mind. So the ability to experience both similarities and differences between one's own body states and those of others (by internal imitation) also forms a basis of our capacity for reflexive functioning or mentalization.

Finally, Chapter 9 elaborates more fully on the clinical implications of a two-body psychology. Whereas in previous chapters the focus has been mainly on self and other in one body/mind, on *object relations* in traditional analytic language, in this chapter the focus is on two (or more) bodies in interaction, in accordance with Balint's assertion that the psychoanalytic situation is "essentially a Two-Body Situation" (1952/1985, p. 235).

So, I argue that by attending to these three areas – *embodied subjectivity, intersubjectivity*, and *reflexivity* – clinical interaction can be navigated from the position of embodied experience. Short clinical vignettes and some extended case discussions are included to illustrate how this can be done in practice. I believe that our own and our patient's ability to focus attention on these three aspects of experience is strongly connected with the quality of psychotherapy. These areas also define the geography of the psychotherapeutic setting: the therapist, the patient, and what is created from this meeting. Organizing experience from these three positions therefore also helps focus the immediate here and now of the therapeutic encounter.

However, before elaborating further on this conception, I should make it clear that I do not think the therapist, the patient, and what results from their meeting are all that influences what happens in therapy. Besides and in addition to these factors is, so to speak, the whole world, including cultural and political factors. In no way do I want to minimize their influence. However, they are not the subject of this text, even if they have been touched upon in the historical review. I am therefore happy that other books cover cultural and political aspects of psychoanalysis and psychotherapy in excellent ways. Recently, Aron and Starr (2013) have written extensively on important historical and political aspects of psychoanalysis and psychotherapy. Jeremy Safran (2012), in his new introductory textbook, also highlights the political aspects of psychoanalysis. I highly recommend these books.

Note

1 Stark has also been involved in dialogue with body-oriented psychotherapists, among them Albert Pesso (Pesso & Boyden-Pesso, 2012; Pesso & Crandel, 1991), with whom I also studied for many years and from whom I learned much.

Chapter 6

Embodied subjectivity
Freud's "Ich" and the embodied self

The ego is first and foremost a bodily ego.

(Freud)

In the previous chapter, I explained how I see the mind, as – at its core – an ongoing process of registering, feeling, and sensing what is happening and changing in our body as we interact with our environment. And, furthermore, that we spontaneously tend to organize our perceptions of what is happening in our body as we interact with other human beings around the perceptual poles of self and other. I now turn to the *self* side of this embodied experience: embodied subjectivity. The starting point for these considerations of self-experience will be a reading of Freud's *The Ego and The Id* (Freud, 1923/1961a). I shall carefully reconsider Freud's thinking as it unfolds in this text in order to tease out how Freud was able to "go on . . . theoretically" some 25 years after confessing to Fliess in 1898 that he could not. I attempt to show that Freud sought to make room for "an organic basis" for his psychology in his theorizing on the ego in 1923.

Ich, ego, and self before 1923

After the publication of *The Ego and the Id* in 1923, *ego* became a favored term in psychoanalysis. And after Kohut (1971) initiated what came to be known as psychoanalytic self psychology, the term *self* became a key word of the highest caliber. Psychoanalytic ego psychologists were at great pains to differentiate conceptually between *ego*, *self*, and *self representation*. Interestingly, Freud never cared about these differentiations. James Strachey refers to this in his introduction to *The Ego and the Id*, and his comments are illuminating.

> The term – *das Ich* – had of course been in familiar use before the days of Freud; but the precise sense which he himself attached to it in his earlier writings is not unambiguous. It seems possible to detect two main uses: one in which the term distinguishes a person's self as a whole (including,

perhaps, his body) from other people, and the other in which it denotes a particular part of the mind characterized by special attributes and functions. (pp. 7–8)

Kernberg (1984), picking up on Strachey's observation, reminded us of the fact that Freud preserved throughout his writings the German *Ich – I –* as a mental structure and psychic agency, but also as the personal, subjective, experiential self. In other words, in his use of the term *das Ich*, Freud never separated the system ego from the experiencing self. Kernberg explains:

> There are innumerable examples of the use of *Ich* before 1923 to designate subjective experience and self-esteem. . . . This characteristic of Freud's concept of *Ich* – which I consider a strength, not a weakness – persists throughout his work. The most dramatic example is probably his statement in *Civilization and Its Discontents* (1930) where the *Standard Edition*, faithful to the German original, reads (p. 65): "Normally, there is nothing of which we are more certain than the feeling of our self, of our own ego." The German version says (1930, p. 423), "Normalerweise ist uns nichts gesicherter als das Gefül unseres Selbst, unseres eigenes Ichs". Here self and ego are explicitly equated! (Kernberg, 1984, pp. 227–228)

Freud's concluding remark in *The Ego and the Id*, that "the ego is first and foremost a bodily ego," is often quoted. And yet Freud only rarely refers to the body in this text. It may be because, unlike many of his followers for whom "only the psychological was under consideration," Freud the neurologist saw the body as a given starting point. The notion of self or ego referred not only to subjective experience, it seems also to have been seen "first and foremost [as] a body ego" by many in scientific and medical circles of a century ago. The following, taken from *Psychological Medicine*, a textbook by Maurice Craig (1905) defining the basic concepts of normal psychology, is a telling example.

> By "self" we mean the "ego" composed of a complex of sensations, perceptions, and affections. In early life the idea of self is largely developed from kinaesthetic sensations. . . . Kinaesthetic sensation is derived from voluntary muscles in action, joints, tendons, and skin. As time goes on, the visual centres assist in the production of an idea of self, and also a certain amount is learned about oneself from the remarks that others make. All through life sensation is the important factor in our idea of self, for greatly diminish sensation and you have to a large extent, if not completely, taken away the consciousness of self. There is no doubt that this fact is not as fully realised as it ought to be, and yet it is the basis of many delusions in the insane. Patients who have the belief that they are dead will usually be found to have an almost complete anaesthesia of the body. (p. 14)

Craig goes on to subdivide self-consciousness into subject-consciousness and object-consciousness: "Subject-Consciousness is what I know, what I feel; while object-consciousness is the knowledge of things of the external world. The 'ego' is therefore conjoined subject- and object-consciousness" (p. 15). This view of "the building blocks" of consciousness and self is, as we will see, similar to the ideas Freud set out in *The Ego and the Id*, and, later, to Damasio's more neurobio-logically informed theory, in which he points to the "two key players," i.e., "the organism" and "the object," in the making of self and consciousness. A comment by Damasio (2010) might help explain why Craig's insights, and indeed Freud's, remained undeveloped.

> The remarkable European school of physiology that flourished from the mid-dle of the nineteenth century to the early twentieth described the contours of body-to-brain signaling with admirable accuracy, but the relevance of this general scheme for the understanding of the mind-body problem went unno-ticed. The neuroanatomical and neurophysiological details, not surprisingly, have been uncovered only in the past few years. (2010, p. 96)

The Ego and the Id revisited

In his editorial introduction, Strachey also identifies as the forerunner of the gen-eral picture of the mind as presented in *The Ego and the Id* (1923/1961a) Freud's *Project for a Scientific Psychology* (1895/1950). "After the isolated attempt in the 'Project' of 1895 . . . Freud left the subject almost untouched for some fifteen years" (p. 8). Although Freud in 1923, unlike in the "Project," makes no specific neurobiological assumptions concerning his ideas about embodied experience, for the neurologist Freud it was in a way self-evident that the body constituted the basis of the mind. And so, a bodily basis and point of departure are not fully explicated in *The Ego and the Id*. It is, therefore, probably no accident that it took another neurologist, Antonio Damasio (1999), many years later, to formulate ideas similar to those in *The Ego and the Id*, being able this time to build on con-temporary advances in neurobiology and neuropsychology.

Far more is unconscious than the repressed

In the introductory chapter of *The Ego and the Id*, Freud places the ego at the intersection of the unconscious and the conscious mind. "The division of the psy-chical into what is conscious and what is unconscious is the fundamental premise of psycho-analysis; and it alone makes it possible for psycho-analysis to under-stand the pathological processes in mental life . . . and to find a place for them in the framework of science" (1923/1961a, p. 13). What is most significant in this introduction is Freud's contention that the unconscious mind contains much more than the dynamic or repressed unconscious, which so far had been the main focus of psychoanalytic research.

> We recognize that the *Ucs.* [unconscious] does not coincide with the repressed; it is still true that all that is repressed is *Ucs.*, but not all that is *Ucs.* is repressed. A part of the ego, too – and Heaven knows how important a part – may be *Ucs.*, undoubtedly is *Ucs.* And this *Ucs.* belonging to the ego is not latent like the *Pcs.* [preconscious] . . . we find ourselves thus confronted by the necessity of postulating a third *Ucs.*, which is not repressed. (p. 18)

Freud's insistence that more is unconscious than the repressed turns out to be a critical premise for his conclusion that the ego is first and foremost bodily. Freud opens Chapter 2 of *The Ego and the Id* by stating, "Pathological research has directed our interest too exclusively to the repressed. We should like to learn more about the ego, now that we know that it, too, can be unconscious in the proper sense of the word" (p. 19).

The cognitive science term *implicit* is being increasingly used to denote *non-repressed* unconscious experience in contrast to the Freudian unconscious, construed as the *repressed* unconscious (Schore, 1994, 2003a/b; Modell, 2008; BCPSG, 2010). But as we have seen, Freud was clear that "not all that is *Ucs.* is repressed . . . and Heaven knows how important a part." In spite of this assertion, the notion of the Freudian unconscious as synonymous with the repressed has prevailed. A problem with the use of the adjective *implicit*, as I see it, is that it is used to connote both nonrepressed unconscious and nonverbal conscious experience. This usage blurs "the fundamental premise of psycho-analysis . . . the division of the psychical into what is conscious and what is unconscious" (Freud, 1923/1961a, p. 13).

External and internal perceptions in the formation of the ego

In elucidating the ego, Freud introduces a critical distinction between external and internal perception. "All perceptions which are received from without (sense-perceptions) and from within – what we call sensations and feelings – are *Cs.* [conscious] from the start" (p. 19). For Freud, the sources of perceptions are external *and* internal, i.e., our own body. Freud is making two closely related assumptions. The first is that the ego is formed by an interaction of external and internal perceptions. It is the combined experience of the external world and the state of our own body that somehow lays the foundation for "the feeling of our self, of our own ego" – "das Gefül unseres Selbst, unseres eigenes Ichs." The second assumption is that it is the internal perception of the body state that gives this "feeling of our self" its unique quality. But Freud also emphasizes uncertainty given the state of knowledge when he wrote about the nature of these internal sensations and feelings of the body.

> Whereas the relation of *external* perceptions to the ego is quite perspicuous, that of *internal* perceptions to the ego requires special investigation. . . .

> Internal perceptions yield sensations of processes arising in the most diverse and certainly also in the deepest strata of the mental apparatus. Very little is known about these sensations and feelings; those belonging to the pleasure-unpleasure series may still be regarded as the best examples of them. They are more *primordial*, more elementary, than perceptions arising externally and they can come about even when consciousness is clouded. . . . These sensations are multilocular, like external perceptions; they may come from different places simultaneously and may thus have different or even opposite qualities. (1923/1961a, p. 22, my italics)

The contents of Freud's words here are striking, particularly the accuracy with which they anticipate contemporary views. Most remarkably, Damasio (2010) recently introduced the idea of *primordial feelings* for "the feeling state that I regard as simultaneous foundation of mind and self" (p. 256). Primordial feelings describe "the current state of the body along varied dimensions, for example, along the scale that ranges from pleasure to pain" (p. 21).

So, in Freud's opinion, the roots of the ego or self are to be found in body sensations and feelings, though he had to admit that little was known about these sensations and feelings. Nevertheless, Freud proposed already in *Instincts and their Vicissitudes* (1915/1957a) a model of self-regulation in an organism that can discriminate between outside and inside through "the efficacy of its muscular activity." "Even the most highly evolved mental apparatus is automatically regulated by feelings belonging to the pleasure-pain series" (p. 118). Much later, Damasio (1994) was in a position to state more firmly that feelings are internal sensations, or "images" of the body's internal landscape; "feeling may not be an elusive mental quality attached to an object, but rather the direct perception of a specific landscape: that of the body" (p. xiv).

Immediate feelings and mediated thoughts

Freud goes further in his conceptualization and argues that sensations and feelings of our own body become conscious in a different and more direct way than thoughts, so that feeling and – verbalized – thought therefore constitute two different processes in the ego. He does not pursue this distinction and its possible implications further. However, what Freud grasped here captures the distinction developed in later years between a direct moment by moment registration of an embodied feeling of self and a verbal reflective domain (Knoblauch, 2000; Beebe & Lachmann, 2002; Stern, 2004). Again, consider Freud's words:

> Actually the difference is that, whereas with *Ucs.* [unconscious] *ideas* connecting links must be created before they can be brought into the *Cs.* [conscious], with *feelings*, which are themselves transmitted directly, this does not occur. In other words: the distinctions between *Cs.* and *Pcs.* [preconscious] have no meaning where feelings are concerned; the *Pcs.* here drops out – and feelings

are either conscious or unconscious. Even when they are attached to word-presentations, their becoming conscious is not due to that circumstance, but they become so directly. (pp. 22–23)

Freud further suggests that while feeling is the direct perception of body state, a thought becomes conscious "through becoming connected with word-presentations corresponding to it. These word-presentations are residues of memories; they were at one time perceptions" (p. 20). By memory, Freud here seems to have in mind what we now define as episodic and/or semantic memory, forms of memory usually connected with words, as opposed to nonverbal affect motor memory.

Freud's distinction between word-connected thoughts as stored in preconscious memory before they become conscious, and feelings as internal perceptions of body states, which become conscious directly, is critical and important for the overall perspective developed in this text. Freud actually distinguishes two realms of the ego, of self-experience, the first comprising a continuous sensing and feeling of changing body states, and a second entailing a mediating process of discrete word-connected thoughts. But he also proposes a third level, between body sensations/feelings and verbal representations, an intermediate level of imagistic symbolization resembling what Bucci (1997) describes in her multiple code theory. "The study of dreams and preconscious phantasies . . . can give us an idea of the special character of this visual thinking" (p. 21), Freud says. However, only the concrete subject-matter of the thought can be given visual expression, not the relations between the various elements. "Thinking in pictures is, therefore, only a very incomplete form of becoming conscious. In some way, too, it stands nearer to unconscious processes than does thinking in words, and it is unquestionably older than the latter both ontogenetically and phylogenetically" (p. 21). Bucci (2005) and Fosshage (2005, 2011) identified this recently as a significant realm of nonverbal but symbolic experience.

The ego and the id

Freud builds on the above distinctions when he introduces his new idea of the id [das Es]: "After this clarifying of the relations between external and internal perception and the superficial system *Pcpt.-Cs.* [perception-conscious], we can go on to work out our idea of the ego" (p. 23). He proposes calling the entity that "starts out from the system *Pcpt.* [perception] and begins by being *Pcs.* [preconscious] the 'ego', and, by following Grodeck in calling the other part of the mind into which this entity extends and which behaves as though it were *Ucs.* [unconscious], the 'id'" (p. 23). An important conceptual point here is that Freud in this formulation seems to equate ego and mind, thus extending the ego far beyond "the feeling of our self, of our own ego" (1930/1961b, p. 65). This very extended use of the term *ego* as more or less identical with *mind* created, I believe, problems and confusion, and caused Kohut (1971) much later to reintroduce *the self* to specifically denote "the feeling of our own ego."

Nevertheless, the point here is that Freud divided the mind into two parts, one that is both conscious and unconscious (superego will be included later) *and* one that is completely unconscious, called the id. But Freud also cautions against seeing the two parts as sharply divided, and illustrates what he is thinking with a drawing of the ego and the id (1923/1961a, p. 24, fig. 1) where "[t]he ego is not sharply separated from the id; its lower portion merges into it" (p. 24). Before going on to consider ego-ideal and superego, Freud ends his new reflections on the ego and the id with the following words:

> A person's own body, and above all its surface, is a place from which both external and internal perceptions may spring. It is *seen* like any other object, but to the *touch* it yields two kinds of sensations, one of which may be equivalent to an internal perception. Psychophysiology has fully discussed the manner in which a person's own body attains its special position among other objects in the world of perception. Pain, too, seems to play a part in the process, and the way in which we gain new knowledge of our organs during painful illness is perhaps a model of the way by which in general we arrive at the idea of our body. – The ego is first and foremost a bodily ego. (pp. 25–26)

Here, Freud articulates a view of the double nature of the body that prefigures the thoughts of Merleau-Ponty (1945/1996), discussed in the first chapter. On the one hand, the body is seen as an object, a site to touch, the "*me*." On the other hand, the body is the experiencing subject, the self-sensing/feeling the touch, the "*I*." Freud ends his presentation of the ego and the id by once more asserting that "[i]t is as if we were thus supplied with a proof of what we have just asserted of the conscious ego: that it is first and foremost a body-ego" (p. 27).

Freud's error

Having developed such a compelling argument for the ego as shaped by the interaction of internal perceptions (feelings and sensations of our own body) and external perceptions, thus including both the external (interpersonal) as well as internal (intra-psychic) world, how could Freud subsequently give priority to an intra-psychic conflict? The answer is, it seems, on the very next page: "For the ego, perception plays the part which in the id falls to instinct. The ego represents what may be called reason and common sense, in contrast to the id, which contains the passions" (p. 25). Here ego and id are suddenly assigned antagonistic roles, with the ego alone responsible for perceiving external reality. What brought Freud to this conclusion? In my reading, it is connected to Freud's view of perception as a purely conscious process: "All perceptions . . . are *Cs*.[conscious] from the start" (p. 19). See also the formula *Pcpt.-Cs.* [perception-conscious].

Freud could contradict himself. He did so when he wrote about the ability of the analyst's unconscious to communicate directly with the patient's unconscious

(1912/1958a), and also when he wrote that it is "a very remarkable thing that the *Ucs.* of one human being can react upon that of another, *without passing through the Cs.*" (1915/1957, p. 194, my italics). Freud did not, however, conceptualize unconscious perception, at least not in his theoretical writing.

> It is easy to see that the ego is that part of the id which has been modified by direct influence of the external world through the medium of the *Pcpt.-Cs.* [Perception-Conscious] . . . Moreover, the ego seeks to bring the influence of the external world to bear upon the id and its tendencies, and endeavors to substitute the reality principle for the pleasure principle which reigns unrestrictedly in the id. (p. 25)

Strange as it might seem today to view perception as merely a conscious phenomenon, it was an assumption Freud shared with mainstream philosophers and experimental psychologists. Modern evolutionary thinking, clinical experience, and experimental evidence, however, support a view of humans and other species as necessarily capable of registering not only the internal states of their bodies, but also of perceiving the outer world long before perception becomes conscious. Passions must be basically rational, as stressed by many, Reich among them, before they can become irrational.

In introducing the concept of id – and superego – Freud is careful not to create strict divisions: the one extends into the other, the id being the lower part of the ego, and the superego the higher, as clearly represented in his drawing on page 24. However, having first established the interpenetration of these entities, Freud then goes on to treat them as if they were separate entities with a will of their own, interacting with each other, sometimes struggling and sometimes cooperating. In these scenes, the ego alone has to handle external reality, including other human beings. It sets the stage for an intra-psychic drama within each individual with only minor roles for fellow humans.

This view of warring internal forces caused analysts to grossly overestimate the role of constitutional intra-psychic conflict – and led to repeated attempts by twentieth-century psychoanalysts to rectify the situation. But it was only with the emergence of a comprehensive relational alternative, which recognized the importance of both internal and external forces, in the 1980s and 1990s (Mitchell, 1988 and Aron, 1996), that this rectification was completed.

Although Freud identified the forces shaping the ego as a combination of inner and outer perceptions, he did not, as we have seen, recognize the outside world's direct impact on the bodily and unconscious roots of the ego, i.e., the id. Only later, with the formation of the superego based on identifications with other persons, was Freud able to find a place for the outer world in the formation of the ego. I return to Freud's conceptualization of identification after comparing his thinking on the rooting of the ego/self in the body with contemporary ideas coming from Damasio (2000, 2010).

Freud and Damasio on body and object in the making of self

Having reviewed and discussed Freud's ideas concerning the rooting of the ego in the body, I want to consider the contemporary thinking of neuroscientist Antonio Damasio (2000). We will find a striking resemblance between their respective views. Damasio's choice of starting point complements Freud's of about 75 years earlier.

> The way into a possible answer for the question of self came only after I began seeing the problem of consciousness in terms of two key players, the *organism* and the *object*, and in terms of the *relationships* those players hold in the course of their natural interactions. (Damasio, 2000, p. 19)

Apart from their common points of departure in *internal and external perception*, the body and outer world, another common feature of their thinking is that both see the emergence of self and consciousness as two sides of the same coin; consciousness implies self-consciousness. They also agree that self-consciousness emerges initially as a *feeling*, "the feeling of our self, of our own ego" (Freud, 1930/1961b, p. 65). This feeling is a sensing of the state of our own body, what they both have referred to as *primordial* feelings. For Freud and Damasio alike, body, feeling, self, and consciousness are inseparable.

The critical difference between Freud's and Damasio's respective ideas is that Damasio from the very start stresses *the relationship* of the body to the outer world. The outer world, he argues, causes changes in the body unmediated by conscious processes. "Seen in this perspective, consciousness consists of constructing knowledge about two facts: that the organism is involved in relating to some object, and that the object in the relation causes a change in the organism" (p. 20). In this sense, Damasio agrees with Spinoza and Merleau-Ponty, who also emphasized the unmediated impact of the external world on the body and thereby on subjective experience.

So Damasio explains how interaction with the outer world – not the least of which comprises other bodies – affects the roots of self-experience in the body from the very start. This is a most important revision of what in other respects is a far more relevant and up-to-date view of the body ego by Freud than has generally been acknowledged. Damasio describes his alternative to Freud's formulations of the id in this way.

> The deep roots for the self, including the elaborate self which encompasses identity and personhood, are to be found in the ensemble of brain devices which continuously and *non-consciously* maintain the body state within the narrow range and relative stability required for survival. These devices continually represent, *non-consciously*, the state of the living body, along its many dimensions. I call the state of activity within the ensemble of such devices the *proto-self*, the unconscious forerunner for the levels of self which

appear in our minds as the conscious protagonists of consciousness: core self and autobiographical self. (p. 22)

According to Damasio, the brain has access, moment by moment, to a dynamic representation of the body. Its internal milieu, viscera, and musculoskeletal frame produce a continuous representation in the brain. In essence, the body, with all its parts, produces a continuous, dynamic neural representation within the protoself. Damasio conceives of a second-order neural mapping of our body as it is modified by the perception of an object. This second-order mapping is the mapping of the relationship between two first-order ideas: object perceived *and* body modified by perception.

> As the brain forms images of an object – such as a face, a melody, a tooth-ache, the memory of an event – and as the images of the object affect the state of the organism, yet another level of brain structures creates a swift nonverbal account of the events that are taking place in varied brain regions activated as a consequence of the object-organism interaction. . . . [W]ith the license of metaphor, one might say that the swift second-order nonverbal account nar-rates a story: *that of the organism caught in the act of representing its own changing state as it goes about representing something else.* But the aston-ishing fact is that the knowable entity of the catcher has been created in the narrative of the creative process. (2000, p. 110)

To capture this moment of emergent self-consciousness, Damasio suggests "step-ping into the light" as a metaphor "for the birth of the knowing mind, for the simple and yet momentous coming of the sense of self into the world of the men-tal" (2000, p. 3).

What Damasio suggests is that self-consciousness first appears as a nonver-bal, felt "story" about the changes taking place in our body as we interact with each other and the environment. If this holds true, it might explain why Milner (1960/1987) found "astonishing changes in the quality of one's perceptions, both of oneself and the outside world" resulting from "concentration of the body" and attention to "whole body awareness." Daniel Stern (2000), observing that an idea of the embodied mind and consciousness was lacking in the 1985 edition of *The Interpersonal of the Infant*, puts it this way:

> All mental acts are accompanied by input from the body. . . . This input is what Damasio . . . has called "background feelings," which are similar to the vitality affects introduced in the present book. . . . Primary consciousness is the yoking together, in a present moment, of the intentional object and the vital background input from the body. The body input specifies that it is you who is now having the experience of the intentional object (the intentional object is whatever is "in mind") . . . . This is what I mean by a sense of an emergent self. (Stern, 2000, p. xviii)

Core sense of self and verbal reflective self

So, for Damasio and Stern, consciousness and self first appear in the form of a nonverbal narrative of feelings and images concerning changes in our body as we interact. Only later will consciousness and self also appear in the form of thoughts connected to memories and words. As mentioned earlier, Freud more than hinted at this fundamental distinction within the ego in stating that sensations and feelings become conscious in a way different from thoughts. Let us remind ourselves of what he said:

> Actually the difference is that, whereas with . . . *ideas* connecting links [to words] must be created before they can be brought into the *Cs.* [conscious], with *feelings*, which are themselves transmitted directly, this does not occur. In other words: the distinctions between *Cs.* and *Pcs.* [preconscious] have no meaning where feelings are concerned; the *Pcs.* here drops out – and feelings are either conscious or unconscious. (Freud, 1923/1961a, pp. 22–23)

Thus, Freud makes an essential distinction between the direct perception of body sensations and feelings on the one hand, and thought processes connected to words and memories on the other. This distinction in the ego/self, hinted at by Freud, Damasio clarifies further by the terms *core self* and autobiographical *extended self*. Moreover, developmental and neurobiological research also underpins the idea of a nonverbal core self emerging during the first year of life, with a verbal autobiographical and reflective self mainly developing from the second year (Stern, 2000; Schore, 2003a, 2011). Freud, however, did not develop this idea further nor explore its possible implications for clinical psychoanalysis. As the previous chapters have shown, this conceptual distinction between core embodied and verbal-reflective self-experience is central to my thinking on clinical attention and will be explored and illustrated in the chapters to follow. Here I offer another vignette from the case of Peter, first introduced in Chapter 1.

It turns out that Peter has a well-developed propensity for empathy, but suffers from an underdeveloped ability to feel his own emotions and needs, to feel his core self so to speak. Peter realizes he is interrupting himself and losing the thread as he tries to tell me something. He will gradually recognize this as a typical reaction to issues that evoke strong feelings, particularly irritation and anger. He also becomes aware of how he stops feeling by holding his breath for a second. He further recognizes an inner voice, telling him he is unreasonable and ought to see the matter from the other's point of view. He will gradually learn how his habitual reaction serves to inhibit his own egocentric feelings in a conflict, persuading him instead to see things from the other's vantage point. He notices the sense of weakness and futility brought about by his reaction, a component, he realizes, of the depression he is seeking help to overcome. And when he does manage to become aware and experience acceptance of his own emotional reactions, he starts feeling more alive, empowered. Peter then, characterized by a deeply engrained empathic reaction pattern and an undeveloped ability to feel his own emotions, exemplifies the sort of patient for whom an enhanced awareness of their core emotional self would be a decisive and most helpful step. As he becomes more able "to feel his own self, his own ego" (Freud, 1930/1961b, p. 65), *he also begins to feel anger and a desire to stand up for his own felt needs.*

In Chapter 8, I shall present yet another vignette from the case of Peter, focusing on problems he turned out to have in the realm of his autobiographical verbal-reflective self.

In Damasio's account of the core self, the conscious *you* springs from *primordial feelings* (2010) which arise from the nonconscious protoself as it is changed by what happens; in the words of T. S. Eliot, "you are the music while the music lasts" (Damasio, 2000, p. 172). The autobiographical self on the other hand

> hinges on the consistent reactivation and display of selected sets of autobiographical memories. In core consciousness, the sense of self arises in subtle, fleeting feeling of knowing, constructed anew in each pulse. Instead, in extended consciousness, the sense of self arises in the consistent, reiterated display of some of our own personal memories, the *objects of our personal past*, those that can easily substantiate our identity, moment by moment, and our personhood. (Damasio, 2000, p. 196)

This does not mean that these two forms of self-experience remain separated. According to Damasio, "autobiography memory is architecturally connected, neurally and cognitively speaking, to the nonconscious protoself and to the emergent and conscious core self of each lived instant" (2000, p. 173). As Lichtenberg, Lachmann, and Fosshage observe, "the autobiographic self connects immediately core consciousness with the forms of memory that are explicit – episodic memory and semantic memory. The sense of a biographic self that arises from this bridging permits a child to say to herself and others 'My name is Helen. I live in the yellow house on the corner'" (2002, p. 48).

To highlight the difference between core and verbal-reflective self, I would say that core self-consciousness is what we are looking for when we're looking for any signs at all of consciousness in a person. Can he feel anything? Core self and consciousness are probably genetically determined for the most part, contingent on structures in the brain stem, and, from an evolutionary perspective, far older than verbal-reflective self and consciousness. The core self changes relatively little over the life cycle, barring brain damage or disorders such as Alzheimer's.

There can be no verbal-reflective self without core self. When core self fails, verbal-reflective self also fails. But every aspect of verbal-reflective self can be destroyed (through brain damage) without core self being affected (Damasio, 2000). While core self is a here and now consciousness, verbal-reflective self presupposes autobiographical memory along with working memory, intelligence, and language. Verbal-reflective self and autobiographical memory both depend largely on the neocortex and are also largely shaped by our interactions with each other and the environment.

Before concluding this discussion of the embodied self, I want to stress again that the two levels of self-organization should not be seen as two separate selves. For better or worse, they are integrated. Findings from attachment research can illustrate this point. Fonagy, Steele, and Steele (1991) studied mothers expecting their first child with the Adult Attachment Interview procedure during pregnancy and in the Strange Situation setting when the child was one year of age. They found that it was possible to predict from the AAI – which studies the verbal-reflective self – the pattern of attachment detected by the Strange Situation test, which captures mainly interaction at the core emotional level. This and other studies using both the Strange Situation and the AAI suggest a degree of coherence between these levels of self-organization, irrespective of whether there is a pattern of secure or insecure attachment. Actually, the AAI could be said to rest on the hypothesis of a correlation between nonverbal emotional regulation in early childhood and the development of the verbal-reflective self. The Boston Change Process Study Group (2008) has recently stressed the coherence between implicit experience and its reflective-verbalization, saying that even if there is a an inherent, inevitable disjunction between the lived and verbalized, "[i]n most cases, there is a high degree of coherence between implicit experience and its reflective-verbalization. Indeed we expect and rely on such coherence in conducting relationships within ourselves as well as with others" (p. 143).

Commenting on Stern's (1985) assertion that "[l]anguage causes a split in the experience of the self" (p. 163), the BCPSG (2008) detects an evolution in Stern's position since 1985. I agree with the present position of Stern and the BCPSG that language does not *cause* a split in the self. As I have already argued and will argue again in Chapter 8, thought and language grow "organically" from nonverbal emotional interaction (gestures and images), while, at the same time, feeding back into the body. Freud probably made a wise decision when he refrained from drawing a line of separation between the parts of the ego in his preliminary drawing (1923/1961a, p. 24, fig. 1). All the same, what the BCPSG refers to as the disjunction does make it a relatively easy option to conceive of a split in the self, not only for psychopathological states, but also for our spontaneous tendency to see our self as disembodied and in our difficulty to realize the embodied nature of self.

One body, one self, and many self-states

While the world around changes dramatically, profoundly, and often unpredictably, the brain has constant access to a representation of an entity with a limited range of possible states – the body. This makes the body a good candidate for grounding our sense of a continuous identity. In a changing world, our body stays basically the same, and is thus able to underpin a feeling of staying the same person. Damasio highlights this by stating what he calls a first principle, one person, one body, one mind.

The fact that multiple personalities are not considered normal reflects the general agreement that one body goes with one self. One of the reasons we so admire good actors is that they can convince us that they are other persons, that they have other minds and other selves. . . . A mind is so closely shaped by the body and destined to serve it that only one mind could possibly arise in it. No body, never mind. For any body, never more than one mind. Body minded minds help save the body. (2000, pp. 142–143)

The view that the body grounds our sense of a continuous self is in keeping with the arguments favoring an embodied self and mind. One self goes with one body. A consequence of this is that people around the world recognize themselves and are recognized by others by the same name throughout their entire life.

As I see it, this view need not be at odds with a contemporary focus on many and shifting self-states (Bromberg, 1991; Howell, 2005). A conception of shifting self-states resulted in particular from the increased focus on trauma and dissociative states. While my existence as one body grounds a feeling of being one and the same person throughout life, within each body there are continuously changing emotional states which give rise to different feelings. Usually, changes in feelings are not considered changes in self-states. If I say "*I got angry, then sad, and then happy again*," it is the same "I" that has these different feelings. If, however, I start referring to myself at different times as respectively "*I am an angry person, I am a sad person, I am a happy person*," we might well take it as evidence of shifting self-states rather than just shifting feelings. As long as the shifting emotional body states shift in reasonable contact with changing relations and life conditions, they remain only shifting feelings. When, however, emotional body states become a relatively permanent fixture, there is reason to talk about separate emotional self-states, rather than just different feelings. Such relatively permanently organized and changing self-states are often, as we know, a central feature in cases of dissociation associated with severe trauma. My main point here is that a cohesive core self and shifting self-states are all grounded in ways in which emotional body states are regulated (or dysregulated). This is also demonstrated dramatically in cases that amount to multiple personalities, as not only emotional expression but the whole bodily appearance changes when personality changes.

In accordance with what I have said above, I find the term *multiple selves* misleading if it is taken as referring to nonpathological states. In agreement with Lichtenberg, Lachmann, and Fosshage (2002), I prefer to talk of one – more or less – cohesive sense of self with a multiplicity of self-experiences, and eventually multiple self-states.

Freud and identification in the formation of the ego

Freud was not, as we have seen, able to find a role for the direct influence of other humans in the earliest stages of the formation of the ego and the id. But he definitely saw such a role for others in the infant's subsequent development. Not only did he describe a process of identification, he was also able to explain how a form of imitation made the process possible. In this way, his ideas underpin my thinking on *embodied intersubjectivity,* to be developed in the next chapter. (For contemporary discussions of the roles of others in the formation of the self, I refer the reader to Stern, 2000, and Rochat, 2009.)

In the third section of *The Ego and the Id,* entitled *The Ego and the Super- ego (Ego Ideal),* Freud considers the process of identification and its place in the formation of the ego. He reminds us how he was able to explain melancholia by supposing that an object which was lost had been set up again inside the ego, that it had been replaced by identification.

> At that time, however, we did not appreciate the full significance of this pro- cess and did not know how common and how typical it is. Since then we have come to understand that this kind of substitution has a great share in deter- mining the form taken by the ego and that it makes an essential contribution towards building up what is called its "character." (1923/1961a, p. 28)

Freud describes how he came to see character formation as a result of identifica- tions based on early object relations.

> In women who have had many experiences in love there seems to be no difficulty in finding vestiges of their object-cathexes in the traits of their character. We must also take into consideration cases of simultaneous object-cathexis and identifica- tion – cases, that is, in which the alteration in character occurs before the object has been given up. In such cases the alteration in character has been able to sur- vive the object-relation and in a certain sense to conserve it. (pp. 29–30)

A contemporary perspective allows us to consider the significance of Freud's observations, of course, not just for women. Freud speculates further that if the ego's object-identifications

> obtain the upper hand and become too numerous, unduly powerful and incompatible with one another, a pathological outcome will not be far off. It may come to a disruption of the ego in consequence of the different identifi- cations becoming cut off from one another by resistances; perhaps the secret of the cases of what is described as "multiple personality" is that the different identifications seize hold of consciousness in turn. (pp. 30–31)

It is fascinating to detect in this statement the seeds of what later emerged as our contemporary understanding of splitting, dissociation, and the formation of multiple self-states. The effects of the first identifications made in early childhood Freud stresses will be general and lasting. So here we see Freud allotting a deci- sive place to the specific other in the formation of character and neurosis through the process of identification, creating a conceptual and theoretical foundation in which later relational developments in psychoanalysis would take root. Though

Freud chose to center his theory on intra-psychic processes, he returned on several occasions to the interpersonal source of the identificatory process as reflected in his observation: "[s]ocial feelings rest on identifications with other people, on the basis of having the same ego ideal" (p. 37).

But questions still hang in the air. What kind of process in the interaction between self and other constitutes the experience of identification? It seems that Freud had already provided an answer two years earlier, an answer suggesting a path that Freud, at the time, did not pursue. To recapitulate (see also Chapter 2), "A path leads from identification by way of imitation to empathy, that is, to the comprehension of the mechanism by means of which we are enabled to take up any attitude at all towards another mental life" (1921/1955, p. 110n2).

In contemporary relational thought, Harris (1998) took note of this path when she wrote: "The development of a body ego draws on and demands a range of iden-tificatory processes, one of which arises through complex forms of surface contact or imitation" (p. 46). Using the Greek term *mimesis*, mimetic identifications, she argues, are points of transfer of affective states. "Mimesis is not imitation in a behavioral sense, although physical acts are involved; mimesis is a responsive, imitative encounter with another being that can lead to mutually induced affective experiences" (p. 46). Harris accurately captures an important point and one I shall discuss in the next chapter.

In the following chapter, I investigate this path from the privileged perspective and contexts of the twenty-first century. After considering *the role of the other* in the formation of *self-experience and character*, I turn to *the experience of the other*. For our purposes, this concerns in particular the analyst's experience of the patient and the patient's experience of the analyst. But in any case, Freud seemed aware of the basic processes involved when he highlighted the interrelatedness of identification, imitation, and empathy.

Chapter 7

Embodied intersubjectivity

"You" in mind

A path leads from identification by way of imitation to empathy.

(Freud)

The patient's expressive movements involuntarily bring about an imitation in our own organism.

(Reich)

I ended the last chapter with a discussion of how Freud came to see a decisive role for others in the formation of the ego, in the shaping of character and self-experience. In this chapter, the focus shifts from *self-experience* to *the experience of the other*, to "you in my mind." It is possible, I shall contend, to experience the subjectivity of others through a process of embodied identification. I review recent research in support of this claim. I also argue that we have an ability to shift from self to other and from other to self at an embodied level and that this ability allows us to navigate clinical interaction from embodied experience. I demonstrate this by presenting and discussing a case. But first, I'll provide a brief history of the central terms.

Empathy, imitation, and identification

Approximately 250 years ago, Adam Smith (1759/1976) hypothesized that when we observe a person in a situation that induces a certain feeling, we automatically experience a weaker version of that feeling. An example would be watching an acrobat walking on a tightrope. Smith called the process "sympathy." Lipps (1903) later explained what he termed *einfülung* on the basis of inner imitation and body perception in a book titled *Einfülung, innere Nachamung und Organempfindung* [Empathy, Inner Imitation and Organ Perception]. Empathy, rather than Smith's sympathy, became the English translation of the German *einfülung*, which means literally to *feel into* another. The corresponding Norwegian word is *innlevelse*, meaning to *live into* another. These terms connote an embodied experience, radically different from a conception of empathy as an inferential "theory of mind" stance toward others' minds, i.e., as a re-presented reflective experience.

The terms suggest an embodied basis for the empathic process. It points moreover to an embodied understanding of Freud's statement where he says, "[i]t is only by empathy that we know the existence of psychic life other than our own" (Freud, 1926/1959, p. 104) especially in light of his view of imitation as the means to achieve empathy.

In contemporary theory, Trevarthen (1979) was the first to postulate primary intersubjectivity in infants. He presented "a theory of innate rhythmic motives for active and conscious regulation of companionship in different degrees of intimacy" (2009, p. 509). Bråten (1998b) formulated the idea of *alter-centric participation* to explain this rhythmic regulation. He proposed an innate *virtual other* that makes it possible to participate in the actions of another from their vantage point. The discovery of mirror neurons in monkeys (Gallese, Fadiga, Fogassi, & Rizzolatti, 1996; Rizzolatti, Fadiga, Gallese, & Fogassi, 1996) and of mirroring mechanisms in the human brain (Gallese, 2009; Gallese, Eagle, & Migone, 2007; Gallese, Keyers, & Rizzolatti, 2004) adds neuro-scientific support to Bråten's idea. "Mirror neurons" are pre-motor neurons that fire whether we perform an action ourselves or see the action performed by someone else. When we observe how other individuals act and what emotions they display, a meaningful, emotional link is automatically established with that other person.

Imitation as the key "mechanism"

An expanded understanding of imitation is, in my view, key to an embodied conception of intersubjectivity. According to recent research and theory, an innate ability to imitate might be intrinsic to processes of intersubjectivity, empathy, and alter-centric participation. Meltzoff and Moore (1995, 1998) and Kugiumutzakis (1998) demonstrated the newborn's remarkable ability to imitate. The rapid evolution of the human species was made possible, the biologist Richard Dawkins (1978) hypothesized, by the development of an imitative faculty. Imitation, he suggests, is the second replicator after DNA. He named this second replicator *meme*, from the Greek for imitation, *mimesis*, as a parallel term to *gene*. Since then, evolutionary biology and psychology have supplied growing evidence supportive of this hypothesis (Blackmore, 1999). Hurley and Chater (2005) open their editorial introduction to the two-volume *Perspectives on Imitation: From Neuroscience to Social Science* with the following words.

> Imitation is often thought of as a low-level, cognitively undemanding, even childish form of behaviour, but recent work across a variety of sciences argues that imitation is a rare ability that is fundamentally linked to characteristically human forms of intelligence, in particular to language, culture, and the ability to understand other minds. (p. 1)

Hobson (2002), in his book *The Cradle of Thought*, says there is something about our propensity to imitate others that is as basic as our intellectual process, "something that makes us *Homo imitans* as well as *Homo sapiens*. What is this something? It is the capacity to identify with others – a capacity that autism reveals to be a thinly disguised emotional process" (p. 215).

We can predict from the notion of the embodied self, developed in the previous chapter, that we will feel what another person is feeling to the extent we can induce in our own body the state prevailing in the other person's body, or, as Harris put it: "Only when you are situated as a body ego can you experience the body ego of the other" (Harris, 1998, p. 47). This is precisely what imitation helps us to do. In this way, "replicating" the state of other bodies is essential to intersubjectivity. Imitation makes it possible for us to feel both kinship and difference, as we feel both our own state and some of the states of other bodies.

An important aspect of imitation is our ability to feel and act in light of the perceived bodily position of the other, a capacity to which Bråten (1998b) gives the term *alter-centric participation*. This is very different from "echo talk" and the kind of copying of goal-directed actions observed in people with autism and in animals. *Imitation in humans typically implies "feeling into" and "living into" the other, what Stern (1985) emphasizes with the notion of attunement.* The consequence of this quality of imitation in humans seems above all to be our capacity to become deeply connected to each other emotionally in ways that other species cannot.

There is growing empirical support for the idea of a close link between unconscious muscular imitation and perception of the emotions of others as displayed by facial and body expressions. When people experimentally observe pictures of emotional facial expressions, they show spontaneous unconscious and rapid electromyographic responses in the same facial muscles as the observed person's (Dimberg, Thunberg, & Elmehed, 2000). This very rapid, automatic activation of the facial muscles is consistent with the conceptualization of the mirror neuron system. Empathic processes may be underpinned by the coordinated activation of the mirror neuron system and motor mimicry. The hypothesis that the rapid muscular imitation in the face is a phenomenon intrinsic to empathy is supported by a study in which individuals displaying high levels of empathy also displayed strong automatic facial mimicry (Sonnby-Borgstrom, 2002). The most penetrating implications of this view of the empathic process have to do with the unconscious, automatic, and very rapid nature of the process. In my view, these contributions in support of an embodied basis for empathy have obvious implications for treatment and training. They offer a way to understand how we might automatically and without awareness register in our own body a state prevailing in the body of the patient.

This is not to say that it is only the emotions of the other we come to feel in an encounter. A mirror neuron study by Schulte-Ruther, Markowitsch, Fink, and Piefke (2007) is relevant here. *Participants in this study frequently reported feeling an emotion other than the one they observed, often an emotional reaction to the observed emotion.* Emotional responses to fearful facial expressions revealed a mixture of congruent (e.g., "afraid") and reactive (e.g., "compassionate") emotions, whereas responses to the angry facial expressions were overwhelmingly reactive; most participants reported such reactive feelings as "attacked," "uneasy," or "uncomfortable," while a very few reported such congruent or empathic feelings as "aggressive" or "irritated." *Exposure to emotional facial expressions was not always or only associated with activation of the mirror neuron system, but was frequently associated with a reactive or authentic emotional experience in the observer.*

The Schulte-Ruther et al. study emphasizes a critical point, one we need to consider when we work with embodied experience. The capacity of a patient or therapist to react to the emotion of the other rather than mirroring it quickly becomes difficult both to fathom and to navigate. The problem will be illustrated and discussed in connection with the case history later in this chapter. *The basic point here is that embodied communication and analytic interaction at the embodied level concern more than the experience of something shared, intersubjective attunement, and empathy; they also embrace subjectivity, authenticity, and egocentricity*, and how the experiences of these dimensions can be different for therapist and patient. This places great store on our capacity to reflect upon a mixture of reactive and empathic emotions. That ability is of key importance for therapist and patient alike. In the next chapter, I explore the need to learn how to balance and reflect on reactive and empathic feelings.

Fonagy, Gergely, Jurist, and Target (2002) coined the term *marked mirroring* with reference to "the good enough mother" who attunes to her child, rather than simply mirroring or imitating it. In addition to mirroring, by telling the child she knows how he is feeling by "marking" she also expresses her "opinion" or evaluation of the child's reaction. In parent–child interaction, mirroring without marking occurs when the parent's response simply reinforces the child's reaction. This corresponds to "over-involving" and "over-identifying" parents (and therapists). It is a good point, I believe, and reminds me of Strand's words cited in Chapter 4, "You can never identify too much with people you want to help. But you can forget you are doing it, and that is no good" (1991, p. 165).

However, following my reasoning on subjectivity and intersubjectivity, mirroring will always be marked by the subjectivity of the imitator. Mirroring or imitation can never be an exact copy, because mirroring happens in another body, another embodied subjectivity, and will always in some way be marked by that subjectivity. So the mother (or the analyst) will always mark their mirroring. The question is rather whether the marking is helpful or not.

As a background and introduction to a further discussion of imitation, I shall sum up by reemphasizing what I said above: emotions, by their very nature, seem to be interactively generated and formative of social relations. *An emotional body state is not only an intrinsic psychological property of a subject, but a relational property of subjects in a given social context.* We not only feel our own emotions, we also sense each other's emotions, are moved by them, make them our own, and in this process transform our selves, for better or worse, through identifications with each other. This intensity and depth in our emotional engagement with each other seem to be a hallmark of the human condition.

Inner imitation and embodied simulation

Imitation has often been restricted conceptually to outer, explicit behavioral copying. This might explain the reluctance of some researchers and clinicians to contemplate a fundamental role for imitation. Stern's explanation of affect attunement, built on this narrower conceptualization of imitation, illustrates and highlights my point.

> [T]he actual actions of the other do not become the referent of the attunement (as they would for imitation); rather, the feeling behind the actions becomes the referent. It is a way of imitating, from the inside, what an experience feels like, not how it was expressed in action. (1985, p. 241)

Gallese, researcher and theorist of the mirror neuron system, renamed the experience described by Stern ("imitating from the inside") *embodied simulation*. It is

> a mandatory, non-conscious, and pre-reflexive mechanism that is not the result of a deliberate and conscious effort. . . . When we see the facial expression of someone else, and this perception leads us to experience that expression as a particular affective state, we do not accomplish this type of understanding through an argument by analogy. The other's emotion is constituted, experienced, and therefore directly understood by means of an embodied simulation producing a shared body state. It is the activation of a neural mechanism shared by the observer and the observed that enables experiential understanding. (Gallese, Eagle, & Migone, 2007, pp. 143–144)

Gallese et al. (2007), then, expand the scope of imitation; when we witness the intentional behavior of others, embodied simulation generates directly a shared body state. It generates a peculiar quality of identification with other individuals, producing aspects of these others' intentional relations in ourselves. "By means of embodied simulation," Gallese and colleagues explain,

> we do not just "see" an action, an emotion, or a sensation. Side by side with the sensory description of the observed social stimuli, internal representations of the body states associated with these actions, emotions, and sensations are evoked in the observer, "as if" he/she would be doing a similar action or experiencing a similar emotion or sensation. (p. 148)

The new possibilities opened up by the concept of embodied simulation for our understanding of the clinical process will be discussed below. The concept will also be a fundamental assumption in the training approach to be described in the last section of this book.

Reis (2009) is concerned that Gallese, by introducing the term *simulation*, which derives from Theory of Mind, could be understood as saying that only a neuronal extra copy of the observed act is formed in the mirror neuron system. This may be a misreading of what Gallese (2009) intends. Consider his explanation:

> The discovery of mirror neurons provides a new empirically based notion of intersubjectivity, viewed first and foremost as intercorporeity (p. 523). . . . Anytime we meet someone, we are implicitly aware of his or her similarity to us, because we literally embody it. . . . Before and below mind reading is intercorporeity as the main source of knowledge we directly gather about others. (p. 524)

And so I read, and will use, the term intercorporeity to mean a direct embodied simulation/imitation. Similarly, *embodied simulation* will refer in my usage to an unmediated embodied imitation, including facial mimicry (Dimberg, Thunberg, & Elmehed, 2000; Sonnby-Borgstrom, 2002) and, to varying degrees, inner physiological changes throughout the body (Ekman, 1985).

Not long ago, Vivona (2009) published a critique of mirror neuron explanations of countertransference. Her critique is consistent with what I said above concerning the complexity involved in reading the emotional expressions of others. Contemporary psychoanalysis has become infatuated with neuroscience, she argues. Analysts, as a consequence of what mirror neuron research seems to explain, draw the – in her view, untenable – conclusion, that we can know the state of the patient immediately from what we are feeling within ourselves, from the countertransference. I have not drawn the same conclusion. Analysts have for decades conceptualized how we come to feel some of our patients' – unconscious – emotional states and even proclivity to act, within ourselves. These sensations are variously called concordant and complementary countertransference and projective identification.

Until recently, empirical investigations have fallen short of explaining these phenomena. Recent advances in neuroscience, and indeed imitation research not based on neuroscience, corroborate suggestions by Freud, Reich, and others to the effect that we can feel the state of others through a kind of inner imitation. These developments naturally enhance the confidence of many analysts in our embodied nonverbal experiences, thereby justifying "a distinct therapeutic role for nonverbal processes in the psychoanalytic situation, which rivals the primacy of verbal processes" (Vivona, 2009, p. 541).

Again, I want to advise caution: this is a complex process. While we may not know the state of the patient immediately from what we are feeling within ourselves, attention to embodied dimensions of our own experience can augment and enhance our clinical "hunches" and enrich our interactive participation with our patients both verbally and nonverbally.

Clearly, this kind of awareness can create many moments of shared emotional experience and understanding. But the process, as noted above, will also involve reactive or ego-centric forms of self-experience and even states whose ambiguity makes it difficult to place on either side of this emotional array. Following a suggestion by Fromm Reichman (Shapiro, 1996; Harris, 1998), I prefer to encourage colleagues and candidates to explore the embodied, affective processes in themselves by assuming a patient's posture. In the section on training and supervision, this technique will be elaborated further. I demonstrate some of the complexities and challenges involved in this combined reactive and imitative process in the case history below.

Explicit and implicit imitation

The fundamental role of identificatory processes has always been central to psychoanalytic theory. Emphasis since Freud has been on the centrality of these processes to the formation of character and neuroses, the formation of internal "object relations," concordant and complementary identifications, and countertransference experiences. What is new is that "the mechanisms" by which these experiences are formed have lost much of their mystery. The "mechanism," as I understand it, facilitates close relatedness between internal and external imitation.

As explained above, central to my approach to clinical practice and training is the wider concept of imitation. This expanded formulation includes *embodied simulation*, the sensing of another's emotions, and *matching* (or at least approximately matching) the behavioral gestures of others, what Stern calls the actual actions of the other. Nebbiosi and Federici-Nebbiosi have recently described a process of *miming* as a form of imitation by which the explicit behavioral gestures or actual actions provide an embodied basis for capturing the patient's feelings (2008, p. 223). These different ideas expand the scope of the concept of imitation by including both explicit *and* implicit imitation (as in embodied simulation). In fact, mirror neuron research suggests a very close relationship between inner and outer, implicit and explicit imitation. The same brain areas are activated when we observe someone doing something as if we were performing the action ourselves. "In humans, there is a kind of direct resonance between the observation and execution of actions, and the possible relation to monkey mirror neurons has been discussed" (Meltzoff & Decety, 2003, p. 493). This observation has important implications for psychoanalysis and psychotherapy. In any therapeutic encounter, when therapist and patient attend to each other's embodied presence, they are already participating in each other's respective actions, feelings, and thoughts.

Imitation, then, is largely an internal process, an embodied simulation by necessity. It is the most economic process, saving much time and energy. It is not coincidental that we talk about gut feeling rather than arm or leg feeling. Reich hit the nail on the head when he suggested that the patient's expressive movements "involuntarily bring about *an imitation* in our own organism." By imitating these movements, he adds, "we 'sense' and understand the expression in ourselves and, consequently, in the patient" (p. 362). Damasio (2000) underlines the centrality of the somatosensory system concerned with mapping the continuously changing internal milieu and viscera, and cites Cole Porter's "I've got you under my skin" as unwittingly capturing this important idea.

The strong connection between inner and outer imitation is also demonstrated by the ease with which embodied simulation is converted into outer motor imitation. It is striking to see how readily analysts and therapists imitate patients during training sessions. Empirical evidence for the innate link between the perception and production of human acts in shared neural representations is consistent with these observations (Meltzoff & Decety, 2003). Meltzoff and Decety report another related finding. The pattern of cortical activation under observation with *an intention* to imitate is more akin to that of motor action than the mere observation of actions (p. 493).

I started the presentation of this conceptual and clinical perspective by reviewing the work of the philosophers Spinoza and Merleau-Ponty. Merleau-Ponty belonged to the phenomenological/existentialist school of twentieth-century European philosophy. I shall now make use of the philosopher Ludwig Wittgenstein, whose background was in analytical philosophy, to round off my discussion of contributions to our understanding of intersubjectivity. The following, from *Remarks on the Philosophy of Psychology*, reminds us that we might have what Hobson (2002) calls a "direct route into the minds of others" (p. 244):

> "We *see* emotion." – As opposed to what? – We do not see facial contortions and *make the inference* that he is feeling joy, grief, boredom. We describe a face immediately as sad, radiant, bored, even when we are unable to give any other description of the features. (Wittgenstein, 1980, vol. 2, p. 570)

> "I see that the child wants to touch the dog, but doesn't dare." How can I see that? – Is this description of what is seen on the same level as a description of moving shapes and colours? Is an interpretation in question? Well, remember that you may also *mimic* a human being who would like to touch something, but doesn't dare. (Wittgenstein, 1980, vol. 1, p. 1066)

Following Wittgenstein, I want to add to the Boston Change Process Study Group's (1998, 2010) observation and suggest that there is not only "something *more* than interpretation," there is also something *before* interpretation.

A clinical illustration – the case of Astrid

The rest of this chapter on intersubjectivity will be devoted to a presentation and discussion of a patient, Astrid. Her case also shows that there really might be something before interpretation.

When Astrid contacted me wanting to start therapy, she was 25. She found it increasingly difficult to be social, to meet and spend time with others. These spaces were coming at shorter and shorter intervals, and she was isolating herself more and more at home. She was interested in the theater and acting and wanted to express herself artistically. She studied history, but made her living working in a store. Arriving for our first session, she was a smiling and friendly young woman, possibly a little bit shy, but not a person I would imagine who found her social life so difficult. At our second session Astrid told me she had just started taking the anti-depressive medication Zoloft. She used to be against medication for mental problems, but in view of her worsening condition, she asked her doctor to give her a prescription. It was already helping a little, she confided. The physician noted in the referral note that she had thought of committing suicide.

Astrid grew up with her parents, a two-year younger brother and a younger sister, six years her junior. Her childhood had been normal and good until her parents' relationship changed for the worse when she was about 10 years old. They stopped doing things with the children and eventually separated. By then, Astrid was about 12. Astrid's life now became very difficult. Her parents continued to live in the same house, but on different floors. Her father was often very depressed and sometimes angry; he seemed to lose control, but was never physically violent. She was afraid and ashamed of the situation at home, and concealed it from her friends by not letting them visit. She continued to do well at school, however.

In her second year in high school, her attitude to food changed. She felt she had grown fat, had alternating periods of hardly eating and overeating. She did not tell anybody about this. By her third year, she realized she had become too thin; it was affecting her skin. She was very embarrassed about this, felt ugly and repulsive. She started dropping classes, avoided friends and isolated herself. She continued, however, with her drama activities and took part in performances at school. On stage, she felt safe and well. She did not graduate from high school because her attendance record in some subjects was below the threshold. She was referred to the local mental health outpatient clinic and had a few appointments there.

This was when her father moved to an apartment of his own in the same neighborhood. Astrid stayed with her mother; her parents had shared custody of her younger siblings. After high school, Astrid stayed at home for a while; her mother encouraged her to get a job, which she did, at a warehouse. She started to be more social again. She and a female friend wrote and staged a cabaret. At the age of 20, she got her first boyfriend. She moved into an apartment with some friends, continued to perform on stage, completed high school and started studying at college. She still felt depressed, and her social anxiety fluctuated in quite unpredictable ways. As time passed, the number of people she felt she could relax with diminished. By the time she decided to seek therapy, it was difficult for her even to be with her mother. Her brother was the only person she could relax with. Anxiety was the dominant feature of her life.

Review of the first 3 1/2 years of the therapy

Astrid and I soon established a good working relationship. We agreed to work together until she regained confidence and felt she could continue on her own. We decided on a twice-weekly therapy plan. But the second weekly session had to wait until an hour became available. During our second session, Astrid said she recognized the mood inside her: It was how she had felt after her parents separated. We both came to see that period as a particularly crucial event in the development of the difficulties she was struggling with. Although Astrid at that time found it difficult to be with either parent, relations with her father were particularly fraught. She felt a strong attachment and sense of care and responsibility for him, but her feelings could also be intensely negative. I recalled the kind of identification first described by Freud (1923/1961a; see the previous chapter), and particularly the type of identification discussed by Philipson (1951; see Chapter 4), where the identification captures specifically what the child finds most disturbing about the parent. When I shared these thoughts with Astrid, they seemed to make good sense to her.

A few months after starting therapy, Astrid spent a holiday visiting her father. She experienced the same sense of gloom, a reminder of the time her parents were separated but lived in the same house. The father shut himself off, and neither wanted nor appreciated contact. Shortly after this holiday, Astrid changed rather dramatically for the better. It was after her stay with her father that she realized how much his attitude to life had rubbed off on her. She started to look at her situation as if from the outside, and felt that her identification with her father had lost its hold on her. She stopped taking the anti-depressives, found a boyfriend, R., and fell in love. She feels extremely happy, she tells me, and she doesn't seem manic to me at all. Astrid's therapy looks as if it will be over very soon indeed. Nonetheless, I recall other cases, where what appeared to be a quick and strong recovery at an early date of therapy didn't last, especially when the patient had fallen in love and feelings were reciprocated.

This turned out to be the case this time too. After a couple of months, Astrid's state of mind again changed. The weather was warmer, but Astrid continued to wrap herself up as if it were still winter. When I mentioned this to her, she started talking about her complexes and how she felt about her body and sexuality. While her parents lived in separate parts of the house, she discovered that her father watched porn on the TV. Now she finds it difficult to be naked with her boyfriend. Her admiration for him grows, but at the same time she loses her own interests. She stops studying for the rest of the term. "I'll play the role of wife like my mother did."

About half a year after the start of the relationship, Astrid ends it. But she wants to keep R. as a friend, and have him play a part in her life. Following this decision, though, she increasingly feels despair, living in a state of crisis. She loses her self-esteem, starts taking Zoloft again. This reaction, she tells me, reminds her of how she felt when earlier relationships ended. Her reaction indicates, I tell her, a strong tendency to idealize the other and downgrade herself. She remembers how she kept her own feelings locked away inside when her parents bickered on end, and that she was afraid her father would end his own life.

Her social anxiety returns. In her reverie, R. is much better than her, more successful. She contemplates suicide again, believing she will never succeed with anything in life. "Half a year ago I felt like a grown up, now I feel like a child again." "Thinking of R., I feel like I am him." "I lose myself, feel like different persons." During this period we, of course, focus on how bad she feels. She also feels less secure in our sessions. When she allows herself to feel her sense of insecurity, tears tend to flow. Astrid says she can't take herself seriously, or go after what she wants. Her crying, however, brings her closer to herself. "It was better last week after I managed to admit that it is difficult for me to come here." She has been able to feel her anger toward R., and has enjoyed being together with friends. She seems, I suggest, ready to pay more attention to her own needs and feelings.

Over the following weeks – we were approaching the end of the first year of therapy – Astrid starts immersing herself in her artistic work. From having played a secondary role, it becomes the most important aspect of her life. It is challenging in a good way, she feels, getting together with others on a stage, and being able to express herself. She visits her father again, but it is difficult. "I am not a separate person when I'm with dad, not a woman of 26 but small and unfinished." "I don't like the girl inside me. I don't feel like a boy, but I lack identity as a girl."

She still senses her tendency to idealize others. And she finds it difficult to sit face to face with me in our sessions. But she wants to address the difficult feelings as she experiences them here and now in the therapy room. This includes eye contact. Her anxiety and tears resurface. "I've got a bad conscience because I think too much instead of just experiencing. I can't enjoy a social setting." Would she prefer to lie down, I ask her, to avoid challenging eye contact all the time. Although she agrees, we don't put the idea into practice just yet.

By the start of her second year of therapy, Astrid is talking about her difficulties with her family. It's not only a question of her father this time. She has "caught" her mother's insecurity. And she still has the tendency to idealize her ex-boyfriend, R. But apart from these difficult areas, the main thing in her life now is the breakthrough in her artistic work. She lands a job with a government-supported and highly respected ensemble.

Throughout the second half of the second year, Astrid faces new challenges as she takes on more responsibilities in connection with her work. It is difficult to give herself the space she needs, and to accept responsibility as the head of the company although it is clearly the right thing to do. She sometimes feels used by others, and that there are no limits to her empathy. She also feels alone at times, and that she can't trust either her mother or her father. Her experience of the therapy has varied over the past half year. She tells me on one occasion she has lost trust in the treatment. That trust returns, however, when she manages to confront her feelings of vulnerability.

Astrid continues to progress professionally in the first half of the third year of therapy. She falls in love with a colleague, K. They start a relationship but he, they discover, still hasn't got his ex-girlfriend out of his system. She senses a small, nagging tendency to idealize K. and has a nasty dream about her mother and father being together again. She wonders what true love is. She is on the lookout for men. After a time, she meets L., and they start a relationship. Her relationship with L. deteriorates during the second half of year three. He can be sarcastic and hurtful. For the first time I get the impression that Astrid has a relationship with a man who actually hurts her. The difficulties and conflicts of her previous relationships have come across, to me, more in the shape of "ghosts." By the end of year three, Astrid has terminated the relationship. It was difficult, but different from earlier "endings." She hardly idealized L. at all.

She continues to progress in her career during the first half of year four. The company tours abroad. She starts writing, and performs her own work. But she also feels anxious and has a bad conscience because she's not good enough, doesn't work hard enough, etc. It's hard to stay with her feelings, her gut feelings. She stops taking Zoloft. She meets a new man, N., and they soon fall in love. This relationship is very satisfactory, Astrid reports. I get a good impression of N. from what she tells me. But she is concerned about losing herself and her interests. The company goes on a new tour abroad.

By the start of the next half year – after a pause of more than a month – Astrid tells me to my surprise that she has broken off her relationship with N., though they're still in touch. She's been having a very tough time, she tells me. She started to feel lonely in the relationship, she explains. N. didn't seem capable or willing to understand her situation or anxieties. But above all, she was increasingly feeling she couldn't be herself in N.'s company. She felt small and helpless, and was unable to find anything interesting to talk about. She doesn't want to lose him as a friend, however, and the idea of N. no longer thinking about her is very scary. But even if life is painful, she manages to go on touring and performing. She sees N. now and then; to her, he is big and she small. Astrid continues to feel her life is difficult; it is dark, she feels abandoned and alone. Her thoughts are increasingly negative. She takes sick leave for a period. She wants to be everything for others, she feels, but always fails, is never good enough. She also failed to make her dad happy.

There is a pattern to all this, I find. Astrid ends relationships because they become impossible, too painful. But ending relationships results in an even more painful emotional state. It is my belief, I tell her, that there is a golden opportunity to get to grips with this pattern, and problems she is facing whether she is in a relationship with N., or not. Astrid seems to appreciate this as a challenge, and decides to embark on a more intimate relationship with N. again. That sparks the return of her self-criticism with full force. She again expresses doubts as to whether the treatment has helped her at all. She has gone through lengthy depressive periods since she was 17–18, she protests, which had nothing to do with external events. The subtext here is possibly this: the therapeutic focus on relationships may never solve her problems. She blames herself for this, at least, she does so verbally. At therapy sessions, she sees herself as having been too politely analytical, avoiding her most difficult feelings.

My process – countertransference – from the middle of year four

So, after having ended – or at least tried to end – her relationship with N., Astrid looks back on nearly four years of therapy as fruitless. She has made no progress at all, she insists. Was there something fundamentally wrong with the way we were working, she wonders. Confronted with these disturbing but possibly revealing questions, my reactions, I realized, were telling me that Astrid might be right.

In our sessions, Astrid tended to sit huddled in her chair with her legs curled up underneath, and her arms resting in her lap. It is a well-known defensive posture, an attempt to ward off and control difficult and painful feelings. However, I gradually became aware that this was not how I had seen her (sitting this way). I had to admit to myself that I had perceived Astrid taking a position that was quite comfortable and relaxing for her; a good starting point for a mutually beneficial session. We often in fact began sessions exchanging what we had been thinking about since the last time. Astrid had more than once told me that she saw herself as good at and very engaged with psychological analysis. Only gradually did I sense a possible subtext to her remarks, saying that her analytical ability and interest might be as much an obstacle to her as a resource. Indeed, I become more convinced of this as I think it over. I also get the embarrassing feeling that I probably contributed actively to making our therapeutic conversation cognitively analytical and reflective. The realization prompts a sense of unease in me for failing to sense the intensity of her inner turmoil and desperation.

I have done quite a lot of work in training and supervising contexts on imitation as a means of improving our understanding of a patient's emotional state (see Chapters 10 and 11). However, I have seldom imitated patients – explicitly – in my own sessions. The thinking behind the use of imitation in training and supervision is that it will enhance practitioners' empathic capacity in therapeutic settings when we do not use imitation as a specific technique. But worried that I might have missed something important about Astrid's emotional state, I decide to make use of explicit imitation, and imitate the way she sat. After the end of our next session, I sat myself down in her chair and tried to assume her physical position as best I could. Gravensteen (2009) and Nebbiosi and Federici-Nebbiosi (2008), in earlier reports, have described in similar fashion imitating their own patients after the end of a session.

Sitting in the way Astrid typically did, I in no way experience what I took to be a relatively relaxed, comfortable position. Quite to the contrary, I feel extremely uneasy, almost desperate. But it was difficult for me to say how far my sensations were the same as Astrid's just a moment ago, and how much could be put down to my own concerns and disquiet, both for her and for me with her. Were my feelings reactive or empathic, as previously discussed?

In the next session, I tell Astrid that I've started wondering whether her anxiety and despair might be more intense than I had realized. She expresses some surprise at hearing me saying this, and says that she can't know if I am right or wrong. I feel, nonetheless, that I am on the right track. Even if I'm not completely convinced, I'm still pretty sure that what I came into contact with was connected with her intense feeling of desperation.

After our initial sessions, we had agreed on two sessions a week, as noted above. At the time, though, I didn't have a vacancy, and with Astrid seemingly heading for a rapid recovery, the need for a second session became somewhat academic.

When Astrid's initial recovery proved short lived, increasing the number of sessions, for some reason, was never raised again by either of us.

Now, three and a half years later, and faced with a shattering discovery, the frequency of our sessions becomes a serious problem. We also missed sessions because of Astrid's growing touring activity, and my month-long holidays from my practice summer and winter reduced the number of sessions even more. Considering the challenges we were facing, there was clearly too little time. Astrid agreed unhesitatingly. We therefore decided to meet twice a week. When a vacancy turned up two months later we added a third weekly session.

Meeting twice a week brought immediate rewards, I felt. Indeed, it seemed to be a necessary condition for reestablishing a therapeutic relationship robust and trusting enough to dare address the situation we found ourselves in the middle of. Astrid had started to express how bad she felt, as previously mentioned, rather than reflecting over why her relationship with N. could not continue. As the sessions grow more frequent, she talks less and cries more. She looks down when she cries. She loses contact with herself, she says, and has to stop crying if she looks at me. In the weeks ahead she goes through many dark moments when life doesn't seem worth living. "I can't live the kind of life I want to, being the way I am. There's no hope for me; there's too much that needs to be changed. I don't care about anything." She lets herself cry silently for a long time toward the end of this session. To me it feels good.

When she misses a session without cancelling, which is very unlike her, I become seriously afraid that something might have happened. It takes several hours to get hold of her on the phone. It's a relief to hear that she'd fallen ill. She had a fever, gone to bed and turned her phone off. She had left a message for me, but it was on a cell phone I hadn't brought with me to the office this day. However, my reaction, my countertransference, is clearly stronger and more dramatic than I am used to. It tells me how worried I am about Astrid, but also that I feel far from sure that our relationship is sufficiently robust to carry us through the crisis.

I therefore take the first opportunity to examine my situation together with members of my peer supervision group. This group uses the supervision model developed at the Character Analytic Institute in Oslo (see Chapter 11). In essence, it proceeds as follows. The supervisee imitates his usual physical stance in therapy, seated in the therapist's chair. The supervisee then adopts his patient's posture, before finally moving to a third place, in between therapist and patient, in order to mull over what he experienced in the two former positions. This is different from imitating the patient alone in one's office because it allows one to explore both the patient's and one's own bodily and mental state under the guidance of a colleague.

Having adopted my usual posture as Astrid's therapist, my anxiety for the state of the therapeutic situation with Astrid is confirmed. When I explore Astrid's posture, it brings me into contact with feelings of turmoil, despair, and desperation, feelings of an entirely different quality than my anxiety as her therapist. In the third position, I look at the encounter I have just staged between Astrid and myself, and I feel that we are indeed on the right track. In the past couple of months I have probably managed to appreciate the state Astrid finds herself in a far more pertinent way. Reflecting now from the third position, our present way of engaging with each other seems appropriate given the challenges we face. What I have in mind here is the frame, the number of sessions per week, and how we relate to each other during these sessions. Astrid has just chosen to lie down on the couch in our sessions.

I believe the most important change in me is my attempt to concentrate on *how* it's like to be her, rather than *what* she has to tell me, *what* she thinks the reasons are for her present situation. In other words, I focus now on the vitality affects, the forms of vitality (Stern, 2010), the *how* rather than the *what* and *why*. I say considerably less now than I used to in my sessions with Astrid, and the same goes for her. Most things are already said, I feel. It is not an understanding of the past or the present that is lacking. The challenge is rather to create space for vulnerable and difficult feelings which previously have not really been allowed to surface in relationships, in encounters with others. What Astrid fills this space with is above all silent sorrow and tears.

Astrid goes back to N., who has actually been waiting for her. While this again gives rise to difficult feelings, particularly about not being good enough, they don't overwhelm her or take control. The most important thing is that she seems to be able to enjoy being in love and in a loving relationship.

I asked Astrid to read the text above and told her that I intended to publish it if she had no objections. I quote the part of her written commentary that applies specifically to what she referred to as the "challenge" in our cooperation.

> The accumulated knowledge and insight into my own emotional life certainly provided a rewarding and important reference for me to progress and grow, but at the same time I feel something's missing, an emptiness, and often a meaninglessness. It can often feel like a way of avoiding feeling anything, or even experiencing.
>
> When we shifted focus in the therapy, I felt a sense of emotional anchoring more often. A feeling of arriving in myself, a feeling of openness and freedom to make my own decisions. In these moments the endless interpreting and searching for meaning are transformed, becoming a preference rather than an absolute necessity. I feel it physically. The world doesn't come at me full throttle, I feel free and easy as I wander through life.

Concluding comments on Astrid's therapy

Like Peter in the earlier vignettes, Astrid tended to lose contact with her core self when she was "invited" to be empathic, to identify with a loved "object." Both have highly developed empathic capacities. Astrid's, however, is more cathected, so to speak, to "pathological" identifications than Peter's. Her identification with her father's depressive and pessimistic view of life, the aspect of her father that made her teenage years so difficult and which she likes least about him, recalls Freud's and particularly Philipson's thinking about identification. Gaining an understanding of this mode of identification and its recurrence when Astrid stayed over with her father early in the therapy had an immediate liberating effect. But it failed to get to grips with the emotional and relational tenacity of these identifications. This became clear when they were triggered again by new relationships, particularly with men. A pattern repeated with several boyfriends was not undone by further reflection and more insights. Mutual reflection did not, in Astrid's case, allay the fear associated with an intimate relationship, resulting in "blind" withdrawal and isolation. The turning point came gradually as both Astrid and I reconfigured the therapeutic challenge: to dare to confront amorphous feelings together, rather than continuing to polish a verbal-reflective understanding.

For me, the turning point involved identifying less with the meaning-seeking side of Astrid, and daring to tune into and becoming empathic with her verbally unformulated feelings, and to seek support in this process by means of explicit imitation. The most crucial realization thrown up by the challenges of this case is how the therapeutic potential of an intersubjective encounter relies above all on the depth of emotional contact, as facilitated by empathy and identification (and supported by imitation/embodied simulation). The value of verbal reflection, understanding, and efforts to capture the meaning of things come on top of this. More important than formulating a "correct" verbal understanding, the crucial thing, at least sometimes, is to create a space where repressed or dissociated emotions connected with past relationships can be felt in a therapeutic relationship and setting, sensations that so far have been intolerable to the patient – and perhaps to the therapist as well – and impossible to express in a relationship. This, I believe, may be the great significance of what Freud originally formulated as the need to make the unconscious conscious.

Given my clinical experience and theoretical convictions, I should never have committed the "error" I did with Astrid; that is, giving priority to analyzing dialogue by way of words at the expense of embodied subjectivity and intersubjectivity. But there is a silver lining, I think. It illustrates a well-established and often confirmed "fact" of clinical psychoanalysis: that personal and induced countertransference can in combination upset the best of therapeutic intentions. In the next chapter, the coin is turned upside down; I examine the value of a well-developed capacity for verbal reflection and the problems that ensue when it is lacking.

Chapter 8

Embodied reflexivity

"We" in mind

I have argued that the foundational level of intersubjectivity and communication can be found in embodied, emotional processes of imitation, empathy, and identification. Thus far I have discussed an understanding of analytic interaction mainly as constituted by rapid, bidirectional, nonverbal, *continuous-process exchanges* (Knoblauch, 2000). I now want to consider the slower, unidirectional, verbal, and more *discrete-state exchanges* in the analytical interaction, i.e., exchanges as they are captured in verbal reflective thought. These are the exchanges that traditionally have been considered the "material" of psychoanalysis and psychotherapy. *I shall, however, suggest that the very same processes of emotional interaction – imitation, empathy, and identification – that constitute continuous emotional communication also form the basis on which reflective thought and linguistic communications are grounded.*

Regarding the usually more conscious states captured in the verbal exchange, I shall also focus on the need for and possibility that the analyst can establish a more distant, reflective perspective within the analytic exchange. In discussing the clinical illustration in the previous chapter, on the other hand, I focused on problems caused by a prematurely distant and reflective perspective toward the analytic exchange; thought that is not grounded in, but has become more or less dissociated from embodied intersubjectivity or, in other words, *ideas about ideas.*

It is important for both therapist and patient, in my view, to develop and strengthen a capacity for *body-based verbal reflexivity.* I do not, however, see this distant and "slower" process as contradicting or in opposition to rapid body-emotional exchanges. It is, rather, a verbal-reflective process grounded in the body-emotional. Take, for example, Ammaniti's (2009) reports from neuro-scientific research (Lenzi et al., 2008). Activity in the mirror neuron system changes to activity in the fronto-parietal areas, mostly in the left hemisphere, when mothers watch the unfolding emotions of their children. When the mothers watch the expressions of stress or joy in their children, the activity of the mirror neuron system is intense, while an ambiguous expression of the child activates the fronto-parietal areas, suggesting that the mother begins a process of reflective thinking, like: "I wonder what my child is experiencing now?"

The rooting of thought and language in the body

It is remarkable that no other explanatory factors seem to be needed to explain the emergence of reflective thought and language. According to researchers and theorists, thought and language are rooted in the very same processes of imitation, empathy, and identification that are characteristic of human interaction and emotional engagement. Hobson (1998) explains his understanding in this way.

> I have suggested that early forms of interpersonal responsiveness, identification and imitation are what disengage an infant from a one-track relation with the environment, and enable her to acquire self-consciousness, to distinguish attitudes from the objects of those attitudes, to apply new meanings or descriptions-for-persons to the materials of symbolic play, and to gain insight into the nature of prediction and naming. If the account is correct, it exemplifies Vygotsky's thesis that sophisticated mental capacities arise through the interiorization of interpersonal processes. (p. 296)

Reis (2009) has, in resonance with Hobson, pointed out that "[t]hinking does not occur as a result of the development of a private sphere or hidden mental space that we would call 'mind' so much as from our active sensorimotor and perceptual involvement in the world and with others in it, which shapes the very properties of conceptual inference" (p. 569). So while we have been looking at the possibility for deep emotional connectedness created by imitation and identification, we can now consider another function of the same process, that of *disengaging from a one-track relationship with the environment*. Realizing that we can approach the same situation from more than one angle seems to be a decisive precondition for reflective thought to unfold. For example, consider how Hobson (2002) envisages *The Cradle of Thought* – and language.

> The links that can join one person's mind with the mind of someone else – especially, to begin with, emotional links – are the very links that draw us into thought. To put it crudely: the foundations of thinking were laid at the point when ancestral primates began to connect with each other emotionally in the same ways that human babies connect with their caregivers. (p. 2)

The crucial thing about these emotional connections is their capacity to facilitate the shift in perspective provided by an ability to adopt or imitate the posture of the other. Repeated experience of *moving* from the one psychological position to the other *through someone else* becomes critically important.

> The mechanism by which all this occurs is the process of identification. As we have seen, normal infants are engaged with other people and with the actions and feelings that are expressed through people's bodies. Their subjective experiences are coordinated with those of their mothers or other

caregivers. Then infants reach a stage in which they identify with the attitudes of others. To identify with someone is to assume the other person's stance or characteristics. (Hobson, 2002, p. 105)

It is through this process of imitation and identification that infants are affected by another person's attitudes to something, and to themselves, in such a way that they assume or adopt the other's emotional stance toward that something, while still maintaining some awareness of their own initial state. It is probably fair to say that the essence of thinking can be boiled down to this: allowing ourselves to be affected by another's attitude toward something while at the same time remaining aware of our own stance. The capacity for reflection can emerge in this way in children and caregivers as well as in therapists and patients.[1]

Siri Hustvedt (2011) asks: "Is it not reasonable . . . that 'self-processing' cannot be distinguished from 'other-processing' at the explicit, conscious level of story-telling?" (p. 191). She provides the following answer: "At the explicit representational level of episodic and imaginative narration, a distinction between self- and other-processing strikes me as entirely artificial" (p. 191). Akhtar and Tomasello (1998) summarize their view concerning the intersubjective basis of language in the following way:

> The more we think about processes of linguistic communication, the less we like saying such things as intersubjectivity 'facilitates' or 'play a role' in early language. Indeed, we believe it is more accurate to say simply that language is an inherently intersubjective phenomenon through and through. Conventional linguistic symbols are nothing more or less than tools that human beings have collaboratively invented for establishing, regulating and maintaining intersubjective interactions with fellow human beings. (p. 334)

Implicit in a view of thought as based on simultaneous self and other-processing is that it originates in bodies in interaction; moving and acting bodies. Discussing rhythmic experience, Nebbiosi and Federici-Nebbiosi (2008) reflect on the conflicting conceptions of action and thought in psychoanalysis.

> Many of the most famous psychoanalytical models – e.g., Freudian, Kleinian, Bionian – consider thought as a function that originates from the ability to tolerate frustration and therefore ascribe to action a function of thoughtless burst that is antithetic of thought. . . . It has been contemporary psychoanalysis – influenced by the research on early childhood – that recognized the importance of the body's motor activity and took an interest in the implicit language of movements (facial expressions, postures, etc.), which these days seems to play an important role in the psychoanalytic dialogue. (pp. 217–218)

Nebbiosi and Federici-Nebbiosi point to implications of the discovery of the mirror neuron. The motor system seems to be closely interconnected with the visual, auditory and tactile systems, perception appears to be directly immersed in the dynamics of action.

> As can be seen, this research on the neural bases of human interaction offers us the extraordinary discovery that thought originates in the body in movement. As the sequence of movements always gives rise to a rhythm, it becomes clear that the latter lies at the basis of building of meaning. Every time that an attempt is made at understanding body and movement language, the rhythmic experience shows its unique function as a bridge between the movement of bodies and the building of the emotional meaning in the relationship. (pp. 219–220)

Referring to the gradual acceptance of action as enabling, as opposed to obstructing, thought we are, say Nebbiosi and Federici-Nebbiosi, in psychoanalysis still far from considering movement on an equal footing with language, and more specifically an emotional language. In order to understand movement in its linguistic function, it must be conceived of as the language of a relationship, not just of an individual. In their view, it was conceiving of the psyche in a mainly intra-psychic way that moved classical psychoanalysis away from the idea of movement as language.

Hobson (2002) suggests that social engagement is also what provides the foundation for language by motivating the appearance of language in the first place. In his view, it was precisely this change in the nature of primate social engagement that led to the kinds of thinking with language that is the hallmark of being human. The need for verbal expression and communication, in Hobson's view, is closely linked to a strong need for and engagement in bodily emotional expression and communication. The connection is made as follows: "If bodily expressions of feeling are such a vital part of our existence, then so is human expressiveness in language" (Hobson, 2002, p. 85). Here again I find the reflections of the novelist Siri Hustvedt illuminating:

> I have often asked myself, why tell one fictional story and not another? Theoretically, a novelist can write about anything, but doesn't. It is as if the *fabula* is already waiting and must be laboriously unearthed or suddenly unleashed from memory. That process is not exclusively the result of so-called higher cognition; it is not purely cognitive or linguistic. When I write, I see images in my mind, and I feel the rhythms of my sentences, embodied temporal expectancies, and I am guided by gut feelings of rightness and wrongness, feelings not unlike what happened to me in psychotherapy as a patient. After my analyst's interpretation, I have felt a jolt of recognition, which is never merely an intellectualization but always a felt meaning: *Oh, my God, that's true, I have to rewrite my story.* (2011, pp. 194–195)

This linkage between embodied temporal expectancies and language was anticipated by Loewald in his paper, *Primary Process, Secondary Process and Language.* He writes,

> The mother's flow of words does not convey meaning to or symbolize "things" for the infant . . . but the sounds, tone of voice, and rhythm of speech are suffused within the apprehended global event . . . while the mother utters words, the infant does not perceive words but is bathed in sound, rhythm, etc. as accentuating ingredients of a uniform experience. (Loewald, 1980, p. 187)

Loewald further suggests that the sensory-motor elements of speech remain bodily ingredients of language, lending to words and sentences the aspect of concrete acts and entities also considered by Ferenczi. "This aspect continues to dwell in language, although unattended to, even in its most abstract use, and in written and read language and 'inner speech' as well" (p. 203).

Lakoff and Johnson (1980) offered extensive evidence on linguistic and philosophical grounds for the rooting of thought and language in the body. They have shown how our abstract verbal concepts are not given a priori but are derived from images of bodily interaction with other people and the environment. Lakoff (1987) wrote:

> Thought is embodied, that is, the structures used to put together our conceptual systems grow out of bodily experience and make sense in terms of it; moreover, the core of our conceptual systems is directly grounded in perception, body movements, and experiences of a physical and social character. (p. xiv)

A simple illustration: "up" and "down" refer to directions as seen from the present position of our body. Added significance comes from the way the body is affected by emotional interaction, as when "up" comes to mean joy and happiness and "down" sorrow and depression. Referring to his cooperation with Lakoff (Gallese & Lakoff, 2005), Gallese (2009) contemplates meaning. It does not, he says, "inhabit a pre-given Platonic world of ideal and eternal truths to which mental representations connect and conform. The body is the main source of meaning, because it not only structures the experiential aspects of interpersonal relations, but also their linguistic representations" (p. 533). Reich also saw language as derived from bodily experience.

> Evidently, language derives from the sensations perceived by body organs. For example, the German word *Ausdruck* and its English equivalent "expression" exactly describe the language of the living organism: *the living organism expresses itself in movements;* we therefore speak of "expressive movements." . . . Language is clearly derived from the perception of inner movements and organ sensations, and the words that describe emotional conditions *directly* reflect the corresponding expressive movement of the living organism (1949/1972, pp. 358–359).

I share with these theorists the position that the very language we and our patients rely on to describe psychological states is itself grounded in embodied experience. Our ability to find words to describe and contemplate intersubjective experience seems largely dependent on our capacity to stay in contact with the embodied emotional processes of self and other. In other words, our ability to imitate and simulate the actions and emotions of the other might, while we remain in contact with our own feelings, also facilitate verbal dialogue. The anatomical proximity of the mirror neuron system and speech centers has been interpreted as evidence of the development of language from dialogical gesture language (Gallese & Lakoff, 2005). Gesture and speech language in humans may still be closely related, as argued by Fonagy and Target (2007a). A critical aspect of the training approach discussed later is the oscillating movement between implicit *and* explicit imitation *and* verbalization. It allows the candidate to accumulate experience of explicit imitation for use in the therapeutic situation in which implicit imitation predominates over explicit. Gianni Nebbiosi and Susanna Federici-Nebbiosi (2008; Federici-Nebbiosi & Nebbiosi, 2012) have similarly reported on the combination of explicit imitation outside the therapeutic situation and implicit imitation in the analytical interaction. Studies by Carr, Iacoboni, Dubeau, Mazziotta, and Lenzi (2003), along with my own observations of analytic therapy, training, and supervision, suggest that explicit, motor imitation intensifies feelings as compared to simply watching a behavior take place; it thereby also facilitates verbalization.

But a cautionary note is called for. Clinically, it can be a relatively simple issue to facilitate verbalization by paying attention to embodied experience. But it can also be very difficult and challenging as when trauma has constituted states of dissociation in patient and/or analyst. Philip Bromberg (1998) and others have described how embodied experience fails to latch into the reflective function and verbalization. It occurs when the power of emotions, first registered bodily, becomes unbearable, causing dissociation and a consequent erasure of the opportunity to verbalize.

Before closing this consideration of arguments in support of the embodied basis of thought and language, I want to again stress that I do not see verbal communication as less important than nonlinguistic interaction. It is not only embodied interaction that shapes language; as noted previously, language also shapes the body. There have been many examples in the psychoanalytic literature of the profound effect words can exert on us physically. Gallese (2009) reports recent research corroborating the hypothesis of a close relationship between bodily activation and the processing of language with an emotional content. Understanding happy sentences activates muscles associated with smiling, while understanding sad and angry sentences activates muscles associated with frowning. This resonates with Merleau-Ponty's views, who also emphasized the primary effect of words on the body, as previously reviewed.

Gut feeling, morality and decision-making

Descartes' Error (Damasio, 1994) is essentially about the relationship between gut feelings and thoughts, particularly as it affects the capacity for social behavior and rational decision-making. Damasio discusses the extraordinary case of Phineas Gage, a 25-year-old railway construction foreman from Vermont, New England. In 1848, he was preparing a charge, i.e., "tamping" or pressing the dynamite, fuse, and sand into a hole in the rock. The unstable mixture suddenly exploded, driving the metal stamping rod, 40 inches long, 1 inch in diameter, and tapered at one end, through Gage's left cheek, past his left eye, and out through the top of his skull where it came to rest. Amazingly, Gage survived. He lost sight in his left eye, but apart from that seemed remarkably unscathed. Soon, however, his behavior changed. He had been a bright, responsible young man. Now, he couldn't keep down a responsible job and hardly worked at all. His conduct deteriorated to the extent "that women were advised not to stay long in his presence, lest their sensibilities be offended" (p. 8). These character traits were the polar opposite of the "temperate habits" and "considerable energy of character" of pre-accident days. Friends and acquaintances could hardly recognize him. "Gage was no longer Gage." "The problem was not lack of physical ability or skill; it was his new character" (p. 8).

Damasio (1994) and his colleagues examined several patients presenting with prefrontal brain damage of the kind suffered by Phineas Cage. Neither intelligence tests nor traditional neuropsychological tests revealed anything amiss with any of these patients. But they seemed emotionally detached or cold, apart from sudden "primitive" outbursts. They found it difficult to make choices, decisions, and act in line with ordinary social and moral precepts. The injury to this part of the brain in these cases has two closely related outcomes: it changes the continual neural updating of the state of the body, and feelings associated with social and personal experience. Inherent emotions, however, are not affected. These patients are literally unable to receive information from their bodies concerning the bodily changes that normally accompany interaction with other people; social and moral emotions become severely hampered.

Feelings, empathy, and moral conduct are not, however, the only things relying on feedback from the body. Purposive thinking is another. Creative thought and problem-solving do not normally proceed according to the strictures of formal logic. What governs our reasoning appears above all to be a bodily/emotional feedback mechanism (the somatic marker hypothesis), helping us to intuitively decide whether we're on the right track or not, whether our gut feeling tells us things are going well or heading for disaster. Antoine Bechara, a colleague of Damasio (1994), developed a card test for patients with ventromedial frontal damage called the Iowa Gambling Test. These patients consistently fail the test because they are unable to distinguish between decks with more reward cards than penalty cards over the long run. The neurological foundation of intuition is about to become well-documented.

Strong feelings are normally considered the enemy of objectivity and rational thought. In many situations, that remains true. But there is growing evidence, as we have seen, that rational thought is impeded or eliminated altogether if we can't monitor our emotional body state. In psychoanalysis and psychotherapy, we see the problem from both vantage points. Put simply, information about the body's emotional state comes through either too strongly, or too feebly.

A philosophical step aside

Before considering contemporary psychoanalytic views on how "disengagement from a one-track relation" makes it possible to reflect on emotional interaction, let us also look at some philosophical views of this process. The American philosopher Teed Rockwell (2005) draws attention to the work of John Dewey, for whom "it is impossible to have experience without a body that interacts with an environment" (1916, p. 180). Dewey further observes that "in well-formed, smooth running functions of any sort – skating, conversing, hearing music, enjoying a landscape – there is no consciousness of separation of the method of the person and of the subject matter" (p. 166).

What Dewey discerned in 1916 was glossed a decade later by the German philosopher Heidegger (1926) who describes the difference between "readiness-to-hand" and "present-at-hand." This readiness-to-hand breaks down when our stance is changed to present-at-hand.

> When we reflect upon experience instead of just having it, we inevitably distinguish between our own attitude and the objects towards which we sustain that attitude . . . such reflection upon experience gives rise to a distinction of what we experience (the experienced) and the experiencing. . . . This distinction is so natural and so important for certain purposes, that we are only apt to regard it as a separation in existence and not as a distinction in thought. Then we make a division between a self and the environment or the world. (p. 167)

Merleau-Ponty put it this way: "Between the self which analyzes perception and the self which perceives, there is always a distance" (1945/1996, p. 43).

In psychoanalysis and psychotherapy, maintaining the separation of "the method of the person (analyst, therapist) and the subject matter (analysand, patient)" has been "so natural and so important for certain purposes" that it was long "regarded as a separation in existence and not as a distinction in thought." With the emergence of relational perspectives came the recognition that the distinction is a separation in thought rather than existence. The ability to shift attention from the experience of ongoing emotional interaction, "readiness-to-hand" to reflection, to the "present-at-hand," is central to the kind of expanded clinical attention that I suggest. The distinction is also critical to my discussion below of "present at hand," "thirdness," and "we-ness."

We-centered reflexivity

I have argued that we as humans seem to have distinct but closely linked systems whereby we get to know our own body and those of others. This is what makes a sense of self – egocentric knowing – and identification with others – alter-centric knowing – possible. However, to ensure a healthy balance and reflexive capacity, a third position is needed, one Benjamin (1998) calls *true observation*. Aron (1996) speaks of *dialectical objectivity*, where the observation is based on opposing subjectivities. "This third position is founded in the communicative relationship, which creates a dialogue that is an entity in itself, a potential space outside the web of identifications" (Benjamin, 1998, p. xv). This more observational position has also been termed *the analytic third* (Ogden, 1994). Other concepts related to the notion of the analytic third include *reflexive functioning* (Aron, 1998), *mentalization* (Fonagy, Gergely, Jurist, & Target, 2002) and *intersubjective consciousness* (Stern, 2004). Aron stresses the importance of one's own body feelings for reflexive functioning, while Stern (2004) underlines an intersubjective ability. Emde (2009) coined the term *we-go* inspired by *ego*, and Gallese (2009) the terms *we-centric space* and *we-ness,* prompted by embodied simulation as supported by the mirror neuron system.

Thirdness, we-ness, or whatever we like to call it, rests, I assume, on perceptions of the state of our own body combined with an ability to simulate and imitate aspects of others' bodily states. This assumption seems to be corroborated by developmental and neuro-scientific research. Meltzoff and Decety (2003) review developmental and neuro-scientific research with a bearing on own body knowledge, imitation, mentalization, and theory of mind. They conclude:

> The adult human framework is not simply one of resonance. We are able to recognize that everyone does not share our own desires, emotions, intentions and beliefs. To become a sophisticated mentalizer one needs to analyze both the similarities and differences between one's own state and those of others. That is what makes us human. (p. 498)

According to Gallese (2007, 2009), the philosopher Husserl (1977, 1913/1989a, b) came to emphasize the role of others in making the world "objective." It is through a shared experience of the world, "Lebenswelt," in the presence of other individuals, that objectivity can be constituted.

> [A]ccording to Husserl the bodies of self and others are the primary instruments of our capacity to share experience with each other. What makes the behavior of other agents intelligible is the fact that their body is experienced not as material object (Körper), but as something alive (Leib), something analogous to our own experienced acting body. (Gallese, 2009, p. 525)

Psychoanalysis and psychotherapy would gain, I think, from conceiving of objectivity in this way, i.e., as an ability to sustain to the best of ability a widened awareness of the state of our own body, embodied subjectivity, and those of others, embodied intersubjectivity. I offer in the next section a way of supervising and training therapists specifically designed to enhance this kind of widened attention.

Mental disorders can be seen in terms of the dominance of egocentricity or alter-centricity, of self-regulation, or interpersonal regulation. In many neurotic states, we find a pronounced alter-centric perspective along with an underdeveloped ability to feel one's own emotions and needs. In disorders of mentalization like borderline states, we typically see a pronounced egocentric perspective. Or, as Bateman and Fonagy put it, "[b]orderline patients have knowledge but not belief" (2004, p. 218). In disorders of the self proper, like psychosis, there is sometimes a breakdown of the ability to care for one's self due to a serious disturbance in one's knowledge of one's own body state. In autistic states, there seems to be a basic disturbance in the capacity for imitation and empathy (Hobson, 2002). Most patients with neurotic problems, like most therapists and analysts, have some contact with their affective states, can empathize with others, and can reflect upon similarities and differences. But we also often find imbalances in all three dimensions, diminishing the regulatory capacities of affective processes. I offer here a clinical illustration, another vignette involving Peter, whom I first introduced in Chapter 1 and discussed further in Chapter 6. This time, the focus is on a need to develop reflective capacity.

The analysis of Peter could have ended where the vignette in Chapter 6 ended, that is with Peter's initial depression lifted, and him becoming more aware of his own emotions, his own ego so to speak, and better able to stand up for his own needs. However, Peter still seemed caught in a "web of identifications." He was still vulnerable and likely to lose himself in intimate relationships. So his analysis, rather than coming to a satisfactory conclusion in a relatively short time span, went on for several more years. It should also be added that Peter was successful in his professional life both before and during the analysis. His interpersonal problems were mainly restricted to family and other intimate relationships. It is also part of the story that this was his second analysis. His first, which we both considered to have been a success, dealt with the same interpersonal challenges as we were now addressing. What was new was his awareness of how difficult he found it to pay heed to his own emotions in a relational conflict, especially when he is on intimate terms with the other person, as noted in the previous vignettes.

As it happened, his difficulties were not restricted to his ability to register and stay focused on his own feelings in a conflict. Whenever another relational conflict appeared, he experienced it as something new rather than a repetition of an old pattern. His ability to compare and reflect on these reactions, where he felt as if he had lost himself, was impaired. In his first analysis, his analyst frequently pointed to these episodes of "losing himself" and Peter often reminded himself of this during our analysis. What I gradually realized was that it was not enough to make verbal reference to something that was quite obvious to both of us. For example, I soon found myself explaining at length and in some detail the resemblance between what was now happening in relation to his cousin and what had been going on with his wife. Somewhat contrary to my ideal analytic self, I came to feel more like a traditional analyst giving extended interpretations. This realization turned out to be very fruitful. Peter recognized that what he had missed in his first analysis was precisely these extended explanations. (Following my character analytic bent it could easily have turned out even worse for me.) We discovered that when his experience of himself was undermined, so was his reflective capacity concerning these situations of emotional and relational conflict. This would probably not be a surprising discovery for analysts and therapists with more experience dealing with severe trauma and dissociation than I. But I should add that Peter's reflective capacity generally is excellent, not least in his work, which involves complex human relations.

Peter's empathic abilities were fine from the start. So much so that it actually caused him problems because his propensity to see matters from the point of view of people he was dealing with was not balanced by an equal ability to feel and handle his own emotions. So he really needed to strengthen his capacity for ego-centric self-experience. But this was not enough. He needed to regain his ability to reflect verbally around his relational "danger spots." The first did not come together with the other in this analysis. They had to be addressed separately at different phases of the process.

The vignettes have shown Peter's need to strengthen his (ego-centric) self-experience *and* reflective capacity in respect of his loss of self-feeling. Given his highly developed empathic capacity, our therapeutic alliance was never threatened. I would like here to append another vignette, one from my analysis of Eva. Her empathic capacity is far more fragile. She easily retreats into her ego-centric feelings of herself. She needs to become aware of this reaction pattern. She also needs to develop an ability to think of her way of reacting from a more we-centric position, giving herself space to attend both to her own, my, and others' perspectives.

In Peter's analysis, my reflective capacity is hardly ever threatened. That was not the case with Eva. At times I had to work hard to transcend my own ego-centric reactions, which threatened both my empathic and reflective capacity.

Believing that I am lost in my own thoughts and have become indifferent to her, Eva experiences intense disappointment. Her reaction is not without reason. Inattentiveness is part of my makeup, or at least I seem to adopt a bodily posture that lends itself to that impression. The way Eva expresses her disappointment gives me the feeling I have committed an unforgivable sin. This I experience as grossly unreasonable, and I feel anger welling within me and an impulse to tell her that I think she is being unfair.

In these situations, it is very important that I take responsibility for my contribution to her disappointment (Kohut, 1971). Only after acknowledging and explaining the reaction in me which caused her to feel abandoned will it be possible to restore sufficient trust and security. Having done this she finds an opening to start exploring her own reactions, including things besides my inattentiveness, which might have led her to feel such catastrophic disappointment.

These episodes test both my empathic and reflective capacity. I needed to stay attuned to Eva's perspective on what is happening. Whenever I failed to do so, our reciprocal understanding and emotional connectedness broke down, rupturing the therapeutic alliance (Safran & Muran, 2000.) It is therefore crucial that I am able to take and stay with my part of the responsibility for what was happening. It facilitates a climate of trust and confidence, enabling her to explore her own contribution. She gradually comes to connect her strong sense of disappointment (along with a sense of hopelessness and worthlessness) to childhood memories of situations involving both her mother and father. Eva becomes increasingly aware of the strength of her need for assurance and the interest and concern of others.

When Eva senses my care and concern, it moves her, and her sense of herself is good. For a long period these new, positive sensations recede quickly into the background. But we are now in a position to consciously attend to two different relational modes, indifference and disregard on the one hand, and involvement and concern on the other.

In terms of her physical reactions, Eva's experience of indifference and disregard is evident in her avoidance of eye contact and by communicating with me indirectly. When she senses concern and attentiveness, however, she straightens up and regards me more directly. Progressively, one old affect motor memory and pattern comes to share the space with a new pattern, new implicit relational knowing.

The above vignette illustrates how we as analysts are fated to exist in a "web of identifications" accompanied by unconscious evocations of affect within our bodies. The positive side of this is the wider foundation it provides for understanding a patient; the negative is the risk of being caught in what Aron (2006) termed the "seesaw," the force working on the analyst to move toward or away from the patient.

This state of affairs underlines the decisive importance of the analyst's ability not only to stay in touch with her own needs and feelings and to empathize with the patient, but also to find ways to take a step aside, retreat from "the web of identifications," to adopt a third, more distanced and objective, position, what Gallese (2007, 2009) terms the *we-centric* position. Our ability to be *we-centric* or "objective" is consequently the ability to balance impressions derived from our sense of our own body and our impressions of those of others. It widens the scope of attention to the processes unfolding/emerging in any analytic interaction. Optimizing a capacity to alternate between these three positions, ego-centric, alter-centric, and we-centric, in therapists and patients alike, is a key component of the training and supervision model I will present and discuss in the next section.

The ability to adopt a we-centric view is also central to my understanding of what Fonagy et al. (2002) call mentalization. Without this we-centric possibility, the analyst will be fastened to the "seesaw" (Aron, 2006), in pre-set, one-sided and unbalanced self–other representations. Another implication of Fonagy et al.'s work is that patients also need to achieve a capacity for "mentalization" to free themselves from embeddedness in pre-set, one-sided, and unbalanced self–other representations; to move from "twoness" to "thirdness" (Binder, 2009).

I recognize that this we-centric perspective might provoke a resurgence of idealistic expectations, in the guise of "the classical analyst." The idea of the "return of the classical analyst" in a contemporary context of subjectivity and intersubjectivity was elaborated by Stark (1999) in her book on *three modes of therapeutic action*, previously reviewed. The difference between the "objectivity" of the classical analyst and this revised conceptualization of "objectivity" is that the therapist does not conceptualize herself as capable of bias-free observation. Rather, the conceptualization of the "objectivity," or better dialectal objectivity (Aron, 1996) that I am describing, is only possible as a we-centric dimension within the intersubjective field, issuing from within the shared *Lebenswelt* of living bodies (Husserl). It is inevitably context-sensitive as "objectivity" is emergent rather than just chosen.

A remark on mentalization and mindfulness

Wallin (2007) refers to Fonagy's (1991) description of the reflective self as "the internal observer of mental life" and adds: "Without such an internal observer, we are simply embedded in subjective experiences that we confuse with objective realities" (2007, p. 158). This internal observer – he terms it *the mentalizing stance* – Wallin maintains, merges with what he calls *the mindful stance*.

> The two converge in facilitating the recognition that our subjective experience is largely a psychological construction, and that much of our psychological suffering can consequently be seen as (unconsciously) self-generated. Both have the potential to lift us out of our embeddedness in experience and the quality of automatic responsiveness it imposes. Yet mentalizing and mindfulness is not the same. . . . While mentalization may provide a key route to the establishment of a coherent self, mindfulness has been seen as key to the transcendence of the self. For mindfulness is the centerpiece of a 2,500-year-old Buddhist tradition in which the aim is to undo the self-imposed suffering caused by clinging to illusory images of self. (Wallin, 2007, p. 158)

Seen through the lens of my conceptual and clinical perspective, these two stances, mindfulness and mentalizing, correspond largely with embodied-affective and verbal-reflective forms of self-experience. A common aim of Eastern meditation practices is to bring the activity of the verbal, imagistic, and autobiographic self to a complete halt, concentrating all attention on a particular aspect of the embodied self-experience such as breathing, body "energy" flows, or visually focusing in darkness. These are, in my view, valuable practices that can facilitate the development of a widening of attention to include all aspects of embodied experience.

I share Wallin's appreciation of the complementary value of the mentalizing and mindful stances. Mindfulness and focusing on embodied experience draw attention to the details of here-and-now experiences, with an attitude of acceptance and curiosity about what is being observed, rather than a desire to interpret or change what is being observed. With mentalization and reflection, we take a step back from immediate experience, allowing us to widen our attention to comparing different perspectives and experiences.

Reich wrote, "*Alongside the 'what' of the old Freudian technique, I placed the 'how'.* I already knew that the 'how', i.e., the form of the behaviour and the communications, was far more important than what the patient told the analyst" (1942/1978, p. 152). The idea of mentalization stresses the *ability,* the *how* of mentalizing, rather than *what* is actually mentalized, the content that was the focus of the concept of insight. Taken together, the idea of mentalization and the practice of mindfulness can help us focus on the formal aspects of our mental processes all the way from emotional body states to the highest levels of abstraction, "ideas of ideas." This is important, not because content is unimportant, but because psychoanalytic and psychotherapeutic culture has traditionally paid more attention to content than to form and process. Forms of vitality have tended to remain "hidden in plain view" (Stern, 2010, p. 3). One of the values of the embodied training practices to be discussed is that they prevent clinical seminars and supervision from privileging the contents of the patients' history and problems at the cost of focusing on "the behavior and the form of the communications."

Note

1 While I endorse this idea, I have certain reservations. My focus and interest in this book are on interpersonal relations and the ability to reflect on self-other relationships. The view argued puts decisive weight on our ability to adopt the attitudes of the other by means of imitation and identification. Now although I take this as being true, I am not in a position to say whether it applies to all forms of thinking and advanced intelligence. As many have observed, people with problems in the autism/Asperger range of disorders, deficient in empathy and imitation, may have an excellent ability to study and reflect over nature. It has even been speculated that some of the most outstanding natural scientists might have had problems in this area.

Chapter 9

Clinical perspectives on two-body psychology

The psychoanalytic situation is essentially a Two-Body Situation.

(Balint)

In an afterword to his paper on *Changing Therapeutical Aims and Techniques in Psycho-analysis* (1952/1985), Balint writes:

> I wish to quote here an idea of John Rickman's [like Balint a student of Ferenczi], of which unfortunately I heard only in April 1950, i.e. only after finishing this chapter. . . . "The whole region of psychology may be divided into areas of research according to the number of persons concerned. Thus we may speak of One-Body Psychology, Two-Body, Three-Body, Four-Body and Multi-Body psychology." (pp. 234–235)

Commenting on this idea, Balint goes on to say that almost all terms and concepts in psychoanalytical theory are derived from studying pathological forms hardly going beyond the domain of one-body psychology, which gives in consequence only a clumsy, approximate description of what happens in the psychoanalytical situation, an essentially two-body situation. "We have," he concludes, "only some vague ideas but no exact knowledge about what distortions happen and how much we miss while describing Two-Body experiences (analytical technique) in a language belonging to One-Body situations" (p. 235).

Over the last decades, Rickman's and Balint's ideas have been widely accepted and developed. Rickman's original formulation has however been altered somewhat, turning it into what has become today's popular term "two-person psychology." Even if I see nothing wrong with the term, I shall return to Rickman's original terminology below. As we still live in a culture dominated more by Cartesian conceptions than Spinozan, the body very easily tends to get lost when it is not explicitly referred to.

In the previous chapters, I have focused mainly on one-body psychology, even if "the other body" was conceptually *incorporated*. This incorporation was possible because each body seems to have a space within it for *the virtual other* (Bråten,

1998a), with a "mirror neuron system" as an essential element of the incorporation process. This structural property of each – one – body is, in my view, what makes a two-body psychology possible. In this chapter, I shall engage explicitly with two – or more – body psychology. In other words, the perspective will be on two (or more) bodies in interaction, and the two bodies I will primarily have in mind are those of analyst and analysand, therapist and patient.

I don't see a sharp distinction between one and two (or more) body psychologies, as each is always somehow represented in the other. This is also reflected in contemporary use of the term *intersubjectivity*. It is used to denote both one body/mind's experience of another body/mind (empathy), and the meeting and mutual recognition of two bodies/minds. Even so, I think "two-body psychology" conceptualized as two or more bodies actually interacting is of great importance. The historical emergence of psychoanalysis and psychotherapy in itself testifies to this fact.

From their very beginning more than 100 years ago, psychoanalysis and psychotherapy have been conceived of as an endeavor requiring the presence of at least two bodies. The last hundred years have seen the emergence of additions to the two-body psychotherapies; couples therapy, family therapy, group therapy, milieu therapy, even community and organization therapy. However, work on promoting psychological health and well-being in only one body – meditation, yoga, and self-help practices could be examples – never came to be considered psychotherapy. This is in a way underlined by the history of Freud's self-analysis, which he recommended replacing with a two-body training analysis. I think there is good reason for this, which I hope to underscore more in this chapter.

A dyadic and dynamic systems view

While studying film and video recordings back in the 1970s, Mary Catherine Bateson (1975), daughter of Margaret Mead and Gregory Bateson, found that one-month-old babies had established a pattern of interaction with their mothers, as both took turns to make a gesture, sound, etc. She called this interaction a *protoconversation*. Researchers and theorists today believe this protoconversation is essential for the acquisition of language and verbal communication (Bråten, 1998a). One particular feature of the protoconversation, in comparison with verbal conversation, is the higher rate of alternation. In an analysis of video footage of baby–caregiver interaction, researchers had to lower playback speed to six frames per second to capture interaction units (Beebe & Lachmann, 2002). The protoconversation proceeded, in other words, more or less unconsciously. The importance of this nonverbal protoconversation does not seem to decline as the ability to speak grows (Beebe & Lachmann, 2002). This has a direct bearing on psychoanalysis and psychotherapy, and the implications for the therapeutic dialogue, mentioned previously, seem self-evident.

In their introduction to *Emotional Development* (2005), Nadel and Muir refer to Tronick's concept of "dyadic states of consciousness."

Tronick's focus on dyadic states has important theoretical and methodological implications and leads us to the argument for *a two-body psychology*, which emphasizes the use of an interactive context to study emotional development and regulation. The use of a two-body psychology is shared by many of the contributors in Section I, and all the contributors in Section II. (p. xvi, my italics)

I see the dyadic models presented by Tronick (2005) and Beebe and Lachmann (2002) as very fruitful developments of a two-body psychology. I will therefore apply the dyadic systems model in analysis and discussion of psychotherapeutic interaction. I find it, however, useful to situate the dyadic systems view within a broader context of dynamic systems theory. Defining the theory, Piers (2005) explains first that a

> *system* is a set of components or parts that interact to form an organized and coordinated whole. A *dynamic system* is a system that changes over time, rather than remaining fixed, or static. By this definition, systems such as the weather, a turbulent river, or the stock market, as well as the mind and the psychotherapy dyad, are all considered dynamic systems. . . . Finally, a *nonlinear dynamic system* is a system whose evolution is *discontinuous, nonproportional, and unpredictable.* . . . [E]ven when armed with full knowledge of current state of the system we are unable to predict the future states of a nonlinear system. (pp. 230–231)

The dynamic systems view is a much needed alternative to the linear cause-and-effect view. A conception of psychoanalysis and psychotherapy that is both embodied and relational needs a theoretical model that is nonlinear in its understanding of therapeutic interactions. Dynamic systems theory seems to offer such a conceptual framework. According to Seligman (2005), most contemporary analysts now think of analyst and analysand as immersed in ongoing, complex patterns of mutual influence. "Whatever other assumptions they make, they agree that psychoanalysis is a dyadic and dynamic system. . . . The systems theories provide a window onto a new way to think about psychoanalytic metapsychology – a background theory that orients our basic working assumptions" (p. 287). Thelen (2005), who applied dynamic systems theory to the study of human development, underscores the embodied implications of the dynamic systems view.

> I am particularly interested in the contributions of embodied processes: perception, movement, and their emotional accompaniments in the production and development of behaviour. Humans perceive and move continually during every waking minute, and much of this has an emotional valence. Yet, in many cognitive accounts, the roles of perception, emotion, and especially movement are considered secondary to mental activities. But according to the principles of dynamics, mental activities not only are founded in emotion,

perception, and action but also are part of the causal web of behaviour throughout life. Moreover, I suggest that even small difficulties with these processes early in life can have lifelong consequences. (p. 262)

The Dyadic Systems Model of Beebe and Lachmann (2002, fig. 4, p. 35), as previously described, has proven to represent a very fruitful application of dynamic systems thinking to the psychoanalytic and psychotherapeutic situation. The dyadic systems model is very convenient for my purpose, the two-body psychology of the psychoanalytic situation. My focus here will be on the two-body, dyadic system. It is, however, important to keep in mind that the dyadic system is part of a broader system, encompassing three, four, and more body psychologies, and also the environment of nonliving bodies. The dyadic model has to be broadened when it is applied for instance to couples, family, and group therapy. The basic premises, however, remain the same.

Some of the implications of a dynamic and dyadic systems view appear to me to be the following. The unconscious is, above all, an embodied, interactive unconscious within which we are situated in the beginning and from when consciousness emerges. Before and parallel with the conscious thoughts we are able to have as we enter into the therapeutic dyad, we are already embedded in an unconscious interaction constituted by the embodied and implicit memories of both therapist and patient. In traditional terms, transference and countertransference are in full swing from the very moment at which the two parties approach each other.

Dynamic systems theory and character

From Reich's character analysis (1949/1972), reviewed in Chapter 2, a conception of character emerged, consisting of three layers: the outermost layer, often one of adjustment and contentedness; an intermediate layer comprising neurotic defense reactions and aggressive and negative sentiments; and finally an innermost layer, a core seeking to realize life's best possibilities, possessed of a self-healing and self-regulating force, consonant with genetic or evolutionary memory. I believe this threefold division is still useful, though it needs to be couched in relational language. Character, as "way of being," must embrace "ways of being with." When a smiling, apparently conciliatory patient has his arms and legs in a defensive posture, he may want to run away and at the same time long for a close and trusting relationship. The relational analyst Steven Stern (1994) calls the old "repeated relation" a type 1 transference, and the new "needed relation" a type 2 transference. He defines character as the compromise between these two tendencies.

Character (neuroses) masks two antagonistic forces, then. On the one hand, we meet others with expectations of a rerun of past events, echoing our autobiographical memory; on the other, we meet others with expectations of a new and better outcome this time in keeping with our genetic memory. Wallin (2007) highlights this point in referring to therapists and patients not only engaging in repeating relational patterns, but "also unconsciously (as well as consciously) motivated to experience new ways of being that are more inclusive and expansive than those they learned in their formative relationships" (pp. 279–280).

The change process, in this sense, is about how this engaging with old ways of being together paves the way for new ways of being together, a "new beginning." The two forces are ever present, however, in the therapeutic relationship, and, for that matter, whenever people come together. This process was illustrated in Chapter 8 with the *Eva* vignette. I repeat here the last paragraph of that vignette.

> *In terms of her physical reactions, Eva's experience of indifference and disregard is evident in her avoidance of eye contact and by communicating with me indirectly. When she senses concern and attentiveness, however, she straightens up and regards me more directly. Progressively, one old affect motor memory and pattern comes to share the space with a new pattern, new implicit relational knowing.*

From a dynamic systems view, Piers (2005) sees the mind as a nonlinear system that arranges, coordinates, and organizes subjective experience from a set of predisposing attitudes. He refers to this organization of attitudes as character. Piers further suggests that the complexity of the emergent attractor regime, of the organization of the attitudes of character, is a reflection of the relative health of the system. The consequences of severely restrictive organizing attitudes are observed in cases of character pathology in which "the mind is a periodic system that restrains its own natural tendency toward self-organization by reflexively damping down entire classes of subjectivity in order to forestall anxiety and maintain equilibrium" (2005, p. 252). In the following, I will argue that the "natural tendency toward self-organization" can be restrained in three different directions corresponding to three classes of character neuroses and ways of relating to others.

Three basic character and relational orientations

In the previous chapters, I elaborated on three basic positions (or stances): subjectivity, intersubjectivity, and objectivity. The kind of objectivity described there is what we might call a secondary objectivity as it concerns the kind of relative objectivity that emerges from considering different subjectivities. Infant research indicates that we are also born with a primary "objectivity." Meltzoff and Moore (1998) found in their experiments on infant imitation that infants, from the very beginning, differentiate between physical movements, which they do not imitate, and intentional human actions, which they do imitate. "Evidently," they conclude, "infants are not behaviourists" (p. 52). So, we seem to be born with three information systems, one for self, one for other, and one for things.

Given this three-system structure, it may be that one or two of the systems can be developed and relied on at the cost of one or two of the others. And this is exactly what seems to happen when the development of secure attachments is not optimal. When the circumstances don't allow stable application of any of the patterns of relating, the consequence will be disorganized attachment, and no stable pattern. Severe mental disturbances are, it seems, either disorganized, with little stable character structure, or characterized by a relatively stable but very one-sided coping strategy.

It is common to see the one-sided strategies as basically two-dimensional, enabling the individual to rely on himself or other. Attachment researchers (Wallin, 2007) call the two patterns of deviation from secure attachment the avoidant/dismissing pattern and the ambivalent/preoccupied attachment pattern. The disorganized/unresolved pattern designates a severity dimension, not a third dimension with close to secure attachment variations as do the two basic dimensions of avoidant/dismissing and ambivalent/preoccupied.

Building on clinical experience and theory developed in the previous chapters, I will argue that we probably have three basic coping, defensive, and relational strategies/orientations and subsequent (neurotic) character styles. Within the spectrum of what has been termed self-definition or ambivalent/preoccupied, we find, in my view, two distinct patterns, orientations, and strategies: one, what I term the narcissistic/psychopathic; and two, the compulsive/schizoid character orientations, respectively. These orientations seem to be similar because the affected individuals both rely on themselves rather than on others. They don't seek support and protection from others, and they both give an appearance of self-reliance and self-assurance. But there are at the same time, I believe, fundamental differences.

The compulsive/schizoid orientation is primarily occupied with the world of things rather than the world of human relations. The individual (who is more often a he than a she) seems to have chosen to privilege the information system that informs him about the world of things rather than human company. He dislikes strong emotions of any sort, preferring rational (compulsive) thinking. The normal neurotics with this orientation tend to prefer occupations like engineering and crafts.

The narcissistic/psychopathic individual, on the other hand, is occupied with the human world, primarily himself (still, more often a he than a she). Whereas the compulsive/schizoid wants to avoid relationships, the narcissistic/psychopathic depends on them, but they must be relations that he can control or that feed his need for admiration. Unlike the compulsive, the narcissistic person does not avoid strong emotion. He tends to tolerate significant amounts of aggression both in himself and in others. He feels free to use aggression to control and manipulate others, but runs, of course, the risk of destroying his relationships. The normal/neurotic individuals with this orientation prefer occupations as leaders in businesses and organizations, as officers and politicians.

The relation-oriented preoccupied/ambivalent pattern covers the territory traditionally ascribed to the hysteric character. This orientation is per definition preoccupied with relations. She (and it tends to be a she more often than a he) wants to help and be helped. She will work hard to maintain intimate relationship(s). She is emotional, easily scared, and seeks good feelings, such as flirtatious, sexual feelings. Unlike the narcissistic/psychopathic, she is afraid of aggression and avoids those feelings in herself and others. Her empathy is normally highly developed, but she has little contact with her own needs and feelings. The normal/neurotic individuals with this orientation prefer occupations like nursing and psychotherapy.

From this, admittedly stereotyped, description, it should be clear that the compulsive and the narcissistic orientations have little more in common with each other than with the hysteric. In his book *Character Analysis,* Reich (1949/1972) describes the corresponding character types as *the hysteric, the phallic narcissistic, and the compulsive character.* And Karen Horney (1945) typified the relational nature of these orientations by naming them *moving towards people, moving against people, and moving away from people,* respectively.

Clinical illustration of three character and relational orientations

Horney's *moving away, moving against, and moving towards other people* typology highlights the fact that these strategies operate within the context of at least two-body psychologies. Most people use all three strategies in varying degrees. And when under ordinary circumstances one strategy is dominant, unusual amounts of stress can cause it to switch places with another. The neo-Reichian body-psychotherapist David Boadella (1987) coined the term *schizo-hysteric swing,* for people with a schizoid coping style who switched to a hysteric style under extraordinary stress, and vice versa. For the purpose of clinical illustration, I have chosen three patients with relatively stable one-sided coping strategies, attachment patterns, and ways of self and interactive regulation of emotion. I will call them *David, Roger,* and *Ruth,* and they all had severe problems.

David was referred for therapy when he was in his mid-20s. He had done relatively well at school, but had always been somewhat withdrawn, preferring to do things on his own. The only person that he did things together with was his two-year older brother. After finishing high school, he started studying to become an engineer. Halfway through his studies, he dropped out because he had to do group work for a laboratory course. Two years later, he was referred for therapy. He had not been able to take up other studies or get a job. His chief complaint on entering therapy was that he missed a (female) sexual partner.

Roger sought therapy in the middle of his 40s on the advice of a friend whose experience of an analysis over several years had been good. Roger's life was generally very unsatisfactory. He was without a job; all his attempts at establishing intimate relations with women failed in the end. He was periodically depressed, had pains in his body, and didn't sleep well. Coming from an academic family, he had spent many years studying arts and the humanities, but without focusing on a specific career. He had only been able to keep a job relevant to his academic qualifications for a few years.

Roger started therapy a couple of times in his early 20s. His therapists and analysts didn't really respect and understand him, he felt, so he quit. Deciding after much hesitation to give therapy another try, he had clear ideas about what had made his life difficult and unsatisfying. His parents had a difficult marriage. Although his mother had a successful career, she also had severe bouts of depression. She died when he was seven. After the death of his mother, his father soon married a woman he had been dating for some time, and had a child with her. Roger felt that his father, however eager he was to entertain him, never really saw his grief and loneliness after the loss of his mother. His new stepmother was hostile, he felt. At the beginning of the therapy, he saw the traumas of his childhood and his family's inability to help him as the cause of his troubles. He also felt that people outside the family and society at large had let him down, for not offering him adequate help.

Ruth was referred to therapy in her mid-30s with severe chronic headaches, including migraines, and, according to her referring physician, anxiety. She had also been suffering from severe abdominal bleeding for many years. Two years before starting therapy, the bleeding had been stopped by a hysterectomy (surgical removal of the uterus), since nothing else had worked. Ruth was trained as a nurse and had been successful in her work. She was unable to work anymore because of her headaches. She was married with two children. She had a good marriage and admired her husband. Had it not been for the headaches, and bleeding, her life, she thought, would have been fine. What she hoped therapy would help her with was to alleviate or rid her of her headaches.

What these three persons had in common was an incapacity to work due to severe mental problems. All three were eager to start therapy and were hopeful as to what it could bring them. Apart from this common ground, the three cases turned out very differently. And my countertransference experience was very different with each of them.

David was a slim young man with a somewhat peculiar appearance, long hair, and hippy-like clothing that was not common in his rural community at the time. He wore long sleeve shirts also in summer; he didn't want to expose his body, apart from his head and hair. He was hesitant, but friendly and eager to talk about his life and especially his (sexual) fantasies. Roger dressed casually and had the look of an artistic appearance. He was happy at finding somebody at last who could help him. Ruth was a slim and tastefully dressed young woman with friendly and pleasant manners. She seemed eager to do what she could to help the therapist help her.

The therapy with David

David attended his twice weekly sitting therapy sessions very consistently. When I started to formulate a strategy and goal for our therapeutic collaboration, I soon discovered that we had very different ideas about how the therapy should proceed. I suggested something in the direction of exploring and eventually expanding emotional experience so as to make it easier for him to be in a relationship,

including intimate, sexual relations and relations in the workplace. David disagreed with the strategy. After quite some time he managed to say that he didn't
want changing at all. There was nothing wrong with the way he was. It was society
that was out of step with people like him. After still more time, more than a year,
David said that what he really wanted me to do was to get hold of a sexual partner
for him. He also wished Norway was more like countries he had read about where
parents picked partners for their children. The therapy lasted four years and was
a continuous "negotiation of the therapeutic alliance" (Safran & Muran, 2000)
without ever reaching an explicit agreement on terms, procedures, or goals.

After a couple of years, David told me that he was doing some writing. He also
asked me if I'd like to see some of it. I saw no reason why I shouldn't, and said
yes. It might even help us, I thought. David had written a kind of pornographic
novel. It was full of penetrating and penetrated body parts, and people without any
form of feeling for each other. It was a search for pleasurable physical sensations.
I could see no aggression in his fantasies. Indeed, they were without relational
feelings of any sort. His writing seemed to confirm what my impressions of our
relationship were. It was as if his emotions had never become real feelings. What
he consciously experienced was more like physical sensations. I gradually came
to understand better why David found flirting and the romantic part of dating a girl
so impossible and meaningless. He had little or no contact with the feelings that
could give meaning to that kind of relationship.

At the verbal content level there had been, in my view, very little if any progress
in this therapy. But we met regularly for more than four years and went through our
usual exchanges, not only on the verbal level, but also of course at a more unconscious body interaction level. More now than at that time, I regard this continuous
bodily relational exchange between us as an important emotional and relational
experience for this young man. Judged from the verbal, explicit level (above the
line in the dyadic systems model), the therapy should perhaps have ended much
earlier because we could agree on very little of what we could verbalize to move
the therapy forward. But we continued our regular meetings despite my repeated
insistence that I neither could nor would set him up with a woman. To me it all
the same felt like we in a way enjoyed our time together. The therapy ended on
my suggestion. I believe he was sorry, though he didn't actually express sorrow.
This is many years ago, now. Today, I hope, I would have had more confidence
in my – embodied – countertransference feeling that it was a constructive process
even though we failed to find the words to express it. When I suggested bringing
the therapy to an end, I thought it had never been a proper therapy. By the time we
parted, however, David had succeeded on his own to have more than one date and
with more than one girl. He told me this only later. They were not great successes,
but nor were they disasters.

When David was in therapy I was already considering myself a body-oriented
therapist. However, I was of the opinion that a necessary precondition for therapy
was that the two parties were able to agree upon some verbal formulation as to
the means and ends of therapy. Today, I would have put less stress on this aspect,

given the special nature of David's conceptual world, but attended more consistently to our bodily-emotional interaction, including David's eagerness to turn up for his sessions despite my unwillingness to provide what he verbally asked for. In other words, I would have paid – even – more attention to implicit self- and interactive regulation going on below the line in the dyadic systems model.

The therapy with Roger

The therapy with Roger was also twice weekly. Based on my impression of him and his history, I suggested making one of those sessions a double one. He immediately agreed and added that anything less would have been completely disagreeable. This, I think, was the first clear warning of what was to come. The first year went smoothly; he was very eager to tell me about his dramatic and troubled life, and I was eager to listen.

By the end of the first year, and before summer vacation, he showed me some of the things that were left from his mother, which his father had given him. I felt I was paying reasonable attention to what he was showing me, but later I could see that the time before this summer vacation had been a busy and somewhat troubled time for me privately. It is reasonable to assume that I had not been as present as I should when Roger showed me what to him were clearly important and made him emotionally vulnerable. Sometime after the summer break, Roger launched into what I felt was both a surprising and an angry tirade, accusing me of not helping him to get a better life. He was no better; on the contrary he felt worse. Rather perplexed, I said I was sorry he was getting worse, but added that in my experience, people with a complex traumatic history like his often needed more than a year in therapy before life got better.

In the following sessions, however, new criticisms came repeatedly. I had not been clear about how the therapy was supposed to help him. This criticism was reasonable, I felt, since I had mainly responded emphatically to what he was eager to tell me during the first year. So I now started to formulate in different ways more explicitly how I thought we might work together to get a better life for him. Whatever I said, however, he disagreed with vehemently. For example, when I suggested that we also pay attention to problems in his present life and difficulties with his current relationships, he was convinced that I was suggesting behavioral therapy, which was definitely not what he needed. His problems were rooted in his history, and when that history was cleared up, there would be no more need to bother about present-day problems. He made this clear to me over quite some time. I might add that his background had given him considerable knowledge of the field of psychotherapy.

As this progressed, I felt more and more uncomfortable and took my own defensive measures. Roger immediately detected the change and criticized me for being defensive. After this I asked colleagues to help me out. To make a long history short, it turned out that Roger had felt disastrously disappointed and abandoned by me because I had not, on my own, returned to the issue of the things from his mother that he had shown me before the summer vacation. He was convinced that I would abandon him like everybody else had done, and not be able to help him. The turning point came only after a last-ditch attempt to explain how I imagined we could work profitably together. These suggestions were unacceptable too and he decided he needed another therapist who had a better understanding of people with a background like his. He wanted my help to find this therapist, but until we found a good alternative he wanted to continue his sessions with me. I agreed to this, with mixed but somehow excited feelings. From this point, the basic atmosphere in our relationship changed. It was as if we both relaxed. Roger dropped the idea of changing therapists after a while, and while he didn't shower me with compliments, he showed a friendly side of himself, greeting me with a smile. Whereas he was regularly late for our appointments, he started coming on time. None of us made a point of these changes. But whenever I missed a point or forgot something he believed I should have remembered, he did not hesitate to berate me, though it didn't take long before his friendly manner was back.

As I now understand the process with Roger and myself, the decisive moment for him was when he felt that his history and childhood experiences were seen and accepted. He had got stuck in an experience of not being seen and respected. And so had I. This experience in his case had brought his early attempts at therapy as a young man to a quick end, and it also nearly brought our therapy to an unhappy conclusion, too. When Roger gradually convinced himself that he was both being seen and respected, he was also able to see and respect me, and to start exploring his own emotional and relational reactions. A repeated relation (Stern, 1994) and "object" countertransference (Geltner, 2012) were gradually replaced with a needed relation and an "anaclitic" countertransference.

The therapy with Ruth

Ruth's therapy was also twice weekly to start with. After about a year, it was extended to three times, and during the most intensive period, which lasted about four years of her 10-year analysis, we had three double sessions a week. She worked partly sitting, partly lying. Most of the work on affect motor memories was done with her lying down. In the first year of therapy, we focused much on what turned out to be a kind of "emotional analphabetism." Ruth knew the names of different emotions and feelings, but had great difficulties applying them to her own emotional experiences, of which she had a lot. David, Roger, and Ruth all found it difficult to feel and express their emotions, even though the form of their emotional problems varied widely. Nevertheless, the similarity suggests that some form of disturbance in the body-emotion-feeling process might be a hallmark of all mental disturbances, as I discussed in the previous chapters. Ruth, however, unlike David and Peter, from the very beginning, turned out to be an eager student of her own emotions.

After a little more than a year, the first images of what looked like memories of sexual abuse started to appear together with strong, painful sensations. The work started by attending to painful sensations in her body, later sexual sensations as well. For a while it looked like a never-ending journey revealing sexual abuse involving people both inside and outside her family. The process was very painful and twice she needed hospital care.

But despite the pain, Ruth was always very eager to explore in depth the possible causes of her problems. This process brought her more and more in contact with her feelings and needs, and she started to change her perception of her position and role in her life. She realized that she didn't want to continue as a nurse. Her choice of profession, she experienced, had been a reflexive instance of the strategy she had developed to survive. After several years in therapy, she embarked on an entirely different career. She was very happy with her studies in art and history.

Another area of her life that changed dramatically was her relationship with her husband, whom she had admired and adored. She gradually found him less agreeable, though, and found that they actually had very different interests. They eventually agreed to split up. In her first job in her new profession, she met a man she liked a lot and they decided to live together. After a while, however, their relationship became more problematic. He found it difficult to express his affection in the way she felt in desperate need of.

All in all, Ruth's life changed in several very positive ways, mainly as a consequence of becoming much better at experiencing her own needs and feelings. She was no longer as ready to admire other people, often indeed seeing herself as the wiser. Her body image changed, as she felt she could accept her body, feeling slimmer even though she had gained a few kilos. Her ability to experience good sexual feelings was much better in her new relationship. However, these changes were not stable. Even if she felt she had achieved a new relationship both to herself and others, and in a way had become a person she was much more satisfied with, she still had a special vulnerability. This vulnerability was especially connected to not being seen in relationships, which reminded her of the abuse she had to endure alone as a child. Many situations continued to elicit her old reactions, not least among them her headaches. So in many ways her life continued to be painful and problematic. Her sensitivity to not being seen resembles Roger's, and for both it was connected to severe childhood trauma. But the way they reacted was different, not least in the transference. For Ruth it seemed like the therapeutic relationship quickly became a stable and secure base from where she could explore all her insecurity both in her past and present life.

Discussion of the three therapies

Usually I don't find it necessary to think of patients as belonging to one or the other diagnostic category or preset character/personality type. Most often, in my experience, individual and changing features characterize the clinical picture and the unfolding of the countertransference. David, Roger, and Ruth were chosen for this clinical illustration because they represent an exception to this rule. Thinking back on their therapies, I have the sense that I was moving in separate territories with each of them. These territories never overlapped. In dynamic systems language, it was as if we were moving in three different attractor basins, and we never reached the kind of tipping point at which we moved from one attractor basin to another. All three stayed in their own basic character orientation: David with his tendency to move away from people; Roger with his tendency to move against people; and Ruth with her tendency to move toward people.

With respect to diagnostic categories, character types, or personality disorders, David might be said to be a rather typical schizoid character (today I might also have considered Asperger's, though I don't think that was the case). He was also compulsive; he had to do things his own way, but he did not have overt compulsive rituals or obsessive, preoccupied thoughts. Roger was not a typical narcissist of the kind that is occupied with his own grandiosity and with dominating others and getting their admiration, but these traits were definitely there. And he had not achieved the relative professional success that might be seen as typical of this character formation. From his description of his father, I would place him closer to the narcissistic prototype. Ruth was not a typical hysteric of the type who creates dramatic scenes to get attention and commiseration. In a way, she was more the classic conversion hysteric who falls ill as a consequence of what to others would be minor emotional confrontations with someone.

With each of them, however, I experienced a separate and specific emotional climate and countertransference. The climate and the countertransference feelings changed enormously during the course of their respective therapies. The greatest and most stormy changes for me happened in Roger's therapy. But even though the changes were substantial, I still have the feeling that I remained within separate territories or specific "attractor basins" with each of them.

David was constantly urging me to pay attention to some "thing," most often his fantasies. But he never asked me to pay attention to the relationship between us or his relationship with somebody else. He was like somebody who wants to go on fishing trips with me again and again, but who could only show interest in the fish we caught, none in me. The tension in our relationship, I felt, came from my repeated attempts to draw attention to his emotional/bodily experience, or to what was going on in our relationship or in his other relationships. (At that time I did not think of the possibility of drawing his attention to my emotional experience.)

With Roger, I felt constantly invited to listen to him telling about his relations present and past. And he wanted me to understand his point of view and support him in what he most often saw as others' unjust treatment of him. For some time, I found this invitation reasonable, also because I really felt he had suffered unjust and abusive behavior, especially as a child. But after a while, I felt the challenge in this therapy was to draw Roger's attention to his own emotional/bodily state and reactions. When I made moves in that direction, however, Roger very quickly got irritated. He was angry, as I came to understand it, not so much because he felt I was going in the wrong direction or being irrelevant, but primarily because it made him feel that I was blaming him for his misery, and that I was the same sort of person as members of his family and others he had had negative experience with. So the emotional climate oscillated between two states for a long time: smooth and friendly when I was empathic and supportive, aggressive and hostile when I had been unempathic or brought attention to his own part in the problematic episodes.

Ruth was constantly eager to explore her usually painful emotional body states. Additionally, she was always open for exploring her relations past and present, including her relationship with me. Ours was consistently characterized by what Freud described as the basic positive transference. At times, it was filled with very strong, vulnerable, and positive emotions, an erotic transference and – though less intense – countertransference. So the tension that arose in this therapy and could have threatened the therapeutic process, in this case, was about strong positive feelings; very different from the process and relationship with both David and Peter.

Comparing the three relationships, it is as if David and I were always intended to move in different directions, while Roger and I first moved in the same direction, but disagreed when I wanted to change direction. Ruth and I almost always agreed on the direction we should take, but we had to take care not to drive into each other.

Concluding this clinical illustration, I would like to draw attention to what has been the main focus: the form of the emotional interaction pattern, rather than the content of the verbal discourse. This does not mean that I don't consider the latter important. But it reflects the argument developed throughout this book that I consider the form of the usually unconscious emotional interaction pattern to contain the strongest energy, the strongest force at work both for stopping and promoting change.

In choosing these three cases as illustrations, I also wanted to highlight what seem to be three basic but very different coping and defensive strategies available for humans. Not being able to rely on any of them is catastrophic. But a strategy based on only one of them will also be highly problematic, as the cases reviewed above should illustrate.

Companionship, animals and isolation

Trevarthen, the first to hypothesize primary intersubjectivity, stated

> that we are born to be a character in a community of characters, making art, myths, and cultural history, that our spirit needs stories and storytellers, that we have an innate "communicative musicality" that responds to the touches, sights and sounds of human bodies intending and feeling "emotional" about the rewards and risks inseparable from acting and inventing in human company. I summarize this as a theory of "companionship." (2004, p. 2)

Animal companionship

It seems that humans, when deprived of satisfactory "companionship" with other humans like parents, seek whatever substitutes are available. Animals seem to be a preferred choice after humans. I would therefore like to add some thoughts on attachment to animals. It is my impression that patients with severe traumas and mainly insecure attachments to humans do better than expected when animals, often dogs, play a central part of the lives. The case of Ruth, just discussed, is an example also in this regard. Taking care of dogs has been an important part of her life. It is also my impression that relating to dogs and other animals in childhood seems to foster the development of empathy. Many people also seem to see their dogs and other animals as crucial to their quality of life.

Relating to animals is, however, not a sufficient or satisfactory alternative to secure attachment to other humans. It has struck me that many human tragedies reported in the media concern people who have ended up keeping a lot of animals in their homes. In some cases, the animals are severely mistreated. I will, however, present a case to illustrate the great benefit that in some cases seems to come from interacting with and having an attachment to animals.

Ann was referred to therapy in her mid-50s. She had had a long and successful career as a nurse: after many years in intensive (emergency) care, she had been working over the last years in mental health. In her last job, however, she had a kind of breakdown after prolonged difficulties with superiors and colleagues. The difficulties she experienced at this workplace, I came to understand, resulted from other staff members feeling provoked by Ann's often superior and quicker understanding of the patients on the ward, combined with the way she communicated this understanding. Prior to this last job she had been involved in consultation work with severely disturbed psychotic patients who had committed serious crimes. She was much sought after for this work for her ability to establish contact and gain the confidence of patients who others (including psychologists and psychiatrists) had found difficult or frightening.

Ann grew up as the only child of her parents, respected leaders in their community. She suffered severe physical abuse at the hands of her father who generally treated her harshly. She sustained damage to her neck in early life, probably as the result of the father's habit of lifting her by the hair and throwing her in the cellar. She was not protected by her mother. Her nanny, however, did stand up to the father and was at times able to protect her. She loved her nanny very much. Both her father and mother were eager to tell her to remember she was a privileged child, coming from a family of better standing and economy than most others in the community.

From before school age, Ann had her own dog which she cared for all the time and which followed her everywhere. Ever since childhood, dogs have been an important part of her life.

In her mid-20s, Ann married and had four children. Her husband turned out to be even more dangerously abusive than her father, and nearly strangled her to death. She was hospitalized and some time later managed to get a divorce. She then met a man she had known as a youth. They married and had a satisfying relationship for quite some years before she started therapy.

In therapy, Ann was surprised by a growing awareness of severe pains in her body. The pains had probably been there for many years as a kind of "unthought known" (Bollas, 1987). A thorough medical examination revealed several serious injuries, among other places in her knees. Over the years of therapy, she had extensive surgery to repair the damage both to her knees and back.

Throughout her life, Ann has had great capacity for and interest in helping others both inside and outside her family. She has always had a strong personal religious conviction and has played a leading role in the local church, enjoying challenging religious leaders (priests and bishops) with more orthodox views than her own. During the final years of her therapy, we attempted to find out how she could find more room for her own needs and interests, not least because it was difficult for her to refuse other people's requests for help and understanding.

Like Ruth, Ann developed a positive transference early in the therapy that remained stable over the next 10 years. And, I might add, a "concordant" countertransference developed on my part. Also like Ruth, Ann had suffered severe trauma as a child and also developed strong empathic abilities. I am not arguing here that relating to dogs should be seen as the cause of an empathic capacity. But it seems likely that strong attachments to animals could have been an element in the development of their empathic and attachment abilities.

It seems that animals can act as substitute attachment figures for children – and adults. I also wonder whether the kind of attention children need to interact well with dogs, for instance, might not train their emphatic capacity and stimulate their mirror neuron system.

The denial of companionship

If Trevarthen is right in his "theory of companionship," and I tend to believe he is, isolation, the denial of companionship and attachment, is the ultimate psychological threat and punishment for humans. This seems to have been realized in human societies long ago, as witnessed by the widespread use of social isolation as an alternative to physical punishment. A historical example is Spinoza's excommunication from the Jewish community in Amsterdam on grounds of persistent heresy. This event is extensively reviewed in Damasio (2003). I find the text of the excommunication strongly indicative of the value attributed to attachment and companionship in history. Apart from destroying the body by torture and ultimately causing death, exclusion from relationships has been considered the most dreadful fate to bestow upon a fellow human being. In the case of Spinoza, the punishment by the standards of the time was mild compared to the torture chamber and the burning at the stake of the Catholic inquisition, and the persecution, torturing, and burning of witches in many Protestant countries at the time. "Evil has many degrees, after all" (Damasio, 2003, p. 252).

On July 27, 1656, the Amsterdam synagogue required "that the said Espinoza should be excommunicated and cut off from the nation of Israel." The concluding sentence of this historic text is especially interesting in our context. It forbade any form of human contact with the excommunicated Spinoza. "And we warn you, that none may speak with him by work of mouth nor by writing, nor show any favour to him, nor be under one roof with him, nor come within four cubits of him, nor read any paper composed or written by him" (Damasio, 2003, p. 253; for the full text of the *cherem* see pp. 252–254).

The text illustrates the value historically attributed to attachment and companionship. Apart from incarceration, torture, and the death penalty, exclusion from the fellowship of people has been considered the most dreadful of punishments. This said, if Damasio's portrait is anything to go by, Spinoza was probably well equipped in terms of strength of character to sustain the isolation. His response may therefore not be too surprising: "This compels me to nothing that I should not otherwise have done" (Damasio, 2003, p. 254).

Part III

Embodied training and supervision

Chapter 10

Training to work with unconscious embodied expressions

Analytic training – as well as psychotherapy training generally – has tended to privilege the exchange of words. In this chapter, I suggest that analytic training can be enriched by incorporating embodied practices inspired by fields like acting, dance, music, and singing. In the performing arts (acting, dance, music), expertise in emotional expression is developed by actively engaging the body. Additionally, many body-oriented therapies (Anderson, 2008) have developed useful methods and exercises to help increase awareness of and attention to embodied experience.

An illustration of what training might look like is offered with a description of nonverbal, embodied ways of presenting and working with cases in the training program at the Norwegian Character Analytic Institute. Candidates are asked to present a case, but without using words. Instead, they stand on the floor, adopting a posture of a particular patient. They then play that patient entering the consulting room and finding a place. After this role play, other candidates are asked to move to the position of the therapist vis-à-vis the "patient." The chapter after this describes a complementary supervision model in which the supervisee stages her interaction with a patient. In this model, the supervisee is asked to role-play herself as therapist and as her patient. She will then move to a third position, where she reflects over the experience so far.

So, in this chapter I will discuss implications for training emphasizing the embodied dimension of the psychoanalytical interaction. I want to emphasize that the training guidelines I am presenting here were developed alongside the theoretical framework discussed in the previous chapters. In some ways, the theory inspired the training practices; in others, the practices helped to clarify theory.

Given what we know about the embodied dimensions of emotional experience and interaction, it is surprising to see how many analytic and psychotherapy training programs continue to rely almost exclusively on verbal exchange. An explanation might be the hold of the idea of the "talking cure"[1] throughout the whole culture of psychoanalysis and psychotherapy. However, I think it is reasonable to assume that psychotherapy training can be enriched by incorporating embodied practices from body-work and the performing arts. What the performing arts share with psychoanalysis and psychotherapy is a commitment to emotional communication. Practitioners of the performing arts realized long ago that expertise in emotional communication depends on training the body to express emotion. The seasoned psychotherapy researchers J.L. Binder and W.P. Henry (2010) recently made the following observation:

> A novice musician would not take courses in music theory and then go directly to performing on stage. Yet, the predominant format of psychotherapy training requires the trainee to go directly from coursework to seeing real patients. No matter how talented the supervisor, the supervision of real patients only minimally approximates the requirements of "deliberate practice." (p. 300)

Muran, Safran, and Eubanks-Carter (2010) observe that for many trainees, the process of establishing an experiential focus involves a partial unlearning of things they have already been taught while doing therapy. The formalized training of therapists often emphasizes the conceptual at the expense of the experiential. And even if conceptual knowledge is essential, they note, it can also serve a defensive function. "It can help them [the therapists] to avoid dealing with the painful and frightening conflictual feelings that inevitably emerge for both patients and therapists" (p. 334). I think the previously discussed case of Astrid can serve as an illustration in this respect.

Personally, when it comes to establishing an experiential focus, I have profited from learning and practicing the *Pesso Boyden System Psychomotor Therapy* (Pesso & Crandell, 1991, www.pbsp.com), a psycho-dramatic and interactive form of group therapy developed by dancers Albert Pesso and Diane Boyden Pesso on the basis of their experience of training dancers in emotional expression through body movements.

Reich (1949/1972) in his – aborted – work to develop an embodied psychoanalysis also stressed the relevance of music and artistic work for an understanding of the pre-linguistic nature of emotional experience and expression. Even if Reich saw language as reflecting the emotional state of the body (as reviewed previously), he believed that it could not represent the deeper feelings of emotional body states.

> The reason is that the beginnings of living functioning lie much *deeper* than and *beyond* language. *Over and above this, the living organism has its own modes of expressing movement which simply cannot be comprehended with words.* Every musically inclined person is familiar with the emotional state evoked by great music. However, if one attempts to translate these emotional experiences into words, one's musical perception rebels. Music is wordless and wants to remain that way. Yet music gives expression to the inner movement of the living organism, and listening to it evokes the "sensation" of some "inner stirring." The wordlessness of music is usually described in one of two ways: (1) as a mark of mystical spirituality, or (2) as the deepest expression of feeling incapable of being put into words. The natural scientific point of view subscribes to the interpretation that musical expression is related to the depths of the living organism. Accordingly, what is regarded as the "spirituality" of

music is merely another way of saying that deep feeling is identical with having contact with the living organism *beyond the limitations of language*. (p. 359)

I believe the incorporation of body practices developed both in traditions of artistic work and traditions of body-work can enhance contact with "deep feeling . . . beyond the limitations of language," especially with regard to countertransference awareness of body sensations and movement. I therefore offer a model for integrating such practices into psychoanalytic and psychotherapy training. However, body practices and body techniques differ in many ways, also with respect to their compatibility with a psychoanalytic or psychotherapeutic framework.

George Downing (1996) suggests a useful tripartite classification of body techniques: experiential interventions, inner techniques, and external techniques. Experiential interventions seek to draw attention to aspects of one's own body experience. An example would be to ask oneself and/or a patient "What do I/you feel in my/your body at this moment?" Most analysts and psychotherapists will be familiar with this type of "body technique," but analysts with a particular interest in the embodied dimensions of analytic interaction will probably use it on a more regular basis. Theoretical and evidence-based arguments for this type of intervention were given in previous chapters.

By inner techniques, Downing refers to experiential intervention follow-ups. When attention is already drawn to something that is going on in the body, it can be followed up by continued attention to the phenomenon, or, if a slight movement is going on, by continuing the movement. Such interventions will often produce heightened awareness of what is going on at more unconscious bodily, emotional levels.

External techniques are techniques and practices employed by body-work therapies. They are "external" inasmuch as the therapist suggests a procedure that is not necessarily grounded in what is already going on in the body. These techniques go beyond "a body that is moving itself" (Shapiro, 1996) and might include adopting specific bodily positions, as in yoga, specific movements, or forms of massage. *Bodies in Treatment*, edited by Anderson (2008), presents and discusses the possible integration or adjunct use of such external techniques (body-work) in psychoanalysis and psychotherapy. It is my belief that the body practices developed in body-work are likely to enhance awareness of body sensations and movement, providing in this way fuller access to countertransference information. I therefore think it is beneficial for analysts and psychotherapists to gain some experience of working with such practices.

The practices described and discussed in this chapter and the previous clinical illustrations include, however, only experiential and inner body techniques. These "techniques," in my opinion, are compatible with an analytical frame. They do not affect the frame such as when one, for example, asks a patient to perform a specific exercise. What the application of experiential and inner body techniques does imply is a shift or expansion of attention on the ongoing analytic interaction.

We got rhythm

In *Bodies in Treatment* (Anderson, 2008) Gianni Nebbiosi and Susanna Federici-Nebbiosi (2008) have a chapter entitled *"We" Got Rhythm. Miming and the Polyphony of Identity in Psychoanalysis*. There they elaborate on the inner connection between body rhythms, relations, and imitation, thereby addressing in practical terms the perspective on analytic therapy and training that is developed in this book. To my knowledge, they are the only analytic practitioners so far to have discussed rhythmic experience *and* applied it to imitation. I will therefore review central aspects of their work before reporting on the application of imitative approaches in clinical training. Nebbiosi and Federici-Nebbiosi want to show how rhythmic experience is basically relational and how it plays a fundamental role in creating dialogue between ourselves and our bodies as well as between us and other people. Furthermore, they explore the way in which the co-creation of rhythm is an important element for the co-creation of meaning, "as well as – through the use of miming – a factor promoting an ability to better get to know and understand the complex implicit languages of body movements and facial expressions to which contemporary psychoanalysis is assigning an increasing value" (2008, p. 214).

Rhythm, I would add, facilitates a view of psychoanalytic interaction as a rhythmic dance for two bodies (Sletvold & Børstad, 2009). In this sense, therapeutic action would depend on the form of this dance, and on how the analyst is able to lead the dance with a particular patient. Everyone with some experience of leading a dance partner will know that different partners present different challenges, and those with experience of being led will know how the dancing experience is shaped by the style of the partner. This brings me to the topic of surrendering to a rhythm. Nebbiosi and Federici-Nebbiosi again:

> To introduce a crucial theme of our discourse, we would like to start precisely by the fact of surrendering to a rhythm and not controlling (counting) our movements to adhere to it. The rhythmic experience always entails surrendering to something other than us and which may become part of us only when we surrender to it. (p. 216)

Rhythm is the way in which we relate bodily to our surroundings, physically and socially, when we breathe, walk, talk, work, make love. We surrender to, or resist, the rhythm of something else, relational fields of embodied simulations and imitations, moving in and out of the spaces of interacting bodies. In rhythmic relations, say Nebbiosi and Federici-Nebbiosi, there is always dialectic between symmetry and asymmetry; it is when symmetry and asymmetry meet that form – the form of emotions – comes into existence.

> Subjective emotions all have special rhythms that give form to particular facial expressions, to a particular breath, heartbeat, muscle tension, and so

on. These rhythmic forms have an exquisitely interactive value and . . . have a specific relational function. (p. 217)

Nebbiosi and Federici-Nebbiosi call attention to the work of Jaffe, Beebe, Feldstein, Crown, and Jasnow (2001) on rhythms of dialogue in infancy. They cite Jaffe et al. in support of their view of rhythm: "When speakers coordinate rhythmic patterns such as sound-silence or look-look-away, they are in fact exchanging important information regarding the perceived warmth, similarity, and empathy of their interaction" (p. 3), and conclude that the study of human interactions and a relational idea of the mind cannot disregard movement as a privileged language for the creation and sharing of affective meanings; "the study of movement as rhythmic experience is the *via regia* to understand implicit affective communication" (pp. 221–222). This echoes what Schjelderup wrote in 1936 (see Chapter 4): *Nicht der traum, sonder das verhalten sind der via regia zum sogenanten unbevussten.* [Not the dream but the behavior is the *via regia* to the so-called unconscious.]

So, when the sharing and communication of emotions take place largely through our own and our patients' body movements, and this process is mainly relational, it raises the issue – say Nebbiosi and Federici-Nebbiosi – for psychoanalysts (and all those who deal with psychotherapy) of a different type of listening.

We must be able to "listen" with all senses to our patients' movements, recognizing the rhythmic forms of posture, facial expressions, alternations of words, and silence. In short, understanding another person and ourselves in relation to another person is achieved not just through verbal and/or visual language, but also through the language of movements that gives form and allows to share the affects of a relationship. (p. 223)

In line with the reasoning offered by Nebbiosi and Federici-Nebbiosi, I suggest that psychoanalytic training should create a place for bodies in rhythmic movement.

This will imply a somewhat radical departure from an exclusive reliance on verbal exchange in training contexts. It has been made possible, in my view, by our growing understanding of the interactive, intersubjective, and embodied basis of the mind, including thought and language. This change has been going on for some time in psychoanalysis, particularly in relational psychoanalysis.

Getting to know by imitation

The centrality of the phenomena variously termed imitation, miming, mirroring, attunement, matching, and embodied simulation in developmental and neuroscientific literature was reviewed and discussed in Chapter 7. These terms are also increasingly finding their way into the psychoanalytic literature. Closely related concepts like identification, internalization, and empathy have, however, always been central to psychoanalytic theorizing. It is surprising, Nebbiosi and Federici-Nebbiosi say, how contemporary psychotherapists and psychoanalysts do not attach any importance to the possibility of miming.

> We believe that the reason for all this, which is deeply rooted in the theoretical and clinical tradition of psychoanalysis, lies in the lack of trust we put in the body – and the excessive trust we put in the mind – as tool for knowing ourselves, the others, and ourselves in relation to the others. Indeed in psychoanalytic literature, it's not unusual to find notations concerning the patient's body (expressions, postures, etc.); however, most of the time, these notations are matched by a reading that does not directly involve *the knowledge process that the analyst's body develops by living these events.* (p. 224, my italics)

To my knowledge, the first – and for a long time the only – analyst to explore the clinical use of imitation was the Danish character analyst Tage Philipson, whose work I reviewed in Chapter 4. Nebbiosi and Federici-Nebbiosi describe their experience of imitating their patients with these words.

> For many years now, we have been using the tool of miming our patients in order to obtain a better understanding of them. This was done for the purpose of using *a knowledge that resides in the analyst's body and of which he is completely unaware.*
>
> However, to have access to this knowledge, we should try and suspend the will and surrender to the knowledge that our body has of the patient. (2008, p. 224, my italics)

In doing so, they do not believe they rule out subjectivity and get direct access to the patient's subjectivity. As Nebbiosi and Federici-Nebbiosi advise, when we imitate patients, we need to avoid the illusion that we have direct access to our patient's subjectivity. At the Character Analytic Institute in Oslo, we ask candidates to mime each other, usually in groups of three, as part of the basic training. When putting words to their experience of imitating each other, we ask them to use expressions like "When I stand like this, I feel . . .", not "You are . . . ." It is also better to let three people do the exercise rather than two; in that way, everyone gets more than one report on what it might feel like to be "like me." They will also be reminded that there is never only one truth. The following description of imitative techniques in training and supervision will hopefully promote awareness of "the knowledge process that the analyst's body develops by living these events."

The training program at the Character Analytic Institute

The background to and the establishment of the Character Analytic Institute were presented in Chapter 4. Here I want to explore in particular the embodied aspects of the training at this institute. Jacobs (2005) points to what he sees as "the neglect of nonverbal phenomena in psychoanalytic education today," while Schore (2003b) calls for the critical nonverbal implicit functions of the right brain to be incorporated into psychoanalytic and psychotherapeutic training programs. The experiences presented below can be seen as a preliminary response to these observations. The program, in addition to focusing on verbal discourse, also attends to embodied dimensions of the psychotherapeutic interaction, especially through the use of imitation.

Trainees are only admitted after two years of supervised clinical practice as licensed psychologists, or two years of psychiatric residency for physicians. The training program consists of a two-year foundation course (seminar and supervision) and an advanced program of training analysis, two-year advanced seminar and supervision. The two-year basic course is also offered as an adjunct to specialization in clinical psychology, and can be taken separately. It takes at least five years to complete the advanced training program.

In the two-year basic seminar, body practices and techniques occupy about half of the time. Priority is given to body practices aimed at exploring the candidates' own embodied experience. This includes exercises developed in schools of body-work focusing on enhancing awareness of one's own body. Body practices also include exercises specifically designed to increase awareness of and sensitivity to aspects of intersubjective experience central to the training program. The same patient is imitated in separate exercises. In one exercise, candidates are asked to focus on their own authentic (egocentric) feelings. In another, they are asked to imitate the "patient" and explore empathic feelings. In a third, they are asked to adopt an observing attitude. In this way, candidates can experience in themselves how quite different and often contradictory reactions can be stimulated in more or less the same embodied encounter depending on the kind of attitude the therapist adopts. The other half of the basic seminar is devoted to the theories of the relational and embodied perspective, with a particular emphasis on how to acknowledge the implicit body emotional *and* the explicit verbal symbolic dimension of the therapeutic interaction.

Whereas the basic seminar gives candidates an opportunity to work on their own embodied experience, the advanced seminar gives priority to working with cases. Downing (1996) demonstrated the basic elements of this approach in his seminars on transference and countertransference in Oslo from the early 1990s. He asked the therapist whose case was under consideration to adopt the patient's position before resuming his own physical stance in relation to the patient. This turned out to be very effective and almost always evoked new and highly relevant feelings and thoughts. The strategy demonstrated that transference and countertransference were indeed basically embodied communication of emotions, and pre-echoed what Wallin (2007) wrote some years later: "In an enactment of transference-counter-transference, what is enacted, verbally and nonverbally, is a particular kind of relationship" (p. 270).

This enacting of the transference/countertransference, as Downing demonstrated it, suggested a new approach to understanding and dealing with the therapeutic impasse. It helped bring into focus the centrality of the nonverbal, embodied dimension of the therapeutic interaction and, above all, was instrumental with other body-oriented traditions in stimulating efforts to refine training practices at the Character Analytic Institute.

The approach to training described here was originally created for candidates in the advanced analytic training program. The guidelines were formulated as ways of working on cases in seminars. Some of the principles were first presented at a conference workshop, "Getting to Know by Imitation" (Nylund & Sletvold, 2002), and more recently by Nylund and Sletvold (2009) and Sletvold (2012a). In the advanced seminar, which follows on from the two-year basic seminar, participants spend half the allotted time presenting and discussing cases from their own therapeutic practice. Prior to this approach, cases were submitted in the shape of written reports, including a brief case history and a full or partial transcript of a session. While case discussions were engaging and candidates came up with lots of ideas, how they understood and addressed the challenges raised by the cases could remain unclear. It was as if the written reports and, not least, the ensuing discussions made the actual interaction between patient and therapist more remote. These experiences reminded me of one of Reich's (1949/1972) more extreme statements.

> If the analyst wants to arrive at a correct appraisal of his patient, he must begin by asking the patient *not* to speak. This measure proves very fruitful, for as soon as the patient ceases to speak, the emotional expressions of his body are brought into much sharper focus. After a few minutes of silence, the analyst will usually have grasped the patient's most conspicuous character trait or, more correctly, will have understood the emotional expression of the *plasmatic* movement. If the patient appeared to laugh in a friendly way while he spoke, his laughter might modulate into an empty grin during his silence, the mask-like character of which the patient himself must readily perceive. If the patient appeared to speak about his life with reserved seriousness, an expression of suppressed anger might easily appear in the chin and neck during his silence.
>
> Let these examples suffice to point out that, apart from its function as communication, *human language also often functions as a defense*. . . . On the basis of repeated experiences, it is my opinion that in many psychoanalyses which have gone on for years the treatment has become stuck in this pathological use of language. (pp. 360–361)

What Reich expresses here is to my mind extreme and one-sided, but nonetheless a relevant antidote to the one-sided privileging of verbal exchange that has prevailed in psychoanalysis for many years. I certainly do not recommend the analyst to "begin by asking the patient *not* to speak." However, adapted to a training situation, Reich's suggestion has turned out to be fruitful.

A basic principle of the experiment introduced in 1999 was that all verbal information concerning a presented case should be initially avoided. Instead of giving written or verbal information, the presenter is asked to stand up and adopt the physical posture of the patient. They are asked neither to accentuate certain traits nor caricature the patient, but to be as faithful as possible to their feeling of how the patient might have stood had she or he been there themselves. In the terminology of Nebbiosi and Federici-Nebbiosi (2008), the instruction is to mime, not to mimic.

> Indeed, the mime does not want to make us laugh: he is not content with some distinctive features. We love mimes because – like poets do with language – they enable us to look at the world and people more in depth and with greater attention. Through mimes we discover the language of bodily rhythms: a world of meaning that would otherwise remain unrecognized. Mimes reveal to us a modality of relational knowledge that we possess and practice, but that we are unaware of. (pp. 223–224)

There are two reasons why candidates are urged not to mimic or caricature. For one, it is not "necessary" to the task of successfully conveying an impression of the patient. It has been amazing to see the accuracy and detail of the information conveyed by relatively ordinary postures of the body. The other reason we don't want candidates to caricature their patients is because they tend to latch on to features of the patient that are already more or less conscious to the therapist/candidate, while downplaying more unconscious features.

Nor are participants asked to focus on particular aspects of the physical posture, like breathing or muscular tension. What we do encourage candidates to do is concentrate on "the total impression" created by "the total expression" (Reich, 1949/1972, p. 362), in agreement with what Jacobs (2005) has suggested.

> Just as the analyst listens with equal attention to all of the patient's verbalizations and tries not to fix any particular aspect of the material in mind . . . so he observes all of the patient's nonverbal behavior. . . . [H]e takes in and registers what he sees, but does not focus on any particular bodily movements or facial expression. (2005, p. 172)

The practical experience we have gained over more than a decade seems to confirm the merits of this approach to case presentation. Indeed, the presenters themselves are often surprised at what they have conveyed about the patient, things they were often not aware of. Traits perceived by participants are also sometimes confirmed by information available elsewhere.

The stricture on not giving any verbal information in the beginning also had a striking effect on the ensuing discussion. As we saw again and again, as soon as verbal information about a case was given, it changed the nature of the discussion. Questions posed by other participants about the patient's life tended to divert attention away from what was actually presented. In this way, we found Reich's suggestion very fruitful to our training situation.

The program focuses on three interrelated aspects of embodied experience. First, the experience of our own body and the bodily foundations of the self.

Second, the embodied basis of intersubjectivity; simulation and imitation of the emotional body states of others. And third, the emergence of a sense of objectivity from reflecting over similarities and differences between one's own state and that of others. The training program thus focuses on 1. embodied subjectivity, self, and authenticity; 2. embodied intersubjectivity, empathy, and identification; and 3. embodied reflexivity, mentalization, and we-centered objectivity. Emphasis varies somewhat if the cases are worked on in a seminar or in supervision. The overall aim of the program is to enhance the relational competence of the candidates.

Nonverbal case presentation

The following is a description of what the nonverbal case presentation looks like.

Step 1. The candidate whose case is to be presented is asked to stand on the floor as she or he imagines the patient would have been standing. While the presenter mimes her patient in a standing position, the rest of the training group is asked to note their own reactions, feelings, and thoughts. They are asked to pay particular attention to their own feelings and what they can see. A little later, they will be asked to stand up and imitate the posture themselves. In other words, they need to focus on three aspects of their experience: 1) their own embodied reactions; 2) what they observe by looking at the presenter; and 3) how they feel by imitating the presenter. After this nonverbal work, participants share their ideas among themselves verbally. The presenter responds to these ideas but is not allowed to add information.

Step 2. In the next step, we ask the presenter to enter the therapy room and sit or lie down as if he or she were the patient. Again the group is asked to observe and make note of their reactions and feelings. No explicit imitation is done at this point. Participants are again asked to share their ideas and the presenter to respond.

Step 3. Once steps 1 and 2 have been completed, the presenter is allowed to tell the group about the patient in speech and/or writing.

Below I present an illustration of how these nonverbal case presentations unfold in practice. No description of the case will be given initially because doing so would miss the point of the exercise, which is that we are looking at embodied, not verbalized experience. Photographs or video might, on the other hand, have been useful. The following vignette includes some of my own notes taken down during one of these presentations.

Mary's case.

Mary (one of the candidates) takes some time to decide how to represent her patient physically. When she's made up her mind, she gives a signal and freezes in the chosen position. The group has been instructed to observe what they see and how they react emotionally. After a few minutes, they are asked to stand and adopt the same posture themselves, continuing to note what they feel. The group then sits down. Mary is not allowed to say anything, but listens and take notes. The others are asked to put their experience into words and share with the group.

Comments:

Note of my own impression: Lost in reverie.

Candidate 1: Splitting, ambition, hiding oneself, "poor me."

Candidate 2: Pulling oneself together, sad, desperate, close to tears.

Candidate 3: Holding, sad and hopeless, wants to be seen and not seen at the same time.

Candidate 4: Resigned, brooding over emptiness, tense and rigid body.

Mary's comment (after the standing sequence):

The different impressions all confirm my own impression and what I know.

Mary is now asked to play her patient entering the room, sitting down, finding a position and moving in the chair for a few seconds (the group is still unaware of the sex of the patient). The group is encouraged again to observe what they see and what they feel. They are not asked to imitate in this sequence themselves.

Comments:

Candidate 1: Looks younger, doesn't give anything away, stays on his own. Difficult to reach, easily hurt. Has no close friends, but is hoping to find some. Strongly dissociating.

Candidate 2: Self-conscious

Candidate 3: Dancing, rocking backward and forward, controlled. In pretty bad shape. Unfriendly, difficult to help. Risk of regression. "I do it my way."

Candidate 4: Moves easily, stays much in his head.

Mary's response (before presenting written information and talking about the patient):

Everything was well observed, felt and thought!

In this case, the observations of the other candidates agreed entirely with what Mary herself knew of her patient. In my experience, this is rarely the case. In most cases, the comments of the group only partly confirm the presenter's impressions.

Candidates find this nonverbal case presentation consistently more meaning-ful than the traditional approach based on verbal information. Many participants are used to a more conventional approach at psychoanalytical case seminars. My experience is that when verbal information about a case is given at the start, it tends to change the nature of the discussion. Participants start asking questions about aspects of the patient's life, something that draws attention away from what was actually presented, away from what Stern has termed *the local level*. So it was particularly rewarding in our training set-up to follow Reich's suggestion to "begin by asking the patient *not* to speak."

The new procedure seems to offer something that isn't available at "talking seminars." There is a different atmosphere, a greater sense of humility and respect for the patient whose case is under examination. There is also a sharper focus on the resources and problems of the patient. The presenters are usually surprised by how much information they actually get across to the group by nonverbal means, and how relevant it is to the case at hand. They are also surprised by their own ability to imitate patients. Many may never have seen their patient standing, and protest ignorance at first. But the procedure is not dependent on explicit knowledge of the patient's physical appearance. What seems decisive for accessing what one knows is to "try and suspend the will and surrender to the knowledge that our body has of the patient" (Nebbiosi & Federici-Nebbiosi, 2008, p. 224).

It is always exciting to see the amount and quality of the information candidates are able to pick up during these two short sessions, i.e., the first in which the presenter stands immobile, and the next when she or he moves for just a few seconds. Participants discuss their ideas about the emotional state of the "patient"; the kind of problems facing them; how it would feel to have this person in therapy; and what the biggest challenges would probably be for the therapist and how they could be addressed. I have been struck by how much unconscious bodily information therapists seem to get from their patients. It confirms experiences reported by Nebbiosi and Federici-Nebbiosi (2008).

> For many years now, we have been using the tool of miming our patients in order to obtain a better understanding of them. This was done for the purpose of using a knowledge that resides in the analyst's body and of which he is completely unaware. (p. 224)

This knowledge, I believe, is relayed by implicit, other-centered participation in the emotional dialogue with our patients, probably due to embodied simulation/ implicit imitation and mirror neuron activity. Additionally, it has been fascinating to witness this unconscious information so easily made conscious and given verbal expression by attention to body feelings and imitation. It is consistent with the close link found between observation, imitation, and verbal reflection reported in Chapters 7 and 8 (Carr et al., 2003; Meltzoff & Decety, 2003).

The training approach gives candidates ample opportunity to experience the transition from observation to embodied simulation and miming, from implicit to explicit imitation. It has also been fascinating to witness the ease with which nonconscious information is made conscious and given verbal expression by attention to body feelings and imitation.

Rehearsing therapeutic interaction

After this "diagnostic" sequence, the next step involves rehearsing therapy interaction. One of the participants plays the therapist, while the presenter continues to imitate his or her patient. They meet at the start of a session and take their positions in the room. After using the procedure on a regular basis for a time, we found that very short interaction sequences seemed to work well. Important things seemed to happen in the first few seconds of the interaction between patient and therapist. I had no clear understanding of what was unfolding at the time. Beebe and Lachmann (2002) showed very convincingly, however, the relevance of microanalytic infant research for adult treatment. And Stern (2004) has systematically analyzed the basic meaningful interactive sequence in psychotherapy, the present moment, to last between one and ten seconds.

Sequences of just a few seconds seem to encapsulate what I will term the basic unit of analysis of psychotherapy interaction. With a total duration of no more than about 30 seconds, it is possible for both the therapist and the "patient" to give an immediate and relatively complete report of their respective experiences. Almost always, both have one or more meaningful stories to tell, often of relevance to the therapeutic challenges. The therapist might tell a story about her impressions of the "patient" and her feelings about herself. The posture she adopted may induce a sense of ease or give her discomfort, an urge to go on from that position or a need to change it. The "patient's" story might be about how it felt to meet this therapist, embarrassment at being looked at, or difficulty with the physical proximity to the therapist. Or she may not have noticed much about the therapist at all. Whatever the reaction, the first few seconds of the encounter between patient and therapist almost always produce meaningful stories. These stories seem to speak directly to key issues for the patient, and to the interaction between the personalities of the therapist and patient. These first few seconds generally pass without verbal communication. Sometimes, however, a sound or some words form a natural element.

After this initial sequence of therapist–patient interaction, extended interaction sequences can be tried. Candidates can experiment with various ways of being with the same "patient." The presenter and "his patient" have an opportunity to experience and compare different therapeutic approaches. Experimenting with verbal comments and interpretations is part of this sequence. But the focus is just as much on the physical posture, the manner in which the therapist moves, and his or her emotional, facial, and body expression in relation to that of the "patient." Again, the strong emotional impact of apparently insignificant changes in the patient's and therapist's postures, ways of moving, expressions, and tone of voice are particularly striking. Enactments could therefore be seen as a constant aspect of therapist–patient relations (Wallin, 2007), and the unconscious as expressed first and foremost in continuous embodied interaction.

When we rehearse therapeutic interaction, we underline the purpose of the exercise: to explore different ways of being with the patient. The seminar work should be considered exploratory. It is not about finding the "right" way. Nonetheless, participants sometimes want to "help" the presenter to tackle issues she has with her patient, or her patient's problems, and the presenter might welcome such help. When this occurs, I find it wise to remind the group of the purpose of the work, which is not group supervision. I also find it fruitful to underline the difference between the work we do in the practical-theoretical seminar, and therapy and supervision. The presenting candidates should in this light be supervised by their ordinary supervisor on the cases they present, which is normally how things proceed anyway because supervision is part of their training.

The therapy rehearsals give seminar participants an opportunity to experiment with different ways of being with a staged patient. Whatever the form and content of these experiments, they won't affect the real patient. And much can be learned from seeing staged interventions which might not seem particularly helpful or promising. On the other hand, it is always a pleasure to observe therapeutic interaction which feels good and promising to the therapist and "patient" as well. Nevertheless, it is always important to keep in mind that we can never know for sure what is the "right" or "best" way to handle a therapeutic situation. One advantage of this type of training in which several therapists work with the same "patient" is the opportunity to see that there is always more than one fruitful way to move ahead.

In conclusion, I will say that our experience since 1999 has convinced my colleagues at the Character Analytic Institute and me that much can be gained from applying these procedures to case seminars/conferences. However, theory is also part of the training; lectures, reading and presenting papers, and verbal theoretical discussions are as important and necessary as before.

Note

1 Ironically, Anna O, who invented the term "talking cure," ended her therapy with Breuer not by talking but by a bodily enactment of the traumatic situation with her father: "On the last day – by the help of re-arranging the room so as to resemble her father's sickroom – she reproduced the terrifying hallucinations which I have described above and which constituted the root of her whole illness" (Breuer & Freud, 1893/1895/1955, p. 40).

Chapter 11

Embodied supervision

Making unconscious relational experience conscious

In this chapter, I present a model of supervision that is complementary to the embodied case work presented in the previous chapter. In this model, the supervisee stages her interaction with a patient. The supervisee is asked to role-play herself as therapist and as her patient. She will then move to a third position, where she will reflect over the experiences gained in the two previous positions. While this way of supervising is an integral part of the training at the Character Analytic Institute, experience has unequivocally shown that the model works just as well also in other settings where supervision is an option. It is not necessary to be in training at the Character Analytic Institute, or indeed to have completed training, to profit from this kind of supervision. But it is an advantage that the supervisor is trained in the model.

Inspired by Aron's (2006) ideas of the seesaw and the triangle (which he presented at a seminar in Oslo in January 2005), we place three extra chairs in a triangle. The first marks the therapist's position, the second (which can also be a couch) the patient's, and the third is where the supervisee reflects over what went on in and between the therapist and patient. This arrangement keeps the "therapy room" and supervision room apart as separate areas. As an introduction to this supervisory "therapy room," the reader might like to repeat the exercise set out in Chapter 5.

I suggest that you envisage yourself sitting with one of your patients. Take some time to let the patient come alive for your inner eye. As you are doing this, shift your attention to what is going on in your body. Pay attention to whatever sensations and feelings you are able to register, and put some of it into words. What I just have asked you to pay special attention to is what I in this text have been referring to as embodied subjectivity.

As a second of two further steps, I ask you to slowly move to the position you have envisioned for your patient/other person. Take your time to feel yourself enter into the patient's emotional expression, posture, and way of moving. Then register what this feels like to you. It is probably quite different from what you experienced in your own position. However, you might have experienced some of these feelings while you were sitting in your own chair as a consequence of automatic inner imitation/embodied simulation. What you sense and feel in this second position is what I have been referring to as embodied intersubjectivity.

The third and last step I invite you to take is to move from the second position to a third position in between and somewhat to the side of the two first positions. Standing or sitting in this position, I suggest that you keep in mind your experiences from both the other positions. Take your time to envision the meeting and interaction between you and the patient. This time I ask you not only to pay attention to sensations and feelings, but also to images and thoughts that might emerge within you. The emergence of images and thoughts from this third position I have been referring to as embodied reflexivity.

When you return to the chair you started from, you can round off if you like by taking "a new look" at the patient, and see if something has changed in the way you experience yourself together with this patient. I suggest that you keep in mind relevant aspects of the experiences you had in this exercise while you go on reading.

The start of a supervision session using this model can be like any other supervision session. However, after the supervisee has given a fair description of the therapy situation she wants to look at and the supervisor has got a fair understanding of it, the supervisee may be asked to move to "the therapy room." Usually we ask her to sit in the therapist's chair first, before proceeding to the patient's position. Supervisees are encouraged to use words to convey their responses in both positions. They will usually include a report on the emotional sensations and thoughts that emerged in the respective positions followed by a short exchange with the supervisor.

This done, we ask the supervisees to move to the third chair placed at right angles to the therapist and patient positions. Seated in the third position, the supervisees are asked to keep their reactions to the two former positions in mind. This tends to generate new perspectives and ideas and generally seems to strengthen the reflective capacity of the supervisee, enhancing a kind of we-centered objectivity.

Often, reflecting from the third position results in new ideas of ways in which the therapist can interact with the patient. We then ask the supervisee to take her seat in the therapist chair again and explore these new ideas, especially their bodily implications.

The next stage gives the supervisee and supervisor an opportunity to experiment with different types of therapeutic interaction. When the supervisee has rehearsed a new way of being interacting with the patient, she can move to the patient position to get a feeling of what it might feel like to be at the receiving end. When the supervisor demonstrates ideas of his own, he sits in the therapist's chair while the supervisee takes up her position in the patient's chair or on the couch, enabling her to feel in her own body how the intervention of the supervisor might be perceived by the patient.

It is not always necessary to use all the chairs, but it is always valuable to have the three positions in mind during supervision and be ready to ask the supervisee to physically assume the different positions. It helps to distinguish between the bodily staging in the here and now and the discussion of the there and then of the analytic process. Body position enhances feelings and changes the basis for reflection.

In my experience, this approach is more likely to trigger personal issues in the supervisee than traditional verbal supervision. If the supervisor does not pay adequate attention to personal emotions activated in the supervisee, supervision will easily become stressful and unproductive. This testifies to the finding that doing usually triggers a stronger emotional response than talking. When the supervisor, however, pays attention to the supervisee's personal emotions, it gives them an opportunity to explore countertransference issues in detail.

The supervisees also have the opportunity to work on their personal issues in the training analysis, alongside the supervision. I think it is valuable for training analysts to be familiar with the kind of training and supervision the candidate is undertaking. All members of the teaching staff at the Character Analytic Institute, including supervisors and training analysts, are invited to a yearly "teachers' seminar." Some, I should add, are accustomed to more traditional forms of supervision.

An important aspect of this supervision model is its alternating focus on the state of the therapist, the state of the patient, and their mutual interaction. When the supervisee occupies the therapist's position, she will empathize with the needs and feelings of the therapist and learn to bring the countertransference into focus and consciousness. In the patient's position, the needs and feelings of the patient and the transference will be highlighted. The third position provides the breathing space needed to work on and strengthen the we-centric and mentalizing capacity of the supervisee, as the focus in this position is on thinking about the relationship while the experiences evoked in the other positions are still fresh.

Supervisory needs obviously vary, and depend not least on the therapeutic process itself, the personality of the supervisee, the patient – and the supervisor. But often, supervisees will display a lack of sensitivity to their own needs and feelings. They may have identified too strongly with certain features of the patient. Or they may have lost their empathic capacity and need to realign. And almost always it will be beneficial to reflect over the therapeutic interaction. So an important aspect of this approach to supervision is that it allows the supervisees to 1. explore their own feelings (countertransference); 2. identify and empathize with the patient; and 3. enhance we-centric reflection. The following snapshots illustrate how this approach to supervision might proceed.

Illustrations of supervision

A candidate in the basic training program is being supervised for the first time. He wants to explore problems in his relations with a female patient. The patient is in her late 50s and started therapy after her husband left her. She felt bitter, hurt, and found it difficult to control her anger. The candidate was unsure about how to work with her uncontrolled anger.

He is asked to sit in the therapist's chair and imagine the client sitting in the other chair. He should observe carefully how his body feels and what comes to mind. After a couple of minutes he reports feeling like something is expected of him, he feels pressured and uncertain how to go on. He also feels irritated with the patient, but sympathizes with her as well.

The supervisee is asked to move slowly over to the patient's chair, and explore in his own time how the patient physically comforts herself. A few minutes later he reports feelings of hope and expectation combined with critical evaluation.

Moving to the third position/chair, the supervisee remains somewhat confused because he expected to face an angry patient. After talking with the supervisor, he realizes that what he experienced was basically a complementary relationship in which the patient expresses, though not in words, how much she expects the therapist to help her, expectations which make the therapist feel uncomfortable.

This vignette illustrates one of the merits of the approach: in a short space of time, the supervisee manages to progress from his explicit thoughts about what is going on in the therapy at the moment to deeper, more unconscious, embodied feelings and sensations of both the patient and therapist. This comes about mainly because the supervisee has explored his own experience, not through the interpretations of the supervisor.

A candidate in the advanced program wants to address her sense of unease before her session with a certain patient. Sitting in the therapist's chair, she feels a mounting sense of discomfort, combined, however, with feelings of sympathy for the patient and a wish to help. Moving to the patient's position she experiences a need to defend herself, to ward off approaching danger. She also experiences strong inner turmoil. In the third chair/position, she is surprised by her experience in the patient's position. Her uneasiness at meeting this patient might be connected to the patient's tumultuous inner world.

Taking the patient position once more she comes into contact with a feeling of shame; her patient might have invested more than she realized in trying to avoid strong feelings of inner turmoil and shame. She understood better her own countertransference and started to think of new ways to address the powerful conflicts and inner turmoil of the patient.

A senior analyst had felt at an impasse with a patient for some time. The patient was apparently afraid of moving forward in his therapy and his life. He had a pronounced resistance to change, so to speak. In the patient position, the therapist, to her surprise, got into contact with a sense of openness and longing to explore new terrain. In the therapist position she recognizes, also to her surprise, her old achievement anxiety. Reflecting over these experiences in the third position, she realizes that her patient's new willingness to change had unconsciously activated her own achievement anxiety, and that the therapeutic impasse probably had more to do with her own countertransference than the patient's.

These two vignettes serve to illustrate how the approach helps the therapist differentiate between her own dominant emotional state and the state of the patient, and to distinguish complementary from concordant countertransference. In the analytic situation, these feelings are necessarily intermingled because we have to deal simultaneously with our experience of the patient (empathy) and our reactions to this experience.

Discussion and summing up on supervision

Generally, I find this approach to supervision to enhance access to unconscious experience. This allows the thinking, reflection, and discussion that follow in the last part of the supervisory session to emerge from a broader and deeper experience, unlike discussions based mainly on what is consciously available at the start of a supervision session.

In summing up, I want to highlight the following advantages of the approach to the supervisee:

- Quicker access to the emotional core of the supervisee's most pressing issue.
- A clearer idea of the most pertinent differences between the supervisee's experience and the patient's.
- Enables candidates to separate egocentric from alter-centric feelings; in other words to differentiate between personal countertransference stemming mainly from one's own past and induced countertransference stemming mainly from identifications with the patient.
- An opportunity for the supervisee to look at how he works with the patient from a we-centric position, and an opportunity to reflect from this third position on the character of their interaction.
- An opportunity to explore in his own time and without interference (from the supervisor) ideas and actions taking form within himself, in contrast to someone else providing the ideas (the supervisor).

The model also underpins and promotes the supervisor's ability to suggest therapeutic options to the supervisee, verbally and by practical demonstration. This way of doing supervision is also gratifying for the supervisor because his alter-centric participation by implicit imitation (and mirror neuron activity) in the supervisee's staging of the way patient and therapist interact widens his experiential horizon.

I will conclude by underlining what seems to be the main difference between this approach and traditional forms of supervision from the standpoint of the supervisor. Traditional supervision has the supervisee present his or her case orally or in writing and the supervisor offering a verbal response, followed by a discussion. Supervision using a one-way screen (popular among family therapists) or video is different, but the role of the supervisor, as a fount of new ideas, is still more or less the same.

The role of the supervisor as described here is markedly different. Instead of focusing on his own understanding of the case, the supervisor looks for ways to help the supervisee *deepen and expand his or her experience and understanding.* In my experience, it is important, especially early in the supervision session, not to discuss the contents of the problem raised by the supervisee too extensively, limiting the discussion to clarifying what the supervisee wants to focus on. Sharing thoughts, however relevant and reasonable, can obstruct rather than facilitate the supervisees' exploration of their experience by drawing attention to what is already available in the conscious mind of both supervisor and supervisee. I advise supervisors not to think too much about the case, but focus on the supervisee's bodily and mental processes, encouraging progress by inviting the supervisee to give herself time to explore her sensations and response to assuming the part of the therapist, the patient, and the reflective position, respectively. However, in the last part of the supervision session, which again looks like a traditional supervision situation, the supervisor (and supervisee) should feel free to share whatever ideas feel relevant.

Throughout the presentation and discussion of this supervision model, I have been referring to central aspects of the conceptual framework (theory) presented in previous chapters. This has been done deliberately. I think it is important to see this way of doing supervision through the lens of theory. It is not simply "chair work." Without adequate theoretical reflection it can, however, easily be seen as such, because the use of chairs and different physical positions has in itself dramatic effects independently of or prior to any theoretical understanding. However, without the theory of embodied subjectivity, intersubjectivy, and reflexivity, one risks losing the opportunity to see the experiences emerging from this way of working in a broader clinical context.

Some concluding thoughts on embodied training and supervision

In the previous chapter, I briefly discussed body/mind practices (body-work), finding them to represent experiences that can be of value for analysts/therapists (as well as for patients). When I refer to body/mind practices, I include methods developed during the last century in Europe and America (Johnson, 1995; Anderson, 2008), alongside traditional practices like yoga and meditation stemming from other parts of the world. In different ways, they foster our ability to focus attention on the body and to use the body more flexibly in self and interactive regulation. As there is a great diversity of such methods, I think candidates in analytic training should make their choice based on individual needs and preferences. What I do favor, however, are practices and methods that focus on exploring embodied experience without a set goal deduced from specific theoretical assumptions.

I consider body-work and art-based therapies as separate modalities from – embodied – psychoanalysis and psychotherapy. These modalities require their own extensive training, sometimes of comparable length to psychoanalytic training (Sletvold, 2012b). So I am not suggesting that these therapies and practices should become an integral part of psychotherapy and psychoanalytic training programs. It is, nonetheless, my impression that many candidates in training – and fully trained analysts – are already practicing various forms of body/mind exercises. These practices are often perceived, however, as something of a private interest or hobby, not a natural element of analytic culture. I want to encourage a change of attitudes here so that body/mind practices and exercises of different kinds along with artistic practices should be considered a natural and valuable aspect of psychoanalytic and psychotherapeutic culture, as indeed they are perceived to be by students and practitioners in the performing arts. It should, however, also be noted that body-work methods belong largely to what Rickman and Balint call One-Body Psychology. Methods derived from the creative and performing arts (Krantz, 2012; Pesso & Boyden-Pesso, 2012) have, on the other hand, always been devoted to embodied communication and interaction.

The embodied training and supervising practices described here, along with those termed *awareness-oriented role plays* by Safran and Muran (2000), were conceived within the scope and frame of relational psychotherapy and "the psychoanalytical situation which is essentially a Two-Body Situation" (Balint, 1952/1985, p. 235). The kind of embodied training and supervising practices described in this and the previous chapter (and those described by Safran and Muran) would benefit in my opinion analytical training programs in general. This applies specifically to the described procedures for case seminars/conferences and supervision. The fruitfulness of these practices depends, I believe, on placing the participants in situations and roles that are relatively realistic insofar as they reproduce essential elements of "the psychoanalytical situation which is essentially a Two-Body Situation." The limited success of neo-Reichian and similar body-work therapies can be explained, I believe, by a failure until recently to consider embodied emotional movements in a truly relational context (Nebbiosi & Federici-Nebbiosi, 2008; Shapiro, 1996). This became possible only with the emergence of relational psychoanalysis and the discoveries of the bodily basis of intersubjectivity over the last decades.

These specific procedures have so far only been adapted for use in analytic training at the Character Analytic Institute in Oslo and Bergen. The results are promising, and I think it would be worthwhile to explore the possibility of adapting them, or similar training procedures, to other training programs and other institutes. So far there has been no systematic evaluation of the long-term impact on analytic practice. Evaluations by some of the candidates who have completed the program are, however, uplifting. They especially underline the experiential quality and focus on details in the approach compared to more conventional training. Two recently published anthologies (Børstad & Sletvold, 2012; Sletvold & Børstad, 2009) contain papers written by several of those who have completed the training. These contributions describe and discuss not least how to overcome therapeutic impasses by focusing in various ways on nonverbal body-emotional interaction.

The way of working on cases and supervision described here should not, however, be taken to imply a recommendation on my part to apply embodied interaction exclusively at case conferences and in supervision. On the contrary, attention to embodied experience should be combined with verbally based evaluations that are adequate for the case, including a thoroughly worked-through life history and/or autobiography. Together with embodied impressions, this verbal narrative should form the basis of a joint (analyst and patient) formulation of working hypotheses. It goes without saying that I also recommend the kind of theory I have presented and discussed in this text as part of a didactic curriculum to accompany the kind of experiential training described.

Generally speaking, when focusing especially on the embodied and affective dimensions of the interaction, it is important, I think, to package this process with verbal reflection/comprehension. Compared with a more traditional approach focusing on interpretation and insight, the approach I am describing can be likened to a reversal of figure and ground, or picture and frame. Behavioral and affective events – enactments – especially at the start and end of the session – have long been recognized for their analytical value, but still remain in the background or frame of the real work, the interpretation of free associations. In the approach I present in this text interpretation, i.e., verbal comprehension, is seen as a means of securing a frame that is as robust as possible for the process, while the process itself is seen as being formed chiefly by moment-to-moment body–emotional interaction.

The embodied procedures described and discussed can, I believe, help analysts and therapists develop their own sensitivity to the various ways in which emotional body states are regulated in the therapeutic encounter, how affect is mutually communicated, and how emotional interaction patterns emerge and change. They help analysts and therapists to be more sensitive to the possibilities of disruption and repair in the ongoing regulation of emotional states in the analytic interaction. The practices could also strengthen the verbal reflective capacity of the analyst.

Concluding remarks and future directions

Chapter 12

The embodied analyst in the twenty-first-century consulting room

I conclude this text by highlighting some implications of the views presented and discussed, and tentatively suggest future directions for analysis and therapy attending to embodied experience. I shall first look at and discuss implications for the analytic room when embodied interaction is seen as central to therapeutic action. I round off by sharing some thoughts on how the activity of the therapist best can be understood and described as a consequence of changing the focus from verbal to emotional communication in psychoanalysis and psychotherapy. I describe this change as a movement from intervention to response.

Therapeutic action and the consulting room

In "The Embodied Analyst in the Victorian Consulting Room," Sue A. Shapiro (1996) explores and discusses "the Victorian consulting room" in the context of a cultural process throughout the nineteenth century to discipline the body, especially in the public sphere. For example, audiences in theatres and concerts were gradually taught not to move or make sounds.

> Not surprisingly, Freud's nineteenth-century patient's body was in knots. It was under so much pressure to be "civilized." It was so corseted. The analyst had no body, except a face which was to be kept without obvious expression. To this end, Freud employed the couch. The patient's body was talked about and interpreted, rarely was the patient expected or encouraged to more fully experience somatic sensations. (Shapiro, 1996, p. 307)

Freud ended up recommending an analytic setting which privileged talking and listening, not moving and looking.[1] Commenting on this state of affairs, Shapiro explores the implications of an analytic room in which looking and moving are basically rejected.

> While much needs to be explored regarding the impact of . . . cultural shifts on psychoanalytic theory I [Shapiro] want to focus here on the impact of the civilizing process and the Cartesian worldview on the form and procedure of

psychoanalysis. As I emphasized at the start of this paper, psychoanalysis is the talking cure. Patients talk, we interpret. We sit quietly in our chairs, seeking to remove our body from our patient's objective experience. The patient may fantasize about our bodily state, but as much as possible our bodily state remains opaque. (1996, p. 308)

However, as we know, two standard settings for conducting psychoanalysis and psychotherapy emerged. First, the analytical setting in which the patient lies on a couch and the analyst sits behind, and weekly sessions numbering three, four, or more. Second, the psychotherapy setting in which therapist and patient sit face to face, with sessions generally at one per week. How and why these complementary psychotherapeutic positions and procedures developed as they did in the twentieth century falls outside the scope of this inquiry.

Whatever positions analyst and therapist decide to adopt in consultation with their patients, the varying impact of the different bodily positions on communication and therapeutic action has not been in the foreground. This seems to be especially true of the "psychotherapy situation" in which therapist and patient sit more or less face to face. As far as I know, very little consideration has been given to the effect of conducting therapy with this arrangement. The classical psychoanalytic setting has, however, been compressively discussed. Much has been thought and written about this setting's propensity to promote regression, foster the development of the transference neurosis, and so on. This discussion has tended, however, to be of an either/or type, restricted to when and with whom the analytic setting is preferable, and when and with whom the face to face arrangement is preferable. Positions have been decided on basis of whether the therapist/analyst was planning psychoanalysis or psychotherapy.

What I want to discuss here is what the chosen position in the consulting room has to say for the subjectivity of each participant and the intersubjective unfolding of affect and thought, conscious as well as unconscious. Throughout this text I have argued that whatever choices the analyst/therapist and patient make with regard to physical positioning and ways of relating/moving in the consulting room, they will generally have a strong impact on how interaction and communication unfold and, consequently, on therapeutic action. So what I want to suggest is that the analyst/therapist explore together with the patient this impact. Instead of letting either the therapist or patient determine the physical arrangement before the therapy starts, it should be a joint decision, taken after mutual exploration. One implication of this procedure is, of course, that it can be changed during a session or analysis. My impression is that what I am suggesting here is not a particularly unusual practice among analysts and therapists. What I want to encourage is an appreciation of these evaluations and explorations as a central element of the unfolding of the analytical process, not just as negotiations and decisions concerning the frame of analysis/therapy. I agree with Jacobs's (2005) suggestion to bring into detailed focus not only auditory but also visual information.

It is a paradox that although the study of transference has been elevated to a fine art, rarely in courses on technique are students taught to observe those small, barely perceptible, and often fleeting interactions between patient and analyst that can be of the greatest significance. (p. 172)

As is well known, Freud experimented with very different positions and ways of relating to patients, including touch and massage, before settling on what became the standard setting, with the patient lying down, the analyst seated behind (Aron & Starr, 2013). Here I want to consider adjustments to this arrangement following Reich's development of the character analytic technique. To my knowledge, Reich himself always worked with patients lying down. He continued this practice not only after developing character analysis, but also later when he practiced vegeto-therapy and orgontherapy. His own position relative to his patients did change, though. In his house in Oslo, he used a rather small room for patient consultations. The size and layout of the room would not allow a chair to be placed behind a couch. And as Reich's descriptions of the physical appearance of patients makes clear, he must have positioned himself in a way that allowed him to observe the whole body of the patient. In this passage, previously quoted in Chapter 2, Reich explicitly says that the patient should be able to see the analyst.

Many psychoanalytic rules had an inherently and strongly taboo character. . . . Such, for instance, was the rule that the analyst should not be seen – should remain, so to speak, a blank sheet of paper upon which the patient inscribed his transference. . . . Under such circumstances, how could the patient dare to express his human criticism? All the same, the patient had a way of knowing about the analysts. But with this kind of technique, they seldom expressed what they knew. (1942/1978, p. 154)

Nic Waal reported the following from her treatment with Reich: "All through this therapeutic attitude to me, he had a loving voice, he sat beside me and made me look at him" (1958, p. 43). Jacobs's (2005) review of his experience of supervision with Annie Reich also speaks to this question.

In my own training I was fortunate to have Dr. Annie Reich as one of my supervisors. Influenced by her former husband, Wilhelm Reich, Annie Reich made a point of positioning her chair so that she could see the patient as he lay on the coach. I was quite amazed, in fact, to see that Dr. Reich's chair was placed at a right angle, rather than behind, the couch. "If you sit behind the patient, you can see nothing," Reich said to me, "and you miss vital mate-rial." In my own work, I prefer to place my chair at a 45-degreee angle from the couch, just out of sight of the patient, but positioned so that I can view the patient's body, and enough of her face so that I can pretty well judge her facial expression.

Braatøy (1954a) makes a similar suggestion. Arguing for the essential importance of being able to see the patient, he comments that analysts who sit behind the patient react "as if I intended a revolution or complete turnabout of their positions; but the analyst can easily sit behind the patient and at the same time observe his face. He has only to place his chair in such a way that its axis forms an angle of about 120° with the couch" (p. 111). So while Reich also stressed the importance of the patient being able to see the analyst, Braatøy and Jacobs focused only on the analyst's ability to see the patient.

In Chapter 4, I reviewed the work of Schjelderup and Philipson with a focus on their contributions to embodied and relational character analysis. The consequences they drew from their work in terms of the analytic setting were somewhat different. As far as I know, Schjelderup always had his patients lying on the couch, but judging from the way he describes his patients, he must have been seated so that he was able to see them. Bjørn Killingmo, who was in analysis with Schjelderup between 1954 and 1959, confirms this (personal communication, March 6, 2013). Schjelderup sat to one side of him, the chair positioned close to the couch. Killingmo remembers sometimes touching Schjelderup physically, though Schjelderup never touched him. However, Schjelderup did bend over his chest and comment on his breathing.

Schjelderup also changed the standard analytic frame by reducing the frequency of weekly hours for training analysis. Analysis, in some cases, could succeed on only two sessions a week, he maintained. This was probably another reason, in addition to the Reichian (character analytic) bias, why IPA refused the application for membership from the Norwegian Psychoanalytic Association in the decades following World War II (Alnaes, 1993).

Schjelderup's position on session frequency was probably influenced by his growing emphasis on the analysis of demeanor and reduced reliance on interpretation of symbolic representations. One of the arguments in favor of the highest possible number of hours per week is that it reduces the risk of disruptions affecting the flow of associations revealing unconscious material. With greater attention to bodily expressions, with potentially unconscious meaning, this situation changes somewhat as they will often be in the form of more stable or repeated embodied expressions. In my experience, working with a focus on embodied rather than symbolic expression will sometimes make the patient feel a need for more than one day to digest whatever's come up before the next analytic session. Steven Stern (2009) recently questioned session frequency in full breadth, arguing that a fixed frequency of weekly hours should no longer be included in the definition of psychoanalysis. His argument is based on current realities of the marketplace, but also on contemporary theory, which emphasizes the co-created, nonlinear nature of the analytic relationship.

Sometime during the 1940s, while he was developing embodied character analysis independently of Reich, Philipson must have reached the conclusion that sitting face to face with the patient is generally the preferable analytic position. By the time Strand (1991) started his training analysis with Philipson in the mid-1950s, sitting face to face was Philipson's standard setting. Marit Nordby (personal communication, August 25, 2013) started analysis with Philipson in the early 1950s after a period of analysis with Raknes. Having been accustomed to lying down for Raknes, she was surprised when Philipson asked her to sit, but she also felt content as this position made her feel more equal. It was in the face to face position that Philipson started miming his patients. Marit Nordby recalls how at one point in her analysis she suddenly recognized her own mother in the way Philipson was sitting, and became aware that she unconsciously, and much against her own wish, had been adopting her mother's way of sitting on the edge of the chair.

Braatøy (1954a) found it ironic that Freud, "the arch-rationalist in the field of irrational behavior" (p. 117), took from hypnosis, which he regarded as an irrational psychotherapy, the supine position of the patient on the coach. And that he did this without questioning why this part of the set-up might be important, saying simply that this is what is left over from hypnotic treatment. The passage Braatøy is referring to reads as follows: "This arrangement has a historical basis; it is the remnant of the hypnotic method out of which psycho-analysis was evolved" (1913/1958c, p. 133). But then Freud adds a personal motive: "I cannot put up with being stared at by people for eight hours a day (or more). . . . I know that many analysts work in a different way, but I do not know whether this deviation is due more to a craving for doing things differently or to some advantage which they find they gain by it" (p. 134). In a footnote, Braatøy adds: "Believe me. Freud was neither intolerant nor dogmatic. He was free from any rigidity. I made a control analysis with him. . . . The analysis of the patient which I carried out under Freud, took place at the house of the patient, she facing me and knitting" (p. 117).

Against this background, Braatøy finds it understandable that Franz Alexander and his group in Chicago could publish a book on psychoanalytic therapy in 1946 where they suddenly, and again without rational explanation, left the couch out of the therapeutic setting altogether. It is nevertheless a curious fact, he says, referring to the Chicago group's strong interest in somatic particulars, because the couch is continually and directly influencing the muscles, literally *the soma* of the patient. From his body-based perspective, Braatøy sees both risks and advantages with the supine position.

> The couch acts by taking away that part of the postural rigidity or tension in the patient's muscles which in standing or sitting position is necessary in overcoming the force of gravity. It makes him literally more pliant and more responsive to the analyst's suggestions. For this reason the couch has its risks. These risks are, as one sees, directly related to the couch being a common factor in hypnotic and psychoanalytic treatment. If, however, the therapist does not exploit this possibility, but sticks to the unbiased, questioning attitude, continues to be interested in the patient's individuality and spontaneity, the relaxation on the coach gives him a specific opportunity to observe the blocking of spontaneous movement determined by *experiences outside* the analytic situation. (p. 119)

Grønseth (1998), a student of Raknes, and reviewed briefly in Chapter 4, practiced character analytic vegetotherapy as it was handed down from Reich to

Raknes, before he developed his own *existential* version in which he no longer massaged the patient or instructed respiratory movements. One of the things he came to emphasize in particular in his new approach was the value, as he saw it, of letting the patient choose his or her own position in the therapy room; sitting or lying, and where to sit. He also took pains with the details of the bodily positioning, and put great emphasis on arranging his consultation room in a way that would not indicate a preference on his part for a particular position for the patient. In a way, Grønseth came to see the positioning of the patient in the consultation room as a kind of "Rorschach test," revealing basic character dynamics. That said, he did not address his own placement (the therapist) with the same assiduity. In his way, then, he maintained a one-body perspective rather than a contemporary, intersubjective, two-body perspective.

Jacobs (1991, 2005), analyzing embodied communication in the analytic setting, asserts that visualization is analogue to phenomena in the auditory sphere known variously as evenly suspended or freely hovering attention. Just as the analyst listens with equal attention to all of the patient's verbalizations, he should also observe all of the patient's nonverbal behavior.

> Looking as he listens, he takes in and registers what he sees, but does not focus on any particular bodily movement or facial expression. The visual imagery that he registers makes contact via associative pathways with visual aspects of memory and stimulates the recall of memories that are linked with the patient's nonverbal communications. Often it stimulates in the analyst kinetic behavior and automatic responses that are reactions on an unconscious level to nonverbal messages. Thus the analyst's visual perceptions join with his auditory perceptions to stimulate in him responses that draw on unconscious visual and auditory memory. (1991, p. 40)

In response to Annie Reich's "If you sit behind the patient . . . you miss vital material," Jacobs's own solution is to sit "out of sight of the patient, but positioned so that I can view the patient's body" (2005, p. 172). This arrangement helps the analyst observe the patient's body; the patients, for their part, might still "miss vital material." The following vignette illustrates this point.

Some years after his training analysis, a psychoanalyst felt a need for further therapy, and, following Freud's (1937/1961c) recommendation, embarked upon another analysis, this time with me. His former training analyst, whom he still valued highly, had in the meantime passed away. In the training analysis, he had lain on the couch, with the analyst seated behind him. In this therapy, he wanted to work sitting face to face. As it turned out, the new analysis essentially continued the exploration of the principal themes of the former training analysis. Many of the comments and interpretations of the training analyst came to mind as keen observations of the process now unfolding. In one such moment, however, what was remembered was not what his former analyst had said, but how he had moved his feet. This brought into focus the fact that during the training analysis the analyst's feet were the only part of his body that he was able to observe. And he realized that his observation of those foot movements provided information on the analyst's emotional engagement.

I should add that in my consultation room I have a chair placed at the end of the couch, explaining to patients that they can use either the couch or the chair or both. My own chair is placed at a right angle to the middle of the couch. It's a position that lets me sit face to face with the patient if he or she prefers to sit in the chair. Emde (2009), in his commentary on implications of research on embodied communication, particularly mirror neuron research (Gallese, 2009), raises the following questions.

> Should face-to-face be the predominant strategic positioning for psychoanalytic work? Does the use of the couch with a distancing of immediate interactions between patient and analyst, and with removal of visual contact, detract or enhance the development of transference experience, and transference-countertransference interactions? Does the use of the couch interfere with the empathic resonance of both partners in the therapeutic enterprise? Does it limit the impacts of interpretive activity? (p. 560)

As Emde contends, much attention has been given in traditional practice to the importance of analyzing the patient's experiences of coming and going in analytic hours; indeed, more and more work seems to be done with the patient and analyst seated, allowing a face to face encounter. And there are schools of psychoanalysis, he continues, that work face to face throughout. In Emde's opinion, questions concerning the use of the couch require systematic empirical study, not least in light of advances in the neurobiology of intersubjectivity. "In terms of therapeutic action, the framing of such questions will turn on how much of adaptive change can be mobilized by pre-reflective, automatic empathic processes (that are evoked and modeled) and how much adaptive change requires reflective conscious processing" (Emde, 2009, p. 560).

In general, I agree with Emde's reasoning. However, knowledge derived from "the neurobiology of intersubjectivity" does not necessarily privilege face to face analysis. The face is the part of the human body that communicates most intensely. Face to face interaction may maximize mirror neuron firing, and might have been one reason why Freud felt he could not stand looking at patients and being looked at by them the whole day long. The following vignette illustrates *a patient* who couldn't abide sitting face to face with the therapist.

This patient felt a desperate need for therapy because her anxiety was so debilitating, it was impossible for her to live a normal social life. She had started therapy several times, but stopped every time after a few sessions. The only kind of therapy she had been able to take part in was in body-work groups. This was because, she explained, she was unable to talk how the therapist expected her to. This time she was hoping the therapist would do the talking. After a few sessions during which we explored our interaction, she was obviously becoming increasingly anxious. What scared her was being looked at for long periods at a time. A preliminary inquiry into this feeling stimulated a memory of the – traumatizing – ways in which her parents had related to her when she was a child. When this became clear, we started exploring different physical positions in relation to each other. The position we finally decided on was close to the classical analytical one, with the patient recumbent and the therapist sitting partly behind making it easy to control observation for both parties. With this arrangement, she found talking to the therapist not that difficult at all. On the contrary, she had much to talk about; things about which there were so little opportunity to talk, she said, in everyday life.

This was a rather special, but not unique, case of a person in desperate need of therapy, and who was about to give up because she couldn't stand the face to face situation. I could review other cases in which highly traumatized persons – especially sexually and physically traumatized – found the very thought of lying down sufficiently provoking and frightening to refuse point blank. In cases where position does not elicit such dramatic reactions, those that are triggered might well be suppressed or judged unreasonable if they reach consciousness at all. It is my experience that reactions elicited by the physical positioning of analyst/therapist and patient should be routinely explored as they often speak to important issues for the patient and affect the working alliance. Decisions concerning choice and change of analytic setting should be made, I suggest, on the basis of such inquiry.

Therapeutic activity: From intervention to response

In my judgment, a change of focus from verbal to emotional communication in psychoanalysis and psychotherapy might change the way in which the activity of the therapist can best be understood and described. Traditionally, this activity has been described in terms of interventions, interpretation being the prototype. If we consider the activity of the therapist in the case of Astrid, described in Chapter 7, during the first four years it could largely be described as interpretation. When the focus shifted to nonverbal emotional attunement in the last part of the process, in my mind it can hardly be described as intervention at all, understood as something consciously formulated. Rather than *intervention,* I see it as an ongoing *response,* verbal and nonverbal, to the patient's mostly nonverbal emotional communication. An intervention or an interpretation is ordinarily seen as an action with a beginning and an end, and based to a degree on conscious thought. The therapist's activity, particularly in the last part of Astrid's therapy, consisted of *reacting and responding* to her verbal and nonverbal emotional communication. These responses required emotional attunement, but were not necessarily preceded by any conscious deliberation. And anyway, thinking can take quite a long time and in many situations will get in the way of an immediate reaction. The activity of the therapist or analyst can in this light be seen as participation in an emotional *jam session* or dance, one that requires abstract, theoretical knowledge as well as bodily-emotional skills, but where the play or dance itself consists of mostly unconscious and spontaneous tunes and steps.

Several schools of psychoanalysis have been developing an understanding of the analyst's contribution such as I have just described. The participating analyst, Balint (1968) said many years ago, is first and foremost focused on sensing and relating to the other mind that is present at the same moment. "All this means consent, participation, and involvement, but *not* necessarily action, only understanding and tolerance; what really matters is the creation and maintenance of conditions in which events can take place internally, in the patient's mind" (p. 145). Inspired by Balint and with reference to Winnicott (1963), Bromberg (1991) observed that

> [t]he act of trying to know the patient . . . is itself forced to become the primary "material" through the powerful enactment of the patient's message that it is his tormented state of mind that is crying to be heard, rather than its contents needing to be understood. In one way, it is as if the patient is communicating that the analyst must somehow "lose" his mind in order to know the patient's. The analyst's ability to make creative use of this disorganized state of relatedness, while keeping his own center of subjectivity without inflicting it on the patient, is the heart of this part of the work. (p. 411)

Finally, the Boston Change Process Study Group (2010) – consisting of analysts and developmental researchers with the late D. N. Stern as the most prominent member – has contributed strongly to this new understanding of the process of change in psychotherapy and psychoanalysis. Over the last 15 years, this group has accumulated evidence that the way the therapist meets the patient (moments of meeting) is at least as important, if not more so, for the change process, than interpretation and intervention. The tenor of the work of the BCPSG was clearly articulated in its first publication: *Non-interpretative Mechanisms in Psychoanalytic Therapy: The "Something More" than Interpretation* (1998). Twelve years and seven publications later, the researchers

> offer a shift in conceptual framework from the notion that therapeutic change depends on the quality of the interventions of the analyst. Working from a dyadic perspective, we would frame conceptions of quality within a relational model that stresses features of the process between two persons. From this vantage point, we located psychotherapeutic quality in an engaged search for directionality and fittedness, in the creative negotiation of sloppiness and indeterminacy, and in efforts to increase the breath of affectively charged experiences that can be brought into the therapeutic relationship. (2010, pp. 210–211)

In my understanding, this was precisely what happened in the case of Astrid: an increase in the breath of affectively charged experiences that could be brought into the therapeutic relationship.

With the BCPSG, I would urge therapists to see their work more in terms of providing verbal and nonverbal emotional responses to the patient's bodily-emotional communications, and to a lesser degree as premeditated intervention. This applies not only to the verbal interventions of traditional talking therapies, but to body-related interventions in body-oriented therapies as well. It isn't a question of either/or, more of a shift in where we anchor our understanding of the therapeutic process. This locus should be flexible and responsive to the kind of problems the patient faces. The case of Astrid illustrated a patient with highly developed reflexive capacity. In patients with borderline problems or an underdeveloped psychological language, as in alexithymia and psychosomatic disorders, the therapeutic challenge will be very different (Bateman & Fonagy, 2004; Lien, 2012; Hyllseth Lien, 2012). In such cases, consciously worked out verbal interpretations and explanations might be of decisive importance. Generally in teaching I have tended to stress in recent years the particular importance of interpretations and formulations at the start of therapy to provide a tentative, shared platform and framing of the therapeutic focus and direction.

Summing up, and still in agreement with BCPSG (2010), I would like to stress that dyadic processes involving mutual emotional recognition seem to have a potential for movement and development marked by increased feeling in the therapeutic relationship of trust and mutual vitalization. These processes seem to strengthen the patient's ability to make his or her emotional experiences relational; to be guided by his or her own feeling in a balanced way in significant exchanges with others.

As stated above, this way of thinking about analytic and therapeutic processes is not new. It might even be fair to say that the mainstream of psychoanalysis and psychotherapy – as it has become increasingly relational – has been sailing in this direction for at least a decade. What I have specifically wanted to set down in this concluding chapter is that this new way of understanding therapeutic action places the consulting room and the two – or more – bodies interacting in it at center stage. No longer seen as an unchanging frame around something going on just between two minds, the consulting room becomes a stage for "the therapeutic dance" (Sletvold & Børstad, 2009). It is my hope that – to paraphrase Shapiro (1996) – the *embodied analyst in the twenty-first century consulting room* will find some inspiration in this text.

Note

1   While I was finishing this manuscript, I read for the first time Theodor Reik's *Listening With the Third Ear* (1948/1991). It is fascinating to see how Reik, one of Freud's first and most loyal students, avoids questioning Freud for recommending that the analyst sit behind the patient, while on the other side he shows a keen interest in observing patients' movements and bodily expressions, a procedure he describes as "listening with the third ear."

References

Akhtar, N., & Tomasello, M. (1998). Intersubjectivity in early language learning and use. In S. Bråten (Ed.), *Intersubjective communication and emotion in early ontogeny* (pp. 316–335). Cambridge: Cambridge University Press.

Alexander, F., & French, T. M. (1946). *Psychoanalytic therapy.* New York: Ronald Press.

Alnæs, A. (1993). Psykoanalysens historie i Norge [The history of psychoanalysis in Norway]. In P. Anthi & S. Varvin (Eds.), *Psykoanalysen i Norge* (s. 13–40). Oslo: Universitetsforlaget.

Ammaniti, M. (2009). Reply to commentaries. *Psychoanalytic Dialogues, 19*, 585–587.

Andersen, C. F. (2007). Vegetativ identifisering: Et interpersonlig nevrobiologisk fenomen. *Tidsskrift for Norsk psykologforening, 44*, 132–138. [Vegetative identification: An interpersonal neurobiological phenomena. *Journal of the Norwegian Psychological Association*].

Anderson, F. S. (Ed.). (2008). *Bodies in treatment: The unspoken dimension.* New York: The Analytic Press.

Anthi, P. (1983). Reconstruction of preverbal experiences. *Journal of the American Psychoanalytic Association, 31*, 33–58.

Anthi, P. (1986). Non-verbal behaviour and body organ fantasies. Their relation to body image formation and symptomatology. *International Journal of Psycho-Analysis, 67*, 417–428.

Anthi, P. (1995). Resistance analysis and psychic reality. *Psychoanalytic Study of the Child, 50*, 032–047.

Anthi, P. (2007, October 1). Commentary on P. Fonagy and M. Target: The rooting of the mind in the body [Letter to the editor]. *Journal of the American Psychoanalytic Association,* online edition.

Anthi, P., & Haugsgjerd, S. (2013). A note on the history of the Norwegian Psychoanalytic Society in the years 1933 to 1945. *The International Journal of Psychoanalysis, 94*, 4, 715–724.

Aron, L. (1996). *A meeting of minds.* Hillsdale, NJ: The Analytic Press.

Aron, L. (1998). The clinical body and the reflexive mind. In L. Aron & F. S. Anderson (Eds.), *Relational perspectives on the body* (pp. 3–37). Hillsdale, NJ and London: The Analytical Press.

Aron, L. (2006). Analytic impasse and the third: Clinical implications of intersubjectivity theory. *International Journal of Psychoanalysis, 87*, 349–368.

Aron, L., & Starr, K. E. (2013). *A psychotherapy for the people. Toward a progressive psychoanalysis.* London and New York: Routledge Taylor & Francis Group.

Balint, M. (1968). *The basic fault. Therapeutic aspects of regression.* London: Tavistock Publications Ltd.

Balint, M. (1985). Changing therapeutical aims and techniques in psycho-analysis. In M. Balint, *Primary love and psycho-analytic technique* (pp. 221–235). London: Marsfield Library. (Original work published 1952.)

Basch, M.F. (1983). Empathic understanding: A review of the concept and some theoretical considerations. *Journal of the American Psychoanalytic Association, 31,* 101–126.

Bateman, A.B., & Fonagy, P. (2004). *Psychotherapy for borderline personality disorder. Mentalization-based treatment.* Oxford: Oxford University Press.

Bateson, M.C. (1975). Mother-infant exchanges: The epigenesis of conversational interaction. In D. Aaronson & R.W. Rieber (Eds.), *Developmental psycholinguistics and communication disorders; Annals of the New York Academy of Sciences* (Vol. CCLXIII, pp. 101–113). New York: New York Academy of Sciences.

Beebe, B., Knoblauch, S., Rustin, J., & Sorter, D. (2005). *Forms of intersubjectivity in infant research and adult treatment.* New York: Other Press.

Beebe, B., & Lachmann, F. (2002). *Infant research and adult treatment.* Hillsdale, NJ: The Analytic Press.

Benjamin, J. (1990). An outline of intersubjectivity: The development of recognition. *Psychoanalytic Psychology, 7,* 33–46.

Benjamin, J. (1998). *Shadow of the other. Intersubjectivity and gender in psychoanalysis.* New York and London: Routledge.

Binder, J.L., & Henry, W.P. (2010). Developing skills in managing negative process. In J.C. Muran & J.P. Barber (Eds.), *The therapeutic alliance: An evidence-based guide to practice* (pp. 285–303). New York and London: The Guilford Press.

Binder, P.E. (2009). Following old paths to new places – thirdness, mentalization, and the search for a transformational meeting. *International Forum of Psychoanalysis, 18,* 168–176.

Blackmore, S. (1999). *The meme machine.* Oxford: Oxford University Press.

Boadella, D. (1987). *Lifestreams. An introduction to biosynthesis.* London and New York: Routledge & Kegan Paul.

Bollas, C. (1987). *The shadow of the object: Psychoanalysis of the unthought known.* New York: Colombia University Press.

Børstad, M., & Sletvold, J. (Eds.). (2012). *Karakteranalytiske dialoger. Kropp og relasjon i psykoterapi II* [Character analytic dialogues. Body and relation in psychotherapy II.] Oslo: Kolofon Forlag.

Boston Change Process Study Group (1998). Non-interpretative mechanisms in psychoanalytic therapy: The "something more" than interpretation. *International Journal of Psychoanalysis, 79,* 908–921.

Boston Change Process Study Group (2007). The foundational level of psychodynamic meaning: Implicit process in relation to conflict, defense, and the dynamic unconscious. *International Journal of Psychoanalysis, 88,* 1–16.

Boston Change Process Study Group (2008). Forms of relational meaning: Issues in the relations between the implicit and reflective-verbal domains. *Psychoanalytic Dialogues, 18,* 125–148.

Boston Change Process Study Group (2010). *Change in psychotherapy. A unifying paradigm.* New York and London: W.W. Norton & Company.

Boyesen, G. (1976). The primary relationship and its relationship to the streaming. In: *In the wake of Reich.* D. Boadella (Ed.). Norwich: Fletcher and Son.

Braatøy, T. (1954a). *Fundamentals of psychoanalytic technique.* New York: John Wiley & Sons.

Braatøy, T. (1954b). Report on the 18th International Psychoanalytic Congress business meeting. *Bulletin of the International Psycho-Analytical Association, 35,* 278.

Bråten, S. (1998a). Introduction. In S. Bråten (Ed.), *Intersubjective communication and emotion in early ontogeny* (pp. 1–12). Cambridge: Cambridge University Press.

Bråten, S. (1998b). Infant learning by altercentric participation: The reverse of egocentric observation in autism. In S. Bråten (Ed.), *Intersubjective communication and emotion in early ontogeny* (pp. 105–124). Cambridge: Cambridge University Press.

Bråten, S. (2000). *Modellmakt og altersentriske spedbarn. Essays on dialogue in infant & adult.* Bergen: Sigma Forlag.

Breuer, J., & Freud, S. (1955). Studies on hysteria. In J. Strachey (Ed. & Trans.), *The standard edition of the complete psychological works of Sigmund Freud* (Vol. 2, pp. 1–251). London: The Hogarth Press. (Original work published 1893/1895.)

Brodal, P. (2010). *The central nervous system: Structure and function* (4th ed.). Oxford: Oxford University Press.

Bromberg, P. M. (1991). On knowing one's patient inside out: The aesthetics of unconscious communication. *Psychoanalytic Dialogues, 1*(4), 399–422.

Bromberg, P. M. (1998). *Standing in the spaces: Essays on clinical process, trauma and dissociation.* Hillsdale, NJ: The Analytic Press.

Bucci, W. (1997). *Psychoanalysis and cognitive science: A multiple code theory.* New York: Guilford Press.

Bucci, W. (2005). The interplay of subsymbolic and symbolic processes in psychoanalytic treatment. Commentary on paper by Steven H. Knoblauch. *Psychoanalytic Dialogues, 15*(6), 855–873.

Bunkan, B. H. (2003). *The comprehensive body examination (CBE). A psychometric evaluation.* Oslo: Unipub.

Carr, L., Iacoboni, M., Dubeau, M., Mazziotta, J., & Lenzi, G. L. (2003). Neural mechanisms of empathy in humans: A relay from neural systems for imitation to limbic areas. *Proceedings of the National Academy of Sciences of the United States of America, 100–9,* 5497–5502.

Cornell, W. F. (2009). Stranger to desire: Entering the erotic field. *Studies in Gender and Sexuality, 10,* 75–92.

Cozolino, L. (2002). *The neuroscience of psychotherapy: Building and rebuilding the human brain.* New York: W.W. Norton & Company.

Craig, M. (1905). *Psychological medicine.* London: J & A Churchill.

Damasio, A. R. (1994). *Descartes' error.* New York: Avon Books.

Damasio, A. R. (1999). *The feeling of what happens: Body and emotion in the making of consciousness.* New York: Harcourt Brace.

Damasio, A. R. (2000). *The feeling of what happens: Body, emotion and the making of consciousness.* London: William Heinemann.

Damasio, A. R. (2003). *Looking for Spinoza.* London: Vintage.

Damasio, A. R. (2010). *Self comes to mind.* London: William Heinemann.

Dannevig, E. T. (1995a). *Tilleggsopplysninger om seminar i karakteranalyse H95 – V97.* Unpublished manuscript at the Norwegian Character Analytic Institute.

Dannevig, E. T. (1995b). Letter from Einar Dannevig to Jon Sletvold, October 29, 1995.

Dawkins, R. (1978). *The selfish gene.* Oxford: Oxford University Press.

Descartes, R. (1992). *Meditations on first philosophy.* G. Hefffernan (Trans.). Notre Dame, IN: University of Notre Dame Press. (Original work published 1641.)

Dewey, J. (1916). *Democracy and education.* New York: Macmillan.

Dimberg, U., Thunberg, M., & Elmehed, K. (2000). Unconscious facial reactions to emotional facial expressions. *Psychological Science, 11*(1), 86–89.

Downing, G. (1996). *Kroppen och ordet* [The body and the word in psychotherapy]. Stockholm: Natur och Kultur.

Downing, G. (2004). Emotion, body and parent-child interaction. In J. Nadel & D. Muir (Eds.), *Emotional development: Recent research advances* (pp. 429–449). Oxford: Oxford University Press.

Downing, G., Wortmann-Fleisher, S., von Einsiedel, R., Jordan, W., & Reck, C. (2014). The basics of video intervention therapy (VIT) and its use with psychiatrically disturbed patients.

In K. Brandt, B. Perry, S. Seligman, & E. Tronick (Eds.), *Infant & early childhood mental health: Core concepts and clinical practice.* Washington, DC: The American Psychiatric Press, Inc.

Edelman, G. (1992). *Bright air, brilliant fire: On the matter of the mind.* New York: Basic Books.

Ekerholt, K. (Ed.). (2010). *Aspects of psychiatric and psychosomatic physiotherapy.* Oslo: Oslo University College.

Ekman, P. (1985). Autonomic nervous system activity distinguishes among emotions. *Science, 221,* 1208–1210.

Emde, R.N. (2009). From ego to "we-go": Neurobiology and questions for psychoanalysis: Commentary on papers by Trevarthen, Gallese, and Ammaniti & Trentini. *Psychoanalytic Dialogues, 19,* 556–564.

Fadnes, B., Leira, K., & Brodal, P. (2010). *Læringsnøkkelen. Om samspillet mellom bevegelser, balanse og læring* [The key to learning. On the interaction between movements, balance and learning] Oslo: Universitetsforlaget.

Federici-Nebbiosi, S., & Nebbiosi, G. (2012). The experience of another body on our body in psychoanalysis: Commentary on paper by Jon Sletvold. *Psychoanalytic Dialogues, 22,* 430–436.

Ferenczi, S. (1950). Technical difficulties in the analysis of a case of hysteria. In J. Rickman (Ed.) & J.I. Suttie (Trans.), *Further contributions to psychoanalysis.* London: The Hogarth Press. (Original work published 1919.)

Ferenczi, S. (1955). Confusion of tongues between adults and the child. In M. Balint (Ed.), *Final contribution to the problems & methods of psycho-analysis,* pp. 156–167. London: Maresfield Reprints. (Original work published 1933.)

Fonagy, P., Gergely, G., Jurist, E.J., & Target, M.I. (2002). *Affect regulation, mentalization, and the development of the self.* New York: Other Press.

Fonagy, P., Steele, H., & Steele, M. (1991). Maternal representations of attachment during pregnancy predict the organization of infant-mother attachment at one year of age. *Child Development, 62,* 891–905.

Fonagy, P., & Target, M. (2007a). The rooting of the mind in the body: New links between attachment theory and psychoanalytic thought. *Journal of the American Psychoanalytic Association, 55*(2), 411–456.

Fonagy, P., & Target, M. (2007b, October 1). Reply to commentary by P. Anthi on: The rooting of the mind in the body [Letter to the editor]. *Journal of the American Psychoanalytic Association,* online edition.

Fosshage, J.L. (2005). Commentary on paper by Steven H. Knoblauch. *Psychoanalytic Dialogues, 15*(6), 875–881.

Fosshage, J.L. (2011). How do we "know" what we "know?" And change what we "know?" *Psychoanalytic Dialogues, 21,* 55–74.

Freud, S. (1950). Project for a scientific psychology. In J. Strachey (Ed. & Trans.), *The standard edition of the complete psychological works of Sigmund Freud* (Vol. 1, pp. 281–391). London: The Hogarth Press. (Original work published 1895.)

Freud, S. (1953a). Psychical (or mental) treatment. In J. Strachey (Ed. & Trans.), *The standard edition of the complete psychological works of Sigmund Freud* (Vol. 7, pp. 281–302). London: The Hogarth Press. (Original work published 1890.)

Freud, S. (1953b). Fragments of an analysis of a case of hysteria. In J. Strachey (Ed. & Trans.), *The standard edition of the complete psychological works of Sigmund Freud* (Vol. 7, pp. 1–122). London: The Hogarth Press. (Original work published 1905.)

Freud, S. (1955a). Beyond the pleasure principle. In J. Strachey (Ed. & Trans.), *The standard edition of the complete psychological works of Sigmund Freud* (Vol. 18, pp. 1 –64). London: The Hogarth Press. (Original work published 1920.)

Freud, S. (1955b). Group psychology and the analysis of the ego. In J. Strachey (Ed. & Trans.), *The standard edition of the complete psychological works of Sigmund Freud* (Vol. 18, pp. 65–144). London: The Hogarth Press. (Original work published 1921.)

Freud, S. (1957a). Instincts and their vicissitudes. In J. Strachey (Ed. & Trans.), *The standard edition of the complete psychological works of Sigmund Freud* (Vol. 14, pp. 109–140). London: The Hogarth Press. (Original work published 1915.)

Freud, S. (1957b). The unconscious. In J. Strachey (Ed. & Trans.), *The standard edition of the complete psychological works of Sigmund Freud* (Vol. 14, pp. 159–216). London: The Hogarth Press. (Original work published 1915.)

Freud, S. (1958a). The dynamics of transference. In J. Strachey (Ed. & Trans.), *The standard edition of the complete psychological works of Sigmund Freud* (Vol. 12, pp. 97–108). London: The Hogarth Press. (Original work published 1912.)

Freud, S. (1958b). Recommendations to physicians practicing psycho-analysis. In J. Strachey (Ed. & Trans.), *The standard edition of the complete psychological works of Sigmund Freud* (Vol. 12, pp. 109–120). London: The Hogarth Press. (Original work published 1912.)

Freud, S. (1958c). On beginning the treatment (Further recommendations on the technique of psychoanalysis I). In J. Strachey (Ed. & Trans.), *The standard edition of the complete psychological works of Sigmund Freud* (Vol. 12, pp. 121–144). London: The Hogarth Press. (Original work published 1913.)

Freud, S. (1958d). Remembering, repeating and working-through (Further recommendations on the technique of psycho-analysis II). In J. Strachey (Ed. & Trans.), *The standard edition of the complete psychological works of Sigmund Freud* (Vol. 12, pp. 145–156). London: The Hogarth Press. (Original work published 1914.)

Freud, S. (1958e). Observations on transference love (Further recommendations on the technique of psycho-analysis III). In J. Strachey (Ed. & Trans.), *The standard edition of the complete psychological works of Sigmund Freud* (Vol. 12, pp. 157–171). London: The Hogarth Press. (Original work published 1914.)

Freud, S. (1958f). The handling of dream-interpretation in psycho-analysis. In J. Strachey (Ed. & Trans.), *The standard edition of the complete psychological works of Sigmund Freud* (Vol. 12, pp. 85–96). London: The Hogarth Press. (Original work published 1911.)

Freud, S. (1959). Inhibitions, symptoms and anxiety. In J. Strachey (Ed. & Trans.), *The standard edition of the complete psychological works of Sigmund Freud* (Vol. 20, pp. 76–175). London: The Hogarth Press. (Original work published 1926.)

Freud, S. (1961a). The ego and the id. In J. Strachey (Ed. & Trans.), *The standard edition of the complete psychological works of Sigmund Freud* (Vol. 19, pp. 1–66). London: The Hogarth Press. (Original work published 1923.)

Freud, S. (1961b). Civilization and its discontents. In J. Strachey (Ed. & Trans.), *The standard edition of the complete psychological works of Sigmund Freud* (Vol. 21, pp. 59–145). London: The Hogarth Press. (Original work published 1930.)

Freud, S. (1961c). Analysis terminable and interminable. In J. Strachey (Ed. & Trans.), *The standard edition of the complete psychological works of Sigmund Freud* (Vol. 23, pp. 209–253). London: The Hogarth Press. (Original work published 1937.)

Freud, S. (1966). The interpretation of dreams. In J. Strachey (Ed. & Trans.), *The standard edition of the complete psychological works of Sigmund Freud* (Vols. 4 & 5, pp. 1–715). London: The Hogarth Press. (Original work published 1900.)

Freud, S. (1991). Gesammelte werke, 13. London: Imago Publishing Co., Ltd.

Gallese, Vittorio. (2007). "Embodied simulation: From mirror neuron systems to interpersonal relations." In G. Bock and J. Goode (Eds.), *Empathy and fairness*. Chicester, UK: John Wiley.

Gallese, V. (2009). Mirror neurons, embodied simulation, and the neuronal basis of social identification. *Psychoanalytic Dialogues, 19*, 519–536.

Gallese, V., Eagle, M.N., & Migone, P. (2007). Intentional attunement: Mirror neurons and the neural underpinnings of interpersonal relations. *Journal of the American Psychoanalytic Association, 55*, 131–176.

Gallese, V., Fadiga, L., Fogassi, L., & Rizzolatti, G. (1996). Action recognition in the premotor cortex. *Brain, 119*, 593–609.

Gallese, V., Keyers, C., & Rizzolatti, G. (2004). A unifying view of the basis of social cognition. *Trends in Cognitive Sciences, 8*, 396–403.

Gallese, V., & Lakoff, G. (2005). The brain's concepts: The role of the sensory-motor system in reason and language. *Cognitive Neuropsychology, 22*, 455–479.

Geltner, P. (2012). *Emotional communication: Countetransference analysis and the use of feeling in psychoanalytic technique*. New York: Routledge.

Gibson, J. J. (1979). *The ecological approach to visual perception*. Boston: Houghton Mifflin.

Gravensteen, H. (2009). Når terapeuten misliker pasienten [When the therapist dislikes the patient]. In J. Sletvold & M. Børstad (Eds.), *Den terapeutiske dansen. Kropp og relasjon i psykoterapi [The therapeutic dance. Body and relation in psychotherapy]* (pp. 109–133). Oslo: Kolofon Forlag.

Grieg, A., Rasmussen, M., & Waal, N. (1957). *Nic Waals metode for somatisk psykodiagnostic* [Nic Waal's method for somatic psychodiagnostics]. Oslo: Nic Waals Institutt.

Grønseth, R. (1991). Eksistensiell karakteranalytisk vegetoterapi [Existential character analytic vegetotherapy]. In A. Faleide, R. Grønseth, & E. Grønseth (Eds.), *Karakteranalytisk vegetoterapi* (pp. 195–230). Oslo: Spartacus.

Grønseth, R. (1998). On the shift of paradigms from characteranalytic vegetotherapy, bioenergetic analysis and psychoanalysis to existential charateranalytic vegetotherapy. *Energy & Character: The Journal of Bioenergetic Research, 29*(2), 48–67.

Gullestad, S.E., & Killingmo, B. (2013). *Underteksten. Psykoanalytisk terapi i praksis [The subtext: Psychoanalytic therapy in praxis]* (2nd ed.). Oslo: Universitetsforlaget.

Harris, A. (1998). Psychic envelopes and sonorous baths: Siting the body in relational theory and clinical practice. In L. Aron & F.S. Anderson (Eds.), *Relational perspectives on the body* (pp. 39–64). Hillsdale, NJ: The Analytic Press.

Hartmann, H. (1954). Report on the 18th International Psychoanalytic Congress business meeting. *Bulletin of the International Psycho-Analytic Association, 35*, 278.

Heidegger, M. (1926). *Being and time*. New York: Harper and Row.

Heller, M.C. (2007a). The golden age of body psychotherapy in Oslo I: From gymnastic to psychoanalysis. *Body, movement and dance in psychotherapy, 2*(1), 5–15.

Heller, M.C. (2007b). The golden age of body psychotherapy in Oslo II: From vegetotherapy to nonverbal communication. *Body, movement and dance in psychotherapy, 2*(2), 81–94.

Heller, M. C. (2012). *Body psychotherapy: History, concepts, and methods*. New York: W. W. Norton.

Higgens, M., & Raphael, C.M. (Eds.). (1972). *Reich speaks of Freud*. New York: Farrar, Straus and Giroux. (Original work published 1967.)

Hobson, P. (1998). The intersubjective foundations of thought. In S. Bråten (Ed.), *Intersubjective communication and emotion in early ontogeny* (pp. 283–296). Cambridge: Cambridge University Press.

Hobson, P. (2002). *The cradle of thought.* London: Pan Books.

Horney, K. (1945). *Our inner conflicts.* New York-London: W. W. Norton & Company.

Howell, E. F. (2005). *The dissociative mind.* Hillsdale, NJ: The Analytic Press.

Hurley, S., & Chater, N. (Eds.). (2005). *Perspectives on imitation: From neuroscience to social science.* Cambridge, MA and London: The MIT Press.

Husserl, E. (1977). *Cartecian meditations* (D. Cairns, Trans.). Dordrecht, The Netherlands: Kluwer: Academic.

Husserl, E. (1989a). *Ideas pertaining to a pure phenomenology and to a phenomenological philosophy.* Dordrecht, The Netherlands: Kluwer: Academic. (Original work published 1913.)

Husserl, E. (1989b). *Ideas pertaining to a pure phenomenology and to a phenomenological philosophy, second book: Studies in the phenomenology of constitution.* Dordrecht, The Netherlands: Kluwer: Academic.

Hustvedt, S. (2011). Three emotional stories: Reflections on memory, the imagination, narrative, and the self. *Neuropsychoanalysis, 13*(2), 187–195.

Hyllseth Lien, M. (2012). Uten ord for følelser. Karakteranalyse ved psykosomatiske tilstander [Without words for feelings. Character analysis of psychosomatic conditions]. In M. Børstad & J. Sletvold (Eds.), *Karakteranalytiske dialoger. Kropp & relasjon i psykoterapi II* [*Character analytic dialogues. Body & relation in psychotherapy II*] (pp. 129–164). Oslo: Kolofon Forlag.

Jacobs, T. (1991). The interplay of enactments: Their role in the analytic press. In T. Jacobs (Ed.), *The use of the self* (pp. 31–49). Madison, CT: International Universities Press.

Jacobs, T. (2005). Discussion of forms of intersubjectivity in infant research and adult treatment. In B. Beebe, S. Knoblauch, J. Rustin, & D. Sorter, *Forms of intersubjectivity in infant research and adult treatment* (pp. 165–189). New York: Other Press.

Jaffe, J., Beebe, B., Feldstein, S., Crown, C., & Jasnow, M. (2001). Rhythms of dialogue in infancy. *Monographs of the society for research in child development, 66*(2). Serial No. 265. Boston: Blackwell.

James, W. (1983). *Principles of psychology.* Cambridge, MA: Harvard University Press. (Original work published 1890.)

Johnson, D. H. (Ed.). (1995). *Bone, breath, & gesture. practices of embodiment.* Berkeley, CA: North Atlantic Books.

Josephs, L. (1995). *Balancing empathy and interpretation. Relational character analysis.* Northwale, NJ and London: Jason Aronson.

Kaplan-Solms, K., & Solms, M. (2002). *Clinical studies in neuro-psychoanalysis: Introduction to a depth neuropsychology.* New York: Karnac.

Kernberg, O. F. (1984). *Severe personality disorders. Psychotherapeutic strategies.* New Haven, CT: Yale University Press.

Killingmo, B. (1990). Beyond semantics: A clinical and theoretical study of isolation. *International Journal of Psychoanalysis, 71,* 113–127.

Killingmo, B. (2007). Relational oriented character analysis: A position in contemporary psychoanalysis. *Scandinavian Psychoanalytic Review, 30,* 76–83.

Knoblauch, S. H. (2000). *The musical edge of therapeutic dialogue.* Hillsdale, NJ: The Analytic Press.

Knoblauch, S. H. (2005). Body rhythms and the unconscious. Toward an expanding of clinical attention. *Psychoanalytic Dialogues, 15,* 807–827.

Knoblauch, S. H. (2008). Tipping points between body, culture, and subjectivity: The tension between passion and custom. In F. S. Anderson (Ed.), *Bodies in treatment. The unspoken dimension* (pp. 193–211). New York: The Analytic Press.

Knoblauch, S. H. (2011). Contextualizing attunement within the polyrhythmic weave: The psychoanalytic samba. *Psychoanalytic Dialogues, 21*, 414–427.

Knutsen, T. (2012). Psykoanalytisk psykoterapi eller psykoterapeutisk psykoanalyse. In R. Ulberg, A. G. Hersoug, & T. Knutsen (Eds.), *Psykoterapi i utvikling* [Psychoanalytic psychotherapy or psychotherapeutic psychoanalysis. In: *Developing Psychotherapy*]. Oslo: Akademika forlag.

Kohut, H. (1971). *The analysis of the self.* New York: International Universities Press, Inc.

Krantz, A. M. (2012). Let the body speak: Commentary on paper by Jon Sletvold. *Psychoanalytic Dialogues, 22*, 434–448.

Kugiumutzakis, G. (1998). Neonatal imitation in the intersubjective companion space. In S. Bråten (Ed.), *Intersubjective communication and emotion in early ontogeny* (pp. 63–88). Cambridge: Cambridge University Press.

Lakoff, G. (1987). *Women, fire and dangerous things: What categories reveal about the mind.* Chicago: University of Chicago Press.

Lakoff, G., & Johnson, M. (1980). *Philosophy in the flesh.* New York: Basic Books.

LeDoux, J. (1996). *The emotional brain: The mysterious underpinnings of emotional life.* New York: Simon & Schuster.

Lenzi, D., Trentini, C., Pantano, P., Macaluso, E., Iacoboni, M., Lenzi, G. L., & Ammaniti, M. (2008). Neural basis of maternal communication and emotional processing during preverbal stage. *Cerebral Cortex, 19*(5), 1124–1133.

Levine, P. (1997). *Waking the tiger. Healing trauma.* Berkeley, CA: North Atlantic Books.

Lichtenberg, J. D., Lachmann, F. M., & Fosshage, J. L. (2002). *A spirit of inquiry: Communication in psychoanalysis.* Hilsdale, NJ and London: The Analytic Press.

Lien, C. (2012). "Det er som om relasjonene er blitt vanvittige." Ubevisst selvdestruktiv relasjonell gjentagelsestvang ["It is as if relations have got crazy." Unconscious self-destructive relational repetition compulsion]. In M. Børstad & J. Sletvold (Eds.), *Karakteranalytiske dialoger. Kropp & relasjon i psykoterapi II* [Character analytic dialogues. Body & relation in psychotherapy II] (pp. 165–202). Oslo: Kolofon Forlag.

Lipps, T. (1903). Einfülung, innere Nachahmung und Organempfindung [Empathy, inner imitation and organ perception]. *Archive fur die Gesamte Psychologie* (Vol. 1, Part 2, pp. 465–519). Leipzig: W. Engelmann.

Loewald, H. (1980). Primary process, secondary process and language. In *Papers on psychoanalysis* (pp. 178–206). New Haven, CT: Yale University Press.

Lowen, A. (1975). *Bioenergetics.* London: Coventure.

Magnussen, S., & Overskeid, G. (2003). Noen sentrale temaer i vitnepsykologisk forskning – anno 2003. *Tidsskrift for Norsk Psykologforening, 40*, 188–203. [Some central themes in forensic psychology – anno 2003. *Journal of the Norwegian Psychological Association.*]

Marcher, L., & Fish, S. (2010). *Body encyclopedia: A guide to the psychological functions of the muscular system.* Berkeley, CA: North Atlantic Books.

Markillie, R. E. (1955). Review of the book: *Fundamentals of psychoanalytic technique*, by Trygve Braatøy. *The International Journal of Psychoanalysis, 36*, 411–412.

Masson, J. M. (Ed. & Trans.). (1985). *The complete letters of Sigmund Freud to Wilhelm Fliess: 1887–1904.* Cambridge, MA: Harvard University Press.

McWilliams, N. (2011). *Psychoanalytic diagnosis: Understanding personality structure in the clinical process* (2nd ed.). New York and London: The Guilford Press.

Meltzoff, A. N., & Decety, J. (2003). What imitation tells us about social cognition: A rapprochement between developmental psychology and cognitive neuroscience. *Philosophical Transactions of the Royal Society of London B., 358*, 491–500.

Meltzoff, A. N., & Moore, M. K. (1995). Infants' understanding of people and things: From body imitation to folk psychology. In J. L. Bermudez, A. Marcel, & N. Eilan (Eds.), *The body and the self* (pp. 43–69). Cambridge, MA: MIT Press.

Meltzoff, A. N., & Moore, M. K. (1998). Infant intersubjectivity: Broadening the dialogue to include imitation, identity and intention. In S. Bråten (Ed.), *Intersubjective communication and emotion in early ontogeny* (pp. 47–62). Cambridge: Cambridge University Press.

Merleau-Ponty, M. (1996). *Phenomenology of perception.* London and New York: Routledge. (Original work published 1945.)

Milner, M. (1987). The concentration of the body. In M. Milner, *The suppressed madness of sane men: Forty-four years of exploring psychoanalysis* (pp. 234–240). London: Tavistock and the Institute of Psychoanalysis. (Original work published 1960.)

Mitchell, S. (1988). *Relational concepts in psychoanalysis.* Cambridge, MA: Harvard University Press.

Modell, A. H. (2008). Implicit or unconscious? Commentary on paper by Boston Change Process Study Group. *Psychoanalytic Dialogues, 18,* 162–167.

Muran, J. C., Safran, J. D., & Eubanks-Carter, C. (2010). Developing therapists' abilities to negotiate alliance ruptures. In J. C. Muran & J. P. Barber (Eds.), *The therapeutic alliance: An evidence-based guide to practice* (pp. 320–340). New York-London: The Guilford Press.

Nadel, J., & Muir, D. (Eds.). (2005). *Emotional development: Recent research advances.* Oxford: Oxford University Press.

Nebbiosi, G., & Federici-Nebbiosi, S. (2008). "We" got rhythm. In F. S. Anderson (Ed.), *Bodies in treatment: The unspoken dimension* (pp. 213–233). New York: The Analytic Press.

Nilsen, H. F. (2013). Resistance in therapy and war: Psychoanalysis before and during the Nazi occupation of Norway, 1933–45. *The International Journal of Psychoanalysis, 94,* 725–746.

Norcross, J. C. (2011). *Psychotherapy relationships that work.* Oxford: Oxford University Press.

Nylund, T., & Sletvold, J. (2002). *Getting to know by imitation: Aspects of training in body-psychotherapy.* Presentation at the 6th International Congress of Body-Psychotherapy. Naples-Ischia, October 27–31, 2002. Unpublished manuscript at the Norwegian Character Analytic Institute.

Nylund, T., & Sletvold, J. (2009). Å få kjennskap til den andre ved hjelp av imitasjon. Aspekter ved opplæring i kroppsorientert psykoterapi [Getting to know the other by means of imitation. Aspects of training in body-oriented psychotherapy]. In J. Sletvold & M. Børstad (Eds.), *Den terapeutiske dansen. Kropp og relasjon i psykoterapi [The therapeutic dance. Body and relation in psychotherapy]* (pp. 53–61). Oslo: Kolofon Forlag.

Ogden, P., Minton, K., & Pain, C. (2006). *Trauma and the body: A sensorimotor approach to psychotherapy.* New York: Norton.

Ogden, T. H. (1994). *Subjects of analysis.* London: Karnac Books.

Orbach, S. (2004). The body in clinical practice, part one: There's no such thing as a body. In K. White (Ed.), *Touch: Attachment and the body,* pp. 17–34. London: Karnac Books.

Panksepp, J. (1998). *Affective neuroscience: The foundations of human and animal emotions.* New York: Oxford University Press.

PDM Task Force (2006). *Psychodynamic diagnostic manual.* Silver Spring, MD: Alliance of Psychoanalytic Organizations.

Pesso, A., & Boyden-Pesso, D. (2012). *Pesso Boyden System Psychomotor: A mind-body approach to emotional well-being & peak performance.* Retrieved from http://www.pbsp.com

Pesso, A., & Crandell, J. (Eds.). (1991). *Moving psychotherapy.* Cambridge, MA: Brookline Books.

Philipson, T. (1951). Identifiseringsprosessenes betydning og mekanisme [Mechanism and meaning in the processes of identification]. *Impuls. 1–2,* 1–4.

Philipson, T. (1952). *Kærlighedslivet. Natur og unatur* [Love life. Natural and unnatural]. København: Lund og Andersens forlag.

Piers, C. (2005). The minds multiplicity and continuity. *Psychoanalytic Dialogues, 15*(2), 229–254.

Racker, H. (1968/2002). *Transference and countertransference.* London: Karnac.

Raknes, O. (1970). *Wilhelm Reich and orgonomy.* Oslo-Bergen-Tromsø: Universitetsforlaget.

Reich, W. (1972). *Character analysis* (3rd ed.). V.R. Carfagno (Trans.). New York: Farrar, Straus and Giroux. (Original work published 1949.)

Reich, W. (1978). *The function of orgasm.* New York: Pocket Books. (Original work published 1942.)

Reich, W. (1988). *The mass psychology of fascism.* New York: Farrar, Straus and Giroux. (Original work published 1946.)

Reich, W. (1994). *Beyond psychology: Letters and journals 1934–1939.* M.B. Higgens (Ed.). New York: Farrar, Straus and Giroux.

Reik, T. (1991). *Listening with the third ear: The inner experience of a psychoanalyst.* New York: Farrar, Straus and Giroux. (Original work published 1948.)

Reis, B. (2009). We: Commentary on papers by Trevarthen, Ammanitti & Trentini, and Gallese. *Psychoanalytic Dialogues, 19*, 565–579.

Rizzolatti, G., Fadiga, L., Gallese, V., & Fogassi, L. (1996). Premotor cortex and the recognition of motor actions. *Cognitive Brain Research, 3*, 131–141.

Rizzolatti, G., Fogassi, L., & Gallese, V. (2001). Neurophysiological mechanisms underlying the understanding and imitation of action. *Nature Reviews Neuroscience, 2*, 661–670.

Rochat, P. (2009). *Others in mind: Social origins of self-consciousness.* Cambridge: Cambridge University Press.

Rockwell, W.T. (2005). *Neither brain nor ghost: A nondualist alternative to the mind-brain identity theory.* Cambridge, MA: The MIT Press.

Rønnestad, M.H., & Skovholt, T.M. (2013). *The developing practitioner: Growth and stagnation of therapists and counsellors.* New York and London: Routledge Taylor & Frances Group.

Rothschild, B. (2000). *The body remembers: The psychophysiology of trauma and trauma treatment.* New York: Norton.

Safran, J.D. (2012). *Psychoanalysis and psychoanalytic therapies.* Washington, DC: American Psychoanalytical Association.

Safran, J.D., & Muran, J.C. (2000). *Negotiating the therapeutic alliance: A relational treatment guide.* New York and London: The Guilford Press.

Schacter, D.L. (1996). *Searching for memory.* New York: Basic Books.

Schafer, R. (1983). *The analytic attitude.* New York: Basic Books.

Schjelderup, H. (1936). Charakterveranderungen durch psychanalytische Behandlung [Character change through psychoanalytic treatment]. *Acta psychiatrica et nevrologica, 11*, 631–650.

Schjelderup, H. (1955). Lasting effects of psychoanalytic treatment. *Psychiatry, 18*, 109–133.

Schjelderup, H. (1956). Personality-changing processes of psychoanalytic treatment. *Acta Psychologica, 12*, 47–64.

Schjelderup, H. (1988). *Nevrosene og den nevrotiske karakter* [The neurosis and the neurotic character]. Oslo: Universitetsforlaget. (Original work published 1941.)

Schore, A.N. (1994). *Affect regulation and the origin of the self: The neurobiology of emotional development.* Hillsdale, NJ: Erlbaum.

Schore, A.N. (2003a). *Affect dysregulation and disorders of the self.* New York: Norton.

Schore, A. N. (2003b). *Affect regulation and the repair of the self.* New York: Norton.

Schore, A. N. (2011). The right brain implicit self lies at the core of psychoanalysis. *Psychoanalytic Dialogues, 21,* 75–100.

Schulte-Ruther, M., Markowitsch, H. J., Fink, G. R., & Piefke, M. (2007). Mirror neuron and theory of mind mechanisms involved on face-to-face interaction: A functional magnetic resonance imaging approach to empathy. *Journal of Cognitive Neuroscience. 19,* 1354–1372.

Seligman, S. (2005). Dynamic systems theories as a metaframework for psychoanalysis. *Psychoanalytic Dialogues, 15*(2), 285–319.

Seligman, S. (2011). Review of the book *Forms of vitality: Exploring dynamic experience in psychology, the arts, psychotherapy, and development,* by D. N. Stern. *Journal of the American Psychoanalytic Association, 59*(4), 859–868.

Shapiro, D. (1965). *Neurotic styles.* New York: Basic Books.

Shapiro, D. (2000). *Dynamics of character: Self-regulation in psychotherapy.* New York: Basic Books.

Shapiro, S. A. (1996). The embodied analyst in the Victorian consulting room. *Gender and Psychoanalysis, 1*(3), 297–321.

Shapiro, S. A. (2009). A rush to action: Embodiment, the analyst's subjectivity, and the interpersonal experience. *Studies in Gender and Sexuality, 10,* 93–103.

Sharaf, M. (1983). *Fury on earth: A biography of Wilhelm Reich.* New York: Da Capo Press.

Sletvold, J. (1996). *Character analysis – The foundation of body psychotherapy.* Paper presented at 4th International Congress of Psycho-Corporal Therapies, 1st U.S. National Conference on Body Oriented Psychotherapy, June 12–16, 1996, Beverly, Massachusetts. Unpublished manuscript at the Norwegian Character Analytic Institute.

Sletvold, J. (2011). "The reading of emotional expression." Wilhelm Reich and the history of embodied analysis. *Psychoanalytic Dialogues, 21,* 453–467.

Sletvold, J. (2012a). Training analysts to work with unconscious embodied expressions. *Psychoanalytic Dialogues, 22,* 410–429.

Sletvold, J. (2012b). Reply to commentaries. *Psychoanalytic Dialogues, 22,* 449–455.

Sletvold, J. (2013). The Ego and the Id revisited. Freud and Damasio on the body ego/self. *The International Journal of Psychoanalysis, 94,* 1019–1032.

Sletvold, J., & Børstad, M. (Eds.). (2009). *Den terapeutiske dansen. Kropp og relasjon ipsykoterapi* [The therapeutic dance: Body and relation in psychotherapy]. Oslo: Kolofon Forlag.

Solms, M., & Turnbull, O. (2002). *The brain and the inner world: An introduction to the neuroscience of subjective experience.* New York: Other Press.

Sonnby-Borgstrom, M. (2002). Automatic mimicry reactions as related to differences in emotional empathy. *Scandinavian Journal of Psychology, 43,* 433–443.

Spezzano, C. (1993). *Affect in psychoanalysis: A clinical synthesis.* Hillsdale, NJ and London: The Analytical Press.

Spinoza, B. (1982). *The ethics.* Indianapolis: Hackett Publishing Co., Inc. (Original work published 1677.)

Stark, M. (1999). *Modes of therapeutic action: Enhancement of knowledge, provision of experience, and engagement in relationship.* Northvale, NJ and London: Jason Aronson Inc.

Starr, K. E., & Aron, L. (2011). Women on the coach: Genital stimulation and the birth of psychoanalysis. *Psychoanalytic Dialogues, 21,* 373–392.

Stern, D. N. (2000). *The interpersonal world of the infant: A view from psychoanalysis and developmental psychology* (2nd ed.). New York: Basic Books.

Stern, D. N. (2004). *The present moment in psychotherapy and everyday life.* New York: Norton.

Stern, D. N. (2010). *Forms of vitality: Exploring dynamic experience in psychology, the arts, psychotherapy, and development.* Oxford: Oxford University Press.

Stern, D. N., Sander, L., Nahum, J., Harrison, A., Lyons-Ruth, K., Morgan, A., Bruschweiler-Stern, N., & Tronick, E. Z. (1998). Non-interpretative mechanisms in psychoanalytic therapy: The "something more" than interpretation. *International Journal of Psycho-Analysis, 79,* 903–922.

Stern, S. (1994). Needed relationship and repeated relationship: An integrated relational perspective. *Psychoanalytic Dialogues, 18,* 317–345.

Stern, S. (2009). Session frequency and the definition of psychoanalysis. *Psychoanalytic Dialogues, 19,* 639–655.

Stolorow, R. D. (2011). *World, affectivity, trauma. Heidegger and post-Cartesian psychoanalysis.* New York and London: Routledge.

Strand, N. H. (1991). På vei mot en "global terapi". Konsekvent karakteranalyse, vegetoterapi og akupunktur [Towards a "global therapy." Consistent character analysis, vegetotherapy and acupuncture]. In A. O. Faleide, R. Grønseth, & E. Grønseth (Eds.), *Karakteranalytisk vegetoterapi. I kjølvannet av Wilhelm Reich* [Character analytic vegetoterapy: In the wake of Wilhelm Reich]. Oslo: Spartacus Forlag.

Sullivan, H. S. (1940). *Conceptions of modern psychiatry.* New York: Norton.

Thelen, E. (2005). Dynamic systems theory and the complexity of change. *Psychoanalytic Dialogues, 15*(2), 255–283.

Totten, N. (1998). *The water in the glass. Body and mind in psychoanalysis.* London: Rebus Press.

Trevarthen, C. (1979). Communication and cooperation in early infancy: A description of primary intersubjectivity. In M. Bullowa (Ed.), *Before speech: The beginning of human communication* (pp. 321–347). London: Cambridge University Press.

Trevarthen, C. (2004). Intimate contact from birth. How we know one another by touch, voice, and expression in movement. In K. White (Ed.), *Touch. Attachment and the body* (pp. 1–15). London: Karnac Books.

Trevarthen, C. (2009). The intersubjective psychobiology of human meaning: Learning of culture depends on interest for co-operative practical work – and affection for the joyful art of good company. *Psychoanalytic Dialogues, 19,* 507–518.

Tronick, E. (2005). Why is connection to others so critical? The formation of dyadic states of consciousness and the expansion of the individuals' states of consciousness: Coherence governed selection and the co-creation of meaning out of messy meaning making. In J. Nadel & D. Muir (Eds.), *Emotional development: Recent research advances* (pp. 293–315). Oxford: Oxford University Press.

van der Kolk, B. A. (1994). The body keeps the score: Memory and the evolving psychobiology of post-traumatic stress. *Harvard Review of Psychiatry, 1,* 253–265.

van der Kolk, B. A., & Saporta, J. (1993). Biological response to psychic trauma. In J. P. Wilson & B. Raphael (Eds.), *International handbook of traumatic stress syndromes* (pp. 25–34). New York: Plenum.

Vivona, J. M. (2009). Leaping from brain to mind: A critique of mirror neuron explanations of countertransference. *Journal of the American Psychoanalytic Association, 57,* 525–550.

Waal, N. (1955). A special technique of psychotherapy with an autistic child. In G. Caplan (Ed.), *Emotional problems of early childhood.* New York: Basic Books.

Waal, N. (1958). On Wilhelm Reich. In P. Ritter (Ed.), *Wilhelm Reich.* Nottingham: The Ritter Press.

Wallerstein, R. (2006). Psychoanalytically based nosology: Historic origins. In PDM Task Force, *Psychodynamic diagnostic manual* (pp. 385–402). Silver Spring, MD: Alliance of Psychoanalytic Organizations.

Wallin, D. J. (2007). *Attachment in psychotherapy.* New York and London: The Guilford Press.

Wampold, B. E., & Brown, J. (2005). Estimating variability in outcomes attributable to thera-pists: A naturalistic study of outcomes in managed care. *Journal of Consulting and Clinical Psychology, 73,* 914–923.

Winnicott, D. W. (1949). Hate in the countertransference. *International Journal of Psychoanaly-sis, 30,* 69–74. (Reprinted from *Through paediatrics to psychoanalysis,* 1975, London: The Hogarth Press).

Winnicott, D. W. (1963). Communicating and not communicating leading to a study of certain opposites. In *The maturational processes and the facilitating environment* (pp. 179–192). New York: International Universities Press.

Wittgenstein, L. (1980). *Remarks on the philosophy of psychology* (Vols. 1 & 2). G. H. von Wright & H. Hyman (Eds.). Oxford: Blackwell.

Index

affect motor memory 62, 63–4
Akhtar, N. 102
alter-centric participation 66–7, 85, 86
analyst/therapist: classical, return of 111–12; focus on xii–xiii; Nazi persecution of 51–2
analytic third 108
analytic training *see* training
Anderson, F. S. 37, 136, 152
animal companionship 127–9
Ann case vignette 128–9
Anthi, Per 32–3, 34, 51, 53–4, 57
Aron, L. xiv, xv, 55, 67, 108, 111, 147
Astrid case illustration 91–9, 164
attachment patterns: animal companionship 127–9; isolation 129–30; levels of self-organization and 80
attending to embodied experience and expressions xiii
autobiographical extended self 78, 79
autobiographical memory 62, 63, 64
awareness-oriented role plays 153

background emotions and background feelings 10
Balint, M. 114, 165
Basch, Michael Franz 25
Bateson, Mary Catherine 115
Becchara, Antoine 106
Beebe, B. 24, 29–30, 116, 117
Benjamin, J. xiii, 108
Bernstein, Lotte 52
Bernstein, Paul 52
Binder, J. F. 134
Binder, P. E. 54
bio-energetic analysis 55
Biosynthesis/Biodynamic Analysis/Bioenergetic Analysis 33–5

Boadella, David 120
body: Cartesian conception of mind and 1, 3–6; double nature of 74; emotional body states 8–9; in making of self 76–81; physical manipulation of 33–5, 37; rooting of thought and language in 101–7; Spinozan conception of mind and 1, 3–6, 13, 76; *see also* one-body psychology; two-body psychology
body-based verbal reflexivity 100
body/mind practices 152–3
Bodynamic Analysis 51
body-oriented psychotherapy 32–7
Boston Change Process Study Group 11, 24, 80, 91, 165, 166
Braatøy, Trygve 47–8, 48–50, 51, 52, 53, 161
Brandt, Willy 52
Brodal, Per 51
Bromberg, Philip 105, 165
Bucci, W. 29
Büllow-Hansen, Adel 51

Cartesian conception of body and mind 1, 3–6
case presentation, approach to 140–4, 153–4
change, processes of xvi
character xiv, 117–18; *see also* character analysis; character and relational orientations
character analysis: described xiv–xv; internationally 28–31; in Norway 38, 53–4; Reich and xv, 10, 21–7, 34, 120
Character Analysis (Reich) xv, 26, 120
Character Analytic Institute: history of 54–7; supervision model of 97;